Edinburgh University Library

Books may be recalled for return earlier than due date;
if so you will be contacted by e-mail or letter.

Due Date	Due Date	Due Date

MARTYRDOM,
MURDER, AND MAGIC

Studies in Church History

William L. Fox
General Editor

Vol. 2

PETER LANG
New York • Washington, D.C./Baltimore • Bern
Frankfurt am Main • Berlin • Brussels • Vienna • Oxford

Patricia Healy Wasyliw

MARTYRDOM, MURDER, AND MAGIC

Child Saints and Their Cults in Medieval Europe

PETER LANG
New York • Washington, D.C./Baltimore • Bern
Frankfurt am Main • Berlin • Brussels • Vienna • Oxford

Library of Congress Cataloging-in-Publication Data

Wasyliw, Patricia Healy.
Martyrdom, murder, and magic: child saints and their cults
in medieval Europe / Patricia Healy Wasyliw.
p. cm. — (Studies in church history; vol. 2)
Includes bibliographical references and index.
1. Christian child saints. 2. Christian saints—Cult—History of doctrines—
Middle Ages, 600–1500. 3. Christian martyrs—Europe—Cult.
4. Murder victims—Europe. I. Title. II. Series.
BX4656.2 .W37   235'.2'083—dc20   94049578
ISBN 978-0-8204-2764-5
ISSN 1074-6749

Bibliographic information published by **Die Deutsche Bibliothek**.
Die Deutsche Bibliothek lists this publication in the "Deutsche
Nationalbibliografie"; detailed bibliographic data is available
on the Internet at http://dnb.ddb.de/.

To my beloved children, Abby and Vika

Contents

Introduction

> The lives of very little children are glaringly told from the standpoint of monks who know nothing about childhood. Their fasting from the breast, their voluntary seclusion, their fondness for church and prayer, their abstinence from all childish amusements and mirth, their ridiculous modesty, their prudery and priggishness, are dwelt on with lingering praise. Indeed, everything said about little children is unchildlike, and very much is utterly repugnant.[1]
>
> —E. C Brewer, *A Dictionary of Miracles*

Childhood and sanctity have long been viewed as profoundly incompatible, if not mutually exclusive, states. Although childhood has been characterized in various historical periods as a time of comparative innocence and purity, qualities often associated with sanctity, examples of child saints do not readily spring to mind. When the *vita* of an adult saint contains a description of childhood, it is usually to draw a contrast between the pious behavior of the young saint and the more rambunctious activities of normal children. Studies of the development of Christianity in a particular era, or of certain types of saints, such as female saints or royal saints, either ignore child saints altogether or treat children within the group as insignificant examples of larger trends. Over the centuries, theologians and scholars have questioned the basic premise that children can be saints at all.[2]

The study of child saints combines the topics of hagiology and the history of childhood. The Catholic Church considers as saints "only those whose lives have been marked by the exercise of heroic virtue."[3] The attributes of sanctity encompassed by this term are not absolute, but adapt to changing historical and cultural conditions. The martyrs, the first saints honored in the church, demonstrated heroic virtue by dying for their faith at the hand of the Romans. With the legitimization of Christianity and the end of official persecution, veneration was also bestowed on confessors, "those...who died peacefully after a life of heroic virtue."[4] The earliest confessors were monks and missionaries, representing two behavioral extremes of isolation and asceticism, or immersion in a surrounding community to inspire conversion through pious behavior. The ensuing centuries have seen many permutations of sanctity and its manifestations. In recognition of this, sociologist Pierre Delooz provides a more functional definition of the saint as "a person whom the Church honors with an official cult."[5]

The literature of sanctity is vast, encompassing the iconography and legends of the saints, accounts of their miracles before and after death, and the physical remains of the saints in the form of shrines and relics, as well as several centuries of scholarly, antiquarian, and devotional writings. While the perceived qualities of sanctity may change over time and locality, worship of saints is widespread within Christianity, and many non-Christian cultures also recognize individuals perceived to be of superior holiness.[6] Historians in recent decades have explored the cultural context and social function of the saints and their cults in the Middle Ages, especially as a manifestation of popular religion.[7] The legends of the saints are not historical documents in any strict sense; their purpose was spiritual edification and their authors were devout and uncritical. In many cases, especially for saints dating from the first millennium, little or nothing of the legend is reliable,[8] but can serve as an indication of popular expectations.

Throughout the history of the Catholic Church, popular expectations have been integral to the recognition of sanctity. For the first millennium of Christianity, no formal canonization process existed, so that all cults were the product of popular canonization through spontaneous local veneration at the tomb of a saint.[9] Martyrs were venerated as early as the second century A.D., and confessors by the fourth century.[10] The first papal endorsement of canonization occurred in 993, but the first substantial papal inquiry into a saint's life was held in 1099 under Urban II.[11] The period between 1099 and 1634, when the canonization process was effectively placed under total papal control,[12] saw an uneasy coexistence of local, regional, and papal influences.[13]

The importance of a saint to any community is often found in the social function of the cult, rather than the identity of the individual who inspired it. A saint does not simply lead a holy life or die a noble death, but also possesses supernatural power which is used to perform miracles.[14] From earliest times, the miraculous powers of the saints were sought in their relics, which could be parts of their bodies or objects that had come in contact with their bodies.[15] The saints, through their shrines and relics, healed the sick, granted prayers, and raised the dead. The power of the saint, centered in the relics, protected the local community and inspired pilgrimages by the faithful. Relics of the saints were venerated dispersed, collected and stolen, elevated and humiliated. The miraculous function of the saints and their shrines was identical whether the saint was a martyr or a confessor, male or female, old or young. The identity of the saint in life was, in reality, secondary to the actions the saint performed in death.

The cults of child saints in medieval society functioned much like those of adult saints, but the subjects of the cults did not. In terms of numbers, the child saints of the Catholic Church constitute an inconsequential subset of the hagiographical pantheon. In recent decades, the history of childhood has received significant scholarly attention, and many formerly neglected sources have been examined for their contributions to this and other related topics. In *Childhood in the Middle Ages*, Shulamith Shahar extensively mines the *Acta Sanctorum* for references to children and childhood found in the *vitae* of adult saints. Although the abundance of *topoi* in the lives of the saints has frequently been cited as a barrier to their effective utilization as historical sources, the narratives contain many details of everyday life, and the behavior described was frequently intended to be plausible, just as the exhaustive miracle lists attached to many cults can provide insights into the problems and priorities of medieval society. Analysis of the *topoi* found in the lives of child saints can contribute substantially to an understanding of medieval concepts of childhood.

A multitude of hagiographical legends reflect the influence of the Gospels on the authors as well their subjects, but the canonical Gospels contain little information on the childhood of Jesus. The only episode of note is found in Luke 2.46-47, "After three days they found him in the temple, sitting among the teachers, listening to them an asking them questions; and all who heard them were amazed at his understanding and answers."[16] No direct parallel to this episode is found in the lives of the child saints, but the holy child who astonishes all with his wisdom and does not act in a childlike manner is a common theme in the lives of adult saints, and finds an echo in the briefer lives of children. The apocryphal Infancy Gospels, which purport to chronicle the exploits of Jesus throughout infancy and childhood, present a less flattering but perhaps more comprehensible picture of a young God who possesses immeasurable powers not yet fully understood and not yet controlled. The infant who bends the palm tree so his mother can be nourished, the young child who fashions clay birds and brings them to life, or the petulant child who strikes an annoying playmate dead and then, chastised by Mary, restores him to life, presents an amusing yet plausible image of supernatural power imperfectly controlled by an immature being.[17]

Virtually all historical treatments of medieval childhood begin with the work of Philippe Ariès, whose famous assertion in *Centuries of Childhood* that the modern age "discovered" childhood, that medieval people had no conception of childhood as a developmental stage, and that high infant mortality precluded medieval parents from feeling love or affection toward their children, creating "a feeling of indifference towards a too fragile childhood.[18] Although his work can be credited with turning scholarly interest to the topic of childhood in history, his thesis has been effectively discredited by all subsequent treatment of the topic, and I will not attempt to re-create the debate here. Several historians of medieval childhood have provided useful historiographical overviews of this subject.[19] No work on childhood can, it seems, avoid using Ariès as a starting-point; Shulamith Shahar, in the opening sentence of *Childhood in the Middle Ages,* states, "The central thesis of this book is that a concept of childhood existed in the Central and Late Middle Ages."[20] Barbara Hanawalt, in her introduction to *Growing up on Medieval London: the Experience of Childhood in History,* similarly notes, "The thesis of this book is simple. The Middle Ages did recognize stages of life that correspond to childhood and adolescence."[21]

Throughout the medieval period, expected behavior was divided into a series of developmental stages derived from classical antiquity known as the "Ages of Man"[22] Different schemes represent Man passing through four, seven, nine, ten or twelve ages, the ages of youth are the most consistently represented and described.[23] The first stage, *infantia* encompassed the first seven years of life. Little children of this age were rightly considered helpless, in need of constant care and oversight, and were seen as weak in body and mind, too young to care for theirselves either physically or morally. *Pueritia* described the years from seven to fourteen, but was often shortened to the age of twelve for girls. The age of seven was considered to mark the beginning of the age of reason, and formal education usually began at this stage. *Pueri* exhibited improved but imperfect physical and moral autonomy. A young girl, called a *puella*, or the diminutive *puellula*, was ready for training in simple household tasks, The end of *pueritia* carried with it certain legal rights and responsibilities. In the Roman world, girls below the age of twelve and boys below the age of fourteen were not considered capable of entering into marriage, or of being charged with adultery. In the medieval West, the age of fourteen to fifteen was often cited as the age at which one could act as a witness in court, enter into a contract, or sell property. Marriages were recognized as valid if the boy was over the age of fourteen, or the girl over the age of twelve.[24] The third stage, *adolescentia*, was less well defined, and generally applied only to males. In the ancient world, a girl at puberty was of marriageable age, and so was considered mature, in contrast to a young male of the same age. In the Middle Ages, daughters of powerful families were betrothed and married young, but unmarried adolescence was more common at the lower levels of society. *Adolescentia,* which usually lasted until the age of twenty-one but sometimes ended at seventeen or eighteen, was the precursor to *iuventus*, the first of several stages of adulthood.[25]

The majority of saints in this study fall under the categories of *infantia* or *pueritia*, but several examples of *adolescentia* are also included. Although specific words such as *infans, puer* or *libera* are used to connote stages of childhood, such usage is not always consistent. Phrases, situations, and other details in the lives of individual saints indicate whether or not a saint was considered a child, even if the exact age was not recorded. These cases, and those of adolescents whose *vitae* closely parallel other child saints, have been included for discussion. On the other hand, just as parents of today speak of their adult offspring as "children," and a man of thirty can still be a "good boy" to his mother, the terminology of youth does not necessarily asssure the identity of a child. The *Martyrology* of Usuard described St. Antoninus as *pueri annorum viginti*,[26] and the martyr Marcellinus, who refused to serve in the Roman army and was cast into the sea, was also described as a *puer*.[27] It seems more appropriate to allow the elements of individual legends to dictate inclusion or exclusion, rather than use of a specific word or an arbitrary chronological terminus.

These criteria have been applied to the adolescent girls from the ages of twelve to eighteen who fall into this marginal category. With few exceptions, female martyrs in this age group died in defense of their chastity. Adolescent virgin martyrs, although quite numerous, were excluded from study unless extraordinary elements of their legends argued for inclusion. Although many were of an age to be considered children by modern readers, and have been so portrayed in the last two centuries, I have taken the societal recognition of sexual maturity as an indication that the subject was no longer considered to be a child in her own culture. Two notable exceptions to this rule are the cults of St. Agnes, who was praised for her youth and innocence before her legend made her a martyr to chastity, and St. Pelagius, an adolescent boy martyred in ninth-century Spain when he spurned the unnatural advances of a Moslem potentate. In the latter case, the youth of the victim was clearly one of his attractions, and so relevant to the martyrdom. Several adolescent girls of the thirteenth and fourteenth centuries, whose reputations for sanctity were founded on pious behavior rather than the preservation of virginity, have also been included.

Even the most casual overview of medieval child saints will support the conclusion that knowledge of a distinct stage of childhood existed, and that childhood was a central component, if indeed not the only factor, in their veneration. Ample scholarship exists for all periods encompassed by this study to confirm that the state of childhood was recognized, and the societal concept of childhood approximated modern conceptions in many ways. Isidore of Seville, following the classical tradition, noted in the *Etymologies*, "They are called *pueri* because of their purity."[28] Children were considered more innocent than adults, especially in the sexual sense, the source of so great a proportion of sin in the Middle Ages. At the same time, their immaturity made them prone to misbehavior because they lacked the moral development essential to virtuous adulthood. Children were both inherently innocent and inherently sinful,[29] but unlike the sinful adult, whose wayward actions were a conscious choice in the face of clear behavioral directives and strict moral training, the child's transgressions were seen as the natural weakness of the childish state. While relevant societal concepts of childhood will be addressed more specifically in each chapter, it will serve as a starting point to note that, while a very few children became saints by controlling their childish impulses to achieve the *virtus heroica* of the adult saint, the vast majority showed no extraordinary moral or spiritual qualities whatsoever-they simply died, occasionally of illness or accident, but usually at the hands of another. The basic attribute of a child saint is first, foremost and always, a premature and usually unexpected death. Whether the killer was a Roman, a relative, or a stranger (most notoriously in the medieval popular imagination, a Jew) the result was the same-veneration as a martyr. Most child saints are correctly considered by modern hagiographers to possess, at best, only marginal qualities of sanctity, and were the product of popular veneration, their cults predating the formal canonization process.

In contrast to the fields this work draws upon, the study of child saints is in its infancy. Prior to the 1980s, child saints attracted little attention of either a scholarly or antiquarian nature. At the end of the nineteenth century, Frances Arnold-Forster devoted a chapter of *Studies in Church Dedications* to child saints with cults established in England, and included gleanings from local folklore, but the principal focus of the work was whether churches and dedications were "ancient," occurring before the Reformation, or modern.[30] Her contemporary, E.C. Brewer, included a list of forty-nine "canonized" child martyrs in his work *A Dictionary of Miracles*, but the list is erroneous and incomplete, including only a few child victims of the persecutions, and some examples of ritual murder victims, of which only one was formally canonized.[31] The cults of a very few child saints, such as the early martyrs Agnes, Faith, and Flocel, and the alleged ritual murder victims William of Norwich and Simon of Trent, have left extensive literary or archaeological records, and have been subject to individual studies. In the later 20th century, scholarly interest in the contributions of the lives of the saints to social history and the history of childhood and the family, but historians most frequently use the term "child saint" in reference to narratives of the childhood of adult saints.[32] *Bambini Santi*, published in 1991 by Anna Benvenuti Papi and Elena Giannarelli, remains the only collection dedicated in its entirety to this subject,[33] but the work is by no means comprehensive. Michael Goodich has produced pioneering work on the spiritual activities of children, especially in the thirteenth century,[34] and Nicholas Orme has profitably explored the role of children in religious culture and spiritual life,[35] as have several authors working under the auspices of the Ecclesiastical History Society.[36]

The outline of this work follows the basic chronological and geographical development of Christianity in Western Europe. Although existing in relative obscurity, child saints have occupied a place in both official and popular devotion that is as old as the cult of the saints itself. The Holy Innocents, considered protomartyrs because they died in place of Christ even before his death on the cross, were widely venerated throughout the Christian west, and their cult was established by the end of the second century.[37] The martyrs of late antiquity numbered scores of children, named and nameless, among their ranks, later augmented by the popularity of the medieval relic trade. Many *passios* portray child martyrs actively confessing Christ and seeking a heroic death in the manner of their adult comrades, but others reflect a sort of accidental martyrdom more in keeping with plausibly childish behavior under such circumstances. As the era of the persecutions ended and Christian missionaries spread throughout Europe in the early Middle Ages, the legends and relics of child martyrs were promoted along with those of more famous adults.

The decline of martyrdom in the fourth century necessitated a modification of early medieval concepts of sanctity. The piety and asceticism expected of saints who were not martyrs was seen at times in children, if the *vitae* of many saints are to be believed, and a few children who died soon after baptism were venerated as confessors. Children continued to be worshipped as martyrs for sustaining a variety of deaths which corresponded to the idea of martyrdom in varying degrees. Societal interest in venerating children was sustained through the creation of indigenous saints and trade in the relics of child martyrs from the era of the persecutions. Christian missionaries, many recognized as saints themselves, spread the teachings of the Church throughout Europe to local populations which accepted Christianity with a more or less imperfect understanding of the underlying doctrinal justification for its practices. One such example was the concept of martyrdom. The popular understanding of martyrdom shifted from dying in defense of the Christian faith to representing an unjust death, and youthful victims of political or domestic violence were venerated as saints, along with their adult counterparts who were frequently members of royal or aristocratic households. These cults represent some of the clearest examples of the intertwining of popular religion with surviving folk practices and magical beliefs.

From the end of the tenth century, the increasing influence of the papacy in the cult of the saints through development of the formal canonization process, accompanied by a growing emphasis upon piety, asceticism and mysticism, acted as a barrier to the recognition of children as saints. The proliferation of medical and pedagogical literature describing the state of childhood in increasingly naturalistic terms discouraged the idealization of childhood, but also demonstrated a growing interest in the state of childhood within medieval society. This interest found a spiritual reflection in the cult of the Holy Family, and particularly in representations of the infant Jesus. The purity and innocence of the holy child was promoted as a goal for the faithful. A small portion of the population emulated this model, and the few who died in childhood were able to achieve sanctity in recognition of their pious activities. The religious reforms of the of the high Middle Ages, marked by increasing papal control over models of sanctity and the institution of a formal canonization process, produced a small but significant group of children who actively sought sainthood through asceticism and prayer in the manner of adult confessors. This group represents the smallest number of child saints, but the highest proportion of those formally endorsed by the Church through the canonization process. In other cases, this theme was adapted by hagiographers who wished to promote more marginal cults. From the twelfth century on, the ranks of the child saints were dominated by the ritual murder victims, young Christian children allegedly murdered for magical purposes by Jews Initial doctrinal objections to the veneration of murder victims rapidly gave way to popular enthusiasm for the cults generated by the alleged crimes.

Among the child saints discussed in this work, violent deaths vastly outnumber death by natural causes. One theme commonly expressed by historians is that the worship of murdered children indicates significant societal value placed on keeping children from harm. Michael Goodich, in discussing cults from the thirteenth century, including the ritual murder victims, suggests that these "deaths reflect the typical bogeyman of the medieval mind."[38] Weinstein and Bell also associate the ritual murder charge with a societal appreciation of childhood. "In their obvious anti-Jewish purpose, these stories tell us something of medieval feelings about children."[39] Barbara Hanawalt acknowledged the significance of the child saint, as exemplified by William of Norwich, Hugh of Lincoln, and similar cases in her work on medieval English peasant families, by noting that "medieval people did value their children in the greatest way they knew: they made saints out of them."[40]

Any discussion of the cult of the saints must confront the question of the gap between popular religion and official doctrine. Although popular religious practice "can be utterly divorced from the official teaching of the Church or the lofty speculations of the theologians,"[41] it is generally recognized that there is no easy separation of the two. Many elements of medieval religious belief properly characterized as popular were shared by the intellectual elite, and the teachings of the clerical hierarchy often found shape in popular practices.[42] The cult of the saints provides a classic example of a popular practice which was accepted and promoted by both church and state in medieval society. The cults of child saints exhibit many examples of popular and elite forces at work, each stronger at different times and for different reasons, but always overlapping. The child saint is a marginal creation of medieval Christianity.[43] An examination of how, when, where and why child saints were created and venerated can provide a window into the elusive realm of medieval popular culture. Their example is not unique; beggars, peasants, and other disenfranchised members of society also fall into the category of marginal saints whose veneration exemplifies a representation of "universal values" to be used in the study of popular culture.[44] The suppressed cult of St. Guinefort, the holy greyhound, is a prominent and singular example.[45] Dogs should not be recognized as saints on any rational doctrinal basis; neither should most of the children venerated as saints in the Middle Ages. Yet the cults existed, and some continue into the modern age.

The study of popular religion frequently embraces the substrata of societal belief in magic, witchcraft, necromancy and other superstitions at work beneath the surface beliefs imposed by the official church.[46] Gábor Klaniczay has postulated a parallel framework for the study of popular religion of religious sensibility which encompasses the saint and the witch, not simply as differently motivated representatives of the same belief in the supernatural, but as both created by the mechanisms of the religious establishment.[47] The powers of the witch were not universally condemned, nor were those of the saint uniformly accepted. This scheme is perhaps the most successful to date in resolving the tension between popular and learned culture and religious practices upon which rocky shores many scholars have dashed their intellectual boats.[48] The marginal status of the child saint hindered the claim to official recognition of sanctity, but facilitated popular devotion. The vast majority of these saints would not have become saints if they had not died as children, and if medieval society did not react with heightened emotion to their deaths. The death of a child, especially a violent death, must have been seen as a greater tragedy than the death of an adult. In these cases, the popular wish to venerate an object of sympathy outweighed official expectations of superior conduct during life. Although the adult victims of violent or unjust death also attracted sympathy, ecclesiastical censure generally put a quick end to the formation of cults. The marginal nature of the child saint allowed at least toleration and sometimes active promotion of these cults.

The attribution of magical properties to the bodies of the dead, and especially to children, may provide an indication of the cultural underpinnings of popular support for such cults. Folkloric beliefs may have flourished more openly in connection with these cults than with more famous and necessarily conventional cults. Folk beliefs frequently reflect magical beliefs held by society, and the legends of medieval child saints contain more than their share of folkloric motifs. Study of the connection between magic and religion is presently a vigorous and burgeoning field, as is the study of medieval childhood. Connections between children, magical practices, and societal beliefs occur only in scattered references, but they do exist. Folk practices in medieval and early modern Europe indicate a role for children not yet adequately explored by historians. Gustav Henningsen, noting the widespread involvement of children in early modern witchcraft accusations in France, Germany, Sweden and the Basque regions, commented, "Here indeed lies an unexplored field awaiting comparative-or still better-interdisciplinary study."[49]

The material for this study is found within the legends of the saints, and the archaeological and liturgical evidence of their cults. Since most of the examples deal with relatively obscure individuals, the hagiological evidence is frequently imperfect. In many instances, especially in the cases of the earlier martyrs, the oldest surviving legend for a saint of the fourth century can be traced only as far back as the sixth, seventh, or eighth century. It is not always possible to assert that the elements of the legend are contemporary with the formation of the cult. I have tried to compensate for this by eliminating from consideration those saints for whom no archaeological or liturgical evidence from the formative period exists. Most legends of child saints change very little over time, once set down, with the exception of early medieval versions of the *passios* of fourth century martyrs, which are embellished with fabulous miracles and litanies of tortures that camouflage the basic story of martyrdom.

Although this study is limited to Western Europe in the Middle Ages, the phenomenon of the child saint is of broader significance, and has been noted in a few sources. Many cults existed within the boundaries of the Roman Empire, but I have generally included only those which developed a following in the West. The Eastern Church maintains examples of similar trends, but these fall outside the scope of the present study. St. Mamas, the holy shepherd, is characterized as a young boy in the Eastern tradition, but appears as a young man in the West. The Russian Orthodox Church venerates the murdered princes, Boris and Gleb, who are sometimes depicted as children, but more usually as young men, as well as little St. Dmitri, the son of Ivan the Terrible who died in 1553. He is one of the patron saints of children in the Russian church. The Georgian Church recognizes the nine martyred children of Kola, pagan children who converted in order to play with the Christian children of the town, and were then murdered by their own parents.[50] Medieval Scandinavia, late to Christianize, exhibited neither imported nor indigenous cults of holy children. Child saints are found in relative profusion in the regions of Italy, France, Spain, Germany, the Low Countries, England, and Cornwall. Scotland, Ireland and Wales, however, possess few examples.

The vast majority of child saints would not be considered saints by the standards applied to adults. That the same standards of piety are not applied equally to children and adults is perhaps not surprising, but it is certainly significant. The suppression of dubious cults has long been a practice of the Catholic Church; the survival and success of so many of these cults dedicated to children is an indication of the need for such beliefs and practices in medieval society. Beyond this, the legends of these saints express significant evidence of attitudes toward childhood and the treatment of children. This work draws on an extensive array of significant achievements by many scholars in various fields. It is difficult and curiously unfashionable at present to label oneself a generalist or produce a general work spanning fifteen centuries and all of Western Europe. The specialist in a particular region or time period may note simplifications or omissions of topics that merit inclusion. This study is intended as an outline of an obscure yet interesting topic that has not to date been comprehensively treated.

CHAPTER 1

Christianus Sum: Child Martyrs of the Early Church

Thus, while anything like a numerical estimate of the number of martyrs is impossible, yet the meager evidence on the subject that exists clearly enough establishes the fact that countless men, women, and even children, in that glorious, though terrible, first age of Christianity, cheerfully sacrificed their goods, their liberties, or their lives, rather than renounce the faith they prized above all.[1]

-Catholic Encyclopedia

Attempts by the Romans to suppress the practice of Christianity from the late first to early fourth centuries provided the Church with its first and largest single group of recognized saints: the martyrs. During what is popularly known as the Age of Persecutions, those who died in defense of their Christian faith were venerated as examples of heroic virtue by the faithful; their stories were preserved and embellished in *passios* and their relics preserved in shrines.[2] Martyrdom was believed to represent the most perfect form of Christianity. Martyrdom erased all sin and allowed direct ascent to heavens, while providing an example to inspire the community of the faithful. The ordeal of voluntarily facing torture and death was considered to require the strength and dedication of an athletic contest, and was not for the weak of mind, body, or spirit. Children might be considered unlikely contestants in such a struggle, yet a number of child martyrs of this era are venerated in the western and eastern traditions. The actual number of martyrs is impossible to determine from existing sources, and is further complicated by the medieval proliferation of questionable relics and spurious legends. A number of such cults, however, are of great antiquity and demonstrable historicity.[3]

In contrast to the picture of martyrdom popularized by devotional literature and Hollywood productions, prosecution of Christians was not the result of Roman objections to any aspect of Christian doctrine, but rather motivated by the perceived threat to the social order seen in the Christian refusal to participate even nominally in the Imperial cult. Roman law and custom were generally tolerant of religious beliefs and practices from all regions of the Empire, although practices thought to be detrimental to society, such as human sacrifice or orgiastic frenzies, were occasionally suppressed.[4] While popular suspicion imputed similar practices to the Christians, such charges do not play a role in official proceedings. The perceived civil crime was contumacy. In the earliest contemporary reference to legal action against Christians, Pliny remarked

> I have asked them in person if they are Christian, and if they admit it, I repeat the question a second and third time, with a warning of the punishment awaiting them. If they persist, I order them to be led away for execution; for, whatever the nature of their admission, I am convinced that their stubbornness and unshakeable obstinacy ought not to go unpunished.[5]

He also noted that anyone who denied or recanted his beliefs should be let go, and that anonymous accusations should be ignored. The evidence of the early *passios* supports this picture of reluctant prosecution. Roman officials provided numerous opportunities for the accused to renounce their faith, make a token sacrifice to the Emperor, and go home. As the vast majority of Christians facing arrest easily avoided punishment by conforming to such requests, providing false documentation, or outright bribery,[6] the behavior of the martyrs was both inspirational and disquieting. Christians viewed such steadfast faith and courage as heroic, while the Romans viewed it as evasive and impudent.[7] Punishment, which included torture, imprisonment, deprivation, and public execution in the arena, could easily be avoided by what the Romans considered to be a minimal concession to the social order.

In outlining the proper conduct toward professed Christians brought before him, Pliny considered "whether any distinction should be made between them on the grounds of age, or if young people and adults should be treated alike."[8] Modern historians have asserted that no such distinction in treatment was made,[9] but the comment itself indicates that children and adolescents represented a noticeable percentage of those arrested, and that the law was prepared to draw a distinction between children and adults accused of the same crime. Accounts of the interrogation of children show attempts by the authorities to treat them more leniently than their adult companions, as though they were not expected to fully understand the consequences of their actions.

Views of childhood in classical antiquity stressed two principal themes, innocence and weakness, which may also be considered as different aspects of one general quality. In ancient Athens, children differed from adults in physical maturity, but perhaps more significantly in terms of moral development, lacking the resolve and purpose of the adult citizen.[10] In the Roman world, childhood was characterized by the dubious quality of *infirmitas,* which referred to both the vulnerability of the child to disease and accident, and the undeveloped capacity for reason. As reason was a quality highly prized among men, children were thus defined as mentally immature, and therefore weak.[11] In both cultures, children were seen as unformed individuals, both physically and morally, who must be educated in order to develop into responsible citizens. The child was a marginal member of society, like women, slaves, old men and barbarians, as opposed to the adult male citizen. In this scheme, the male child was expected to outgrow his *infirmitas,* while the female child never would.[12]

The life-and-death power of the Roman *paterfamilias* over his offspring has fostered the image of a stern and unloving patriarch; one historian of the Roman family has gpne so far as to claim that grief over the death of a child contained an element of selfishness, as the child would no longer be present to support the parents in old age.[13] Numerous sources, in fact, attest to the active role played by Roman fathers in overseeing the welfare of their children, while the influence of Roman mothers over their sons is the stuff of both history and legend.[14] Despite the acceptance of contraception, abortion, and the exposure of infants (the first two of which are regularly practiced in our own age,) parents invested considerable emotional and financial resources in childrearing, and Augustus instituted laws penalizing citizens who either did not marry or remained childless.[15] Parents were directly responsible for the moral education of their children, even in wealthy families.[16] For more practical matters, children of the Roman upper class were normally cared for by a female nurse, the *nutrix,* and a male *paedagogus,* before passing to the control of a tutor.[17] The influence of this surrogate family was recognized as a rival to the parents in contributing to the formation of the child's character and behavior, and the possibility of inferior slaves introducing a subversive influence was recognized by Roman society as well.[18] Several child martyrs were converted to Christianity by their nurse or tutor, and chose to die with them despite the pleas of their fathers.

While the weakness of children was recognized as appropriate to their age, and childish play was allowed and encouraged, the formal training which began at the age of seven carried the aim of replacing the characteristics of the *infans* with those of the adult. Children who exhibited particularly mature behavior were singled out for praise.[19] Since only male children would become citizens, they were the principal recipients of formal education, although females also received training and moral guidance.[20] The second stage of childhood, *pueritia*, ended for boys at the age of fourteen, when they were deemed capable of participating in war.[21] The end of childhood for girls, at approximately the same age, was marriage. While social status did not appreciably influence the stages of physical development common to all children, it dictated the quality of upbringing; the lower classes had few resources to invest in their offspring or their education. The role of the *deliciae,* children of the slave class kept as "pets" by the rich and appreciated for their childish charms but also used for sexual purposes, indicates the extent to which cultural factors influenced the concept and reality of childhood.[22]

The historian Tacitus contrasted the practice of infanticide among Roman matrons to the practices of the Germans, who raised all of their children from birth but invested little effort in their upbringing or education,[23] and the same observation can be made of Christian families. Christianity has been credited by some historians of the family with contributing to a new understanding and appreciation of children in the society of late antiquity, while other studies have emphasized continuity rather than abrupt change in family life and personal behavior.[24] The majority of Christians were vulnerable to the same sins found in pagan society, such as money lending, fornication, and slander, and undoubtedly exhibited failings as parents as well.[25] The Christian rejection of abortion, infanticide, and the exposure of infants[26] might seem to provide obvious affirmation of a higher value placed on childhood, yet Christian parents who raise all of their children from birth, but invested few resources in their development, could be considered poor parents by prevailing social standards. Pagan values which encouraged secular pursuits such as education and the training for public service were often rejected by Christians as irrelevant to the business of salvation.[27] The growth of infant baptism in this period may be evidence of the recognition of the spiritual equality of Christians of all ages,[28] although it may simply testify to parental anxiety over the eternal fate of beloved children in an age of high infant mortality.

Christianity had no power to alter the physical and material limitations affecting children, but it did influence concepts of childhood by increasing attention. "For the first time in history, it seemed important to decide what the moral status of children was. In the midst of this sometimes excessive concern, a new sympathy for children was promoted."[29] The eagerness of

Church leaders to end the practice of exposure of infants has been interpreted as a crucial first step toward the elevation of the status of children in western society.[30] The emphasis on chastity in Christian behavioral standards and the minimization of class distinctions extended the concept of sexual and moral innocence to all children, rather than a privileged few.[31] Ideals, however, do not always reflect reality, and labeling familiar practices as sinful does not always prevent people from sinning. The repeated prohibitions of infanticide and exposure of children throughout the Christian centuries illustrate the fallacy of confusing theory with practice in questions of behavioral control.[32]

Many aspects of the classical characterization of childhood were echoed in Christian thought. Childhood remained a time of physical and moral *infirmitas*. The child who did not act like a child was characterized as *puer senex,* an old child or "little old man." This image of childish superiority was transformed from a description of behavioral maturity to a more spiritual quality of precocity to fit the demands of hagiographical motifs in the *passios* of child martyrs and childhood episodes in the lives of adult saints.[33] The *puer senex* possessed the quality of adult rationality, "the extent to which his spirit was ahead of his years."[34] Christian use of the *puer senex* motif became a common *topos,* a manifestation of the theme of spiritual transcendence over the natural behavior of the age of *pueritia.*[35] Evocation of the *puer senex* was integral to the stories of the early child martyrs, because martyrdom was a manifestation of the grace of God, a difficult and heroic act attainable only by a very few. The child martyr, in overcoming youthful *infirmitas,* demonstrated strength in weakness, and thus attained heroic virtue.

The *passios* of the child martyrs are not in any sense reliable as historical accounts; they tend to be repetitive, derivative, and formulaic, and many minor cults predate their legends by several centuries.[36] In their earliest form, however, the stories exhibit a cohesive set of characteristics that often reveal plausible behavior meant to inspire the faithful. Most accounts of child martyrdoms are relatively undeveloped, reflecting the fact that these children usually did nothing worthy of note or emulation prior to their interrogation and execution. The young martyr must signify in some way that he or she explicitly accepts the consequences of steadfast faith. A brief allusion to the *puer senex* motif was generally used to signify the precocious understanding necessary to validate the legitimacy of martyrdom.

The most widely known child saints from this period are Agnes, Faith, Eulalia of Mérida, and Pancras. All were distinguished by their youth in the earliest records of their cults. Agnes was a girl of twelve or thirteen, Faith and Eulalia were twelve, and Pancras a youth of fourteen. While their ages straddle the boundary between childhood and adulthood, the *passios* of each preserve the theme of heroic and eloquent defense of the faith considered exceptional for one so young. The three girls are also honored as virgin martyrs, but early authors celebrated their martyrdom as a triumph over the weakness of childhood rather than the weakness of womanhood.

The cult of St. Agnes is one of the most ancient and widespread in Christianity. Her tomb was venerated under Constantine and subsequently honored by Popes Liberias, Symmachus, and Honorius, and the cult has left an extensive archaeological and literary record.[37] The antiquity of her cult is one of the most fully documented of all of the martyrs, and she was perhaps the most popular martyr in Rome after Peter and Paul.[38] Prudentius, Ambrose, Tertullian and Augustine each left accounts of her passion which contributed to her fame. Disagreement over the exact age of Agnes dates back to the patristic period; Tertullian and Ambrose identify her as a girl of twelve; Augustine and some manuscripts of Ambrose give her age as thirteen.[39] The story of Agnes was similar to those of many virgin martyrs; sought in marriage by the son of a powerful Roman, she chose virginity, spurned his advances, and was executed, but her bravery was especially noteworthy because of her youth. "Devotion beyond her age, virtue beyond her nature," declared Ambrose;[40] evoking the image of the *puer senex*, he wrote, "She was counted a child in years, but was old in her mind."[41] St. Jerome, acknowledging the popularity of the cult in his own era, wrote, "Agnes is praised in the writings and by the tongues of all nations, especially in the churches. She overcame the weakness of her age, conquered the cruelty of the tyrant, and consecrated her chastity to martyrdom."[42]

Agnes was honored repeatedly for possessing the "double crown" of martyrdom and virginity.[43] Prudentius placed primary emphasis on her martyrdom as a refusal to obey the impious laws and sacrifice to idols, but most writers, including Ambrose, concentrated on her virginity. Beginning with the *Vita Agnetis* of Ambrose, her martyrdom was attributed to her refusal of marriage to the son of a prefect.[44] Medieval versions of her legend embellished the consequences of her choice in lurid detail, but despite the blurring of distinction between youth and adulthood, her childishness continued to be emphasized to a degree not found in the legends of other martyrs to chastity. The lamb became her symbol.

Eulalia of Mérida, a girl of twelve martyred in Spain under Maximian for her refusal to sacrifice to idols, was another young virgin martyr honored by early Fathers of the Church. Like Agnes, she was also praised in a hymn by Prudentius, who referred to her as *puella* and *puellula* in addition to *virgo*.[45] Gregory of Tours provided a description her tomb in Mérida, and repeated the belief first mentioned by Prudentius that when she was martyred her soul ascended to heaven in the shape of a white dove.[46] Later recensions of her legend maintained her childish identity more fully than those of St. Agnes, but the story also became encrusted with fanciful occurrences meant to be manifestations of God's favor. Eulalia miraculously survived numerous tortures; she was stretched on a rack, torn with iron claws, and her sides were burned with flaming torches. She finally expired when fire was forced down her throat.[47]

The antiquity of the cult of St. Faith, or Ste. Foy, of Agen and Conques, another young girl martyr, is attested to by the testimony of Jerome,[48] and her relics were elevated at the beginning of the fifth century by St. Dulcidius, Bishop of Agen.[49] She was also subjected to numerous painful tortures, and miraculously survived being roasted on a brazen bed only to succumb to decapitation. Despite the similarities of her story to those of other child martyrs, however, extant versions of her legend do not predate the sixth century, and her greatest fame was reserved for the medieval dispute over the ownership of her relics.

Pancras was a pagan youth of fourteen who was converted to Christianity and baptized, along with his uncle Dionysius, during a trip made to Rome to claim an inheritance.[50] When Pancras appeared before Diocletian, the emperor was "astounded by his youth," and made a special plea to that effect in asking Pancras to sacrifice in order to save his life.[51] Pancras told Diocletian not to be deceived if he only saw before him a boy of fourteen, since the Lord had given him both knowledge and sense beyond his years. He then denounced the pagan gods before being sentenced to death. The cult of St. Pancras dates from at least the beginning of the sixth century. The basilica dedicated to St. Pancras on the Via Aurelia in Rome was built by Pope Symmachus, and rebuilt in the seventh century by Honorius.[52] His cult was mentioned by Gregory of Tours,[53] and his feast was celebrated by Gregory I.[54] The earliest surviving versions of the *passio* date from this period as well; while so late as to be considered unreliable, they nevertheless preserve the tradition of the child martyr remarkable for his wisdom and resolve.[55]

These young martyrs, although still children, were considered to be on the threshold of adulthood, appearing alone in their *passios* and acting independently. Much younger children also figured as martyrs. So young that they would be under the constant protection of family members, they were tried as part of the family group, and are depicted as showing plausible reactions to their surroundings. Family martyrdoms usually narrate the torture of family members in descending age, as though the sight were meant to dissuade the young child and allow for more lenient treatment. Youth could be considered a mitigating factor under Roman law, allowing children under the age of twelve to escape punishment as they were not of the age of discernment. Youth could also result in a less severe punishment. In an early version of the martyrdom of Agnes, the judge ordered the most mild form of execution, strangulation, in recognition of her reduced responsibility.[56] In a few cases, very young children were dismissed rather than executed. For Christians, the image of divinely inspired courage exhibited by these tiny victims provided an even greater contrast between expected and actual behavior for a young child. Few examples better illustrate the gulf between pagan and Christian values than the veneration of child martyrs whom the Romans tried particularly hard to dissuade from death.

St. Hilarion was still a young child [*infans*] when arrested with his family during the persecutions of Diocletian.[57] As the youngest member of the family, he was questioned last, and exhorted to recant his faith. Hilarion was not interested in the mercy of the court, but declared, "*Christanus sum* [I am a Christian] and I have been at the collect with my father and brothers willingly and of my own accord."[58] The foolish proconsul, who "did not understand that he was not fighting with men, but with God through the Martyrs,"[59] tried to frighten the child, saying "I will cut off your hair,[60] and your nose, and your ears, and so send you away."[61] The harsh threat was clearly intended to dissuade the child and save his life, albeit in a mutilated state. Hilarion refused to be swayed, however, saying, "Do whatever you wish to do, because I am a Christian."[62] The *passio* ends without specifying whether the threats were carried out, but grants eternal glory to the young martyr and his family. The cult of Hilarion and his family is of ancient origin, and is referred to by Augustine.[63]

St. Cyricus or Quiricus, who was martyred with his mother Julitta at Tarsus under Diocletian, met death at the tender age of three, in a manner considered to qualify as martyrdom, by proclaiming "*Christianus sum*" before he died. Although the profession of faith in one so young was, like that of Hilarion, seen as a manifestation of the grace of God, the circumstances in which it occurred could be historically plausible. Cyricus and Julitta were arrested with other Christians, and because Cyricus was so tiny, the prefect Alexander held the little child on his lap while his mother was tortured. To each of Julitta's agonized cries of *Christianus sum*, little Cyricus repeated, "I am a Christian, too."[64] His cries could be seen to demonstrate either the grace of God, or the repetitive language skills developmentally appropriate to a three-year-old. His recorded behavior was also indicative of a normal toddler. When Cyricus tried to run to his mother, the prefect restrained him. He then tried to free himself in typical toddler fashion by kicking and biting, and this display of temper provoked the prefect into dashing the child's brains out on the floor.

The doctrinal question of whether the martyrdom of Cyricus demonstrated a conscious profession of faith pales beside the antiquity and popularity of his cult. His legend, together with the legend of Hilarion, indicates that children were not intended targets of persecution. Children did not have to recant or denounce their faith in order to survive; they simply had to go away. Those children who did make a conscious profession of faith resulting in martyrdom were regarded as even more heroic than adults. The story of Cyricus also illustrates the fine and sometimes questionable line separating martyrdom from other fates. Cyricus was killed, not because he was a Christian, but because he was a naughty child who he misbehaved. Any objections to his veneration that might have been articulated have left no historical record, but a medieval version of the legend amplified his simple declaration to a miraculously learned theological argument, well beyond the natural capacity of any young child.[65] The cult enjoyed official promotion and widespread popularity throughout the Christian world, and similar questionable distinctions continued to be applied to later child saints.

The two most critical elements in the legends of Hilarion and Cyricus, utterance of the phrase *Christianus sum* and the reluctance of the authorities to punish children as severely as adults, occur in other *passios* as well. An unnamed boy, executed with Mark and Mucianus, was at first excluded from punishment because of his youth, but "vehemently" cried out that he, too, was a Christian.[66] He was at first merely beaten, but his persistence eventually resulted in his death.[67] Another young boy, Dioscorus, nearly met a similar fate. Arrested with three adult companions in the persecutions of Decius, he was not executed because of his youth, but simply whipped repeatedly and set free.[68] The child Paulillus, arrested during the Vandal persecutions, was at first excluded from torture because of his youth, but persisted in slipping back into the group to proclaim his faith. The authorities refused to execute a child, so he was beaten with rods and condemned to servitude. He died in captivity.[69] St. Rhais, a catechumen and the daughter of a Christian priest, also voluntarily joined a group of prisoners at Alexandria and was executed for declaring "I too am a Christian."[70] Sanctianus, Augustinus and Beata, three children of Spanish origin martyred in Gaul in the third century, were given several chances to retract their statements by the prefect because they were in the flower of youth, but they refused and so were executed.[71] Their cult dates from the time of Constantine, when a church in their memory was erected at Soissons.[72] Precocious speech is also seen in later stories. The Martyrs of Nagran consisted of some three hundred and forty Christians put to death in Arabia under the Jews in the sixth century. Among the group was a boy "five years old," who "in his lisping voice confessed Christ, and could not be silenced by promises or threats, but threw himself headlong into the fire where his mother was burning."[73]

Attempts by authorities to discourage martyrdom were by no means limited to children; in one of the most famous and reliable martyrdom accounts, Vibia Perpetua was exhorted to think of her newborn baby and her aged father and save her life by performing the sacrifice, but even these appeals did not shake her resolve to die for her faith.[74] Intense religious feelings and the conversion impulse are seen throughout history to occur in adolescence, as can be documented in the *vitae* of many saints;[75] younger children may be similarly inspired by the examples of parents and family. The recurrence of this theme in the hagiography of the child martyrs may represent the actual emotions of child zealots, the logical and tragic result of a close emotional relationship with parents and family, or an attempt to foster appreciation for such dedication within the Christian community, and especially to cultivate similar emotions in less exemplary children.

In several legends of family martyrdom, parents followed the example of the mother of the Maccabees[76] and nobly postponed their own death in order to perform the even more heroic task of encouraging their children to precede them in sanctity. The *passio* of Barulas, who suffered with St. Romanus, described him as a young child of seven years, but Prudentius specified that he was so young that he was not yet weaned.[77] Despite his considerable youth, Barulas was nevertheless able to articulate a surprisingly sophisticated argument in favor of the one true God which astounded his interrogator. When asked who provided him with these words, Barulas responded, "My mother, and the God of my mother."[78] In other words, his mother taught him to talk, and instructed him in faith, but God provided him with the inspiration for his knowledge. Shortly thereafter, his tongue was cut out. In recounting the tale, Prudentius further stressed the youth of Barulas by exhorting the child to drink from the same vessel as the little children of Bethlehem, while forgetting the milk and breasts appropriate to his age.[79] The mother of Barulas, repressing her own feelings during the torture, evoked the example of the mother of the seven Maccabees. She glorified the role of martyrdom for her son, and expressed the belief that, as her son was a part of her, so his death would bring glory on them both.[80] The support of his mother allowed little Barulas to die happily.[81]

St. Justus of Beauvais was a nine-year-old Christian boy who refused to denounce his relatives in hiding to the Roman soldiers. He confessed his own Christianity instead, and was summarily beheaded. His mother, informed of his death, reacted by praising God: "I give thanks to you, God the father of Heaven and Earth, who has taken back this innocent and pure soul." She then asked her son Justus to pray for her.[82] Justus appears in Christian folklore as one of the cephalophores, or head-carrying saints. The oldest surviving version of the legend is though to be from the eighth century; the headless body stood upright, frightening the soldiers away, and the miraculous child thoughtfully carried his head home to his mother. The cult of Justin of Paris, diffused after the ninth century, is a close copy of the cult of Justus of Beauvais.[83]

Theognis, Agapitus, and Pistus, three young boys martyred at Edessa, were sent to martyrdom with the exhortations of their mother, who followed them in that fate shortly thereafter.[84] There is no evidence of any significant western cult for these martyrs, but the story is a common one. The spurious Acts of SS. Faith, Hope, and Charity, and their mother Wisdom (Sophia or Sapientia), composed in the sixth century, parallel this story almost exactly, with a greater smattering of blood and gore.[85] The saga of the young girls is included in the *Golden Legend*. Saints Felicitas and Symphorosa[86] each exhorted their seven sons to martyrdom. The twelve-year-old son of St. Conon shared both torments and martyrdom with his father, who was a deacon in the Church.[87] St. Crescentius was also martyred with his father, St. Euthymius.[88] Eleutherius or Deutherius was a newly-baptized child who was martyred with his father, Longinus, in Gaul.[89] In some versions of the story, Deutherius was a child who died while praying at the tomb of St. Victor of Marseilles, and was honored as a confessor. Many similar stories preserve only the names of children, or include as nameless victims of a group martyrdom, such as the ten children martyred with SS. Philip, Zenon and Narses, or the many children martyred with St. Fort. St. Valens is said to have been martyred with three boys.[90] St. Julianus was martyred with Basilissa, a young girl of marriageable age, Celsus, a young boy, and seven boys who were brothers.[91]

While the family relationship was depicted as an important source of inspiration for the child martyr, and the miraculous courage of the weak and helpless child meant to serve as an example to the larger Christian community, direct interaction with the community occasionally occurred. St. Flocel, a boy martyred at Autun in the third century, was said to have encouraged his companions to accept their fate by telling them not to fear the rack, the whipping, or being thrown to the beasts.[92] An undated *passio* depicted Flocel comforting his companions with the words of Christ to the Apostles, "Do not fear those who can bring death to the body, but rather fear those who can condemn the body and soul to hell."[93] St. Neophytus, the child of Christian parents, gained a reputation for piety in childhood and was an example to his schoolmates, before turning himself in for martyrdom at the age of fifteen.[94]

A number of young boys also found the path to martyrdom away from the direct influence of their parents, in the schoolyard. SS. Justus and Pastor, martyred in Alcalà under Diocletian, were two brothers who ran away from school one day when they heard that a search was being made for Christians. Turning themselves in and boldly confessing their faith, they achieved martyrdom.[95] The cult of the two saints predates the acts by several centuries; their relics were venerated from the late fourth century, while the legend developed in the seventh century.[96] Arezzo in Tuscany claims a similar pair of brothers, Pergentinus and Laurentius, who rose from the schoolyard directly to heaven via the path of martyrdom.[97] St. Artemas, a legendary schoolboy-saint of Puteoli, was harassed by his pagan teacher and classmates, and finally suffered martyrdom when they stabbed him to death with the pens used to inscribe their wax tablets.[98] Although such legends may simply be derived from the story of St. Cassian of Imola, they suggest the relative strength of Christian faith over childish peer pressure, as well as the potential dangers of a classical education.

The intent of such stories may have been to separate Christian children as much possible from the surrounding pagan environment. Although these literary motifs may have produced an atmosphere of turgid Christianity, with a potent effect on children, the child martyr was not necessarily the child of Christian parents. Several belonged to wealthy or aristocratic pagan families, and were converted through the efforts of a nurse or tutor. As Christianity in the early centuries often spread through the lower strata of society, such a situation was no doubt possible, and might have reflected societal fears of the undermining of the integrity of the familia such as that expressed in the story of Vibia Perpetua.

The story of St. Vitus also draws from the narrative of Vibia Perpetua. St. Vitus, martyred in Sicily, was born of pagan parents but was converted to Christianity by his tutor, Modestus, and his nurse, Crescentia. The passio is noteworthy for its description of the conflict between pagan father and Christian son. In trying to force a recantation from Vitus, his father tried affection, tears, persuasion, and finally anger. When these methods failed, Vitus was taken to the prefect by his father in desperation. The prefect, Valerian, was incredulous at the boy's flouting of convention. Why, asked the prefect, since Vitus was no more than a child, did he resist the wishes of his father, and not submit himself to the laws of the emperor?[99] The resolve of the boy in the face of such pressures may be attributed to the power of

God, but it also indicates the disquieting social effects of Christianity. While martyrdom may have promoted solidarity among Christian families, it was a divisive force in pagan households.

The legend of St. Christina of Bolsena, while even less reliable than that of St. Vitus, exhibits the same elements of familial conflict. Despite questionable elements in the legend, the cult of the young martyr can be traced from the fourth century.[100] Converted to Christianity at the age of eleven by a slave in the household, Christina melted down her father's idols and used the proceeds to distribute money to the poor. Her father had her whipped, and finding himself still unable to control her behavior, denounced her to the authorities. His first approach, however, was based upon affection. "'My only daughter, for whom I have labored...''...Don't call me your daughter,'" she responded, claiming instead to be the daughter of God in heaven.[101] His own parental authority challenged, the father appealed to the greater authority of the state, and his daughter was executed.

Several stories pit Christian children, encouraged by Christian slaves, against their pagan parents. St. Devota, patron of Monaco and Corsica, was raised as a Christian by her nurse, and was martyred during the persecutions of Diocletian when she could not be made to sacrifice to idols. Although born of pagan parents, "she was a Christian from early childhood [*ab infantia*]"[102] The *passios* seldom credit slaves with the conversion of the children, rather implying the grace of God. As in the case of Eulalia of Mérida, a white dove flew from her mouth when she died. The brothers Cantius and Cantian, with their sister Cantianilla, were converted to Christianity by their tutor, Protus, and eventually martyred by soldiers of Diocletian. In this case, the tutor was given a prominent position in the *passio*.[103] Tradition held that they were of the blood of the emperor. Other children of noble pagan blood who converted to Christianity and became martyrs were Prisca, Restituta of Sora, Columba of Sens, Potitus, Ansanus, and Cyril of Caesarea. Prisca, Restituta and Columba were of pagan aristocratic background, but engaged in only minimal conflict with their fathers. Prisca is recorded as suffering martyrdom under Claudius I for refusing to sacrifice to idols; although her acts are a forgery, there is evidence of a very early cult in Rome, and she is considered a protomartyr of the West.[104] Restituta "overcame in a combat for the faith the violence of the demons, the caresses of her family, and the cruelty of the executioners."[105] Her family reacted to her conversion more with sadness than with anger. She was converted by St. Cyril, and was martyred under Aurelian. Columba of Sens was born of an aristocratic pagan family, but left them at the age of sixteen to travel to Gaul. A later version of the legend reduced her age to seven. She was martyred near Meaux, under Aurelian.[106]

The conversion of a son may have distressed pagan parents more than the loss of a daughter. Potitus, the only son of a rich man, converted to Christianity while very young and remained Christian despite the threats of his father. Although the legend may not predate the ninth century, the name of Potitus is mentioned in several early martyrologies, including Jerome, Florus and Bede. Florus gave the boy's age as thirteen.[107] St. Ansanus converted at the age of twelve, and was denounced by his father. He fled Rome for Siena, and earned the title of "the Baptizer" before his execution.[108] The young Cyril of Caesarea,[109] like Christina, would no longer adore the idols in his house, and so was expelled by his father. He was later beheaded for his refusal to sacrifice.[110] Pagan parents were not the only victims of the conversion impulse in their children; St. Lucius was a Jewish youth who converted to Christianity and was killed by his Rabbi father. Christians were expected to place allegiance to God above the sense of duty to pagan family members in both theory and practice, but the family tensions revealed in these and other *passios* present a convincing portrait of parental reaction, not only to the worship of different gods, but to the greater problem of the undermining of the authority of the paterfamilias.

Child martyrs also defied community standards by refusing to sacrifice to the gods of their families and actively attacking the public manifestations of pagan cults. St. Glyceris suffered martyrdom as a young girl at Heraclea under Antoninus;[111] as the daughter of Christians, she took an active role in protesting elements of pagan religion. During a pagan feast, she entered a temple and crossed herself; a later version of the *passio* depicts her as a full-fledged idol-smasher.[112] Although her legend contains many fanciful circumstances surrounding her martyrdom, the cult seems to be of genuine antiquity.[113] St. Dominica, said to have suffered martyrdom in the time of Diocletian, was also an iconoclast. "For having destroyed idols, she was condemned to the beasts, but being uninjured by them she was beheaded and went to the Lord."[114] The legend of St. Salsa of Tipasa dates from the late fourth century,[115] and records a detailed series of events which pit the young girl against the local snake-god. Taken by her parents to a festival of the deity, she waited until the others were asleep, then entered the temple, struck off the head of the statue, and threw it into the sea. When the others awoke and saw what she had done, they threw her into the sea. Salsa was included in the Martyrology of Jerome, and her cult was widespread in Spain during the time of the Vandals, when Christians migrated northward from North Africa. The cult of the serpent was known to have been celebrated in the region, and archaeological excavations in Tipasa have uncovered evidence of both pagan and subsequent Christian edifices along the sea coast.[116] If the legend of St. Salsa does no more than embody the conflict between newly-arrived Christians and the indigenous pagan cult, it exemplifies this struggle in the person of a single young girl.

The child martyr, as the earliest manifestation of the child saint, set the tone for later centuries and opened the door to myriad questionable practices. Children were popular images for the promotion of Christian faith, precisely because children were less likely than adults to possess the courage, fortitude, and insight required of martyrdom. For the early Church, divine intervention played a major role. The steadfast faith of the child martyr, although demonstrated in diverse ways, was officially promoted not as a virtue of the individual, but as the gift of God. Popular audiences, on the other hand, granted a more active role to children, as the legends which developed over centuries placed them in a variety of socially significant roles. Plausible behavior, however, ran the risk of clashing with hagiographical intent. While the profession of Christianity through the words *Christianus sum* ensured the legitimacy of martyrdom, the question of intent remained. Legends of a later date mingled the conscious acts of the martyrs with an increasing variety of miraculous deeds and excruciating torments survived by the power of God. The tension between the roles of active champion of the faith and passive conduit of divine grace was never fully resolved. Through the logical extension of the motif of childish passivity, sanctity could even be achieved by that most helpless of creatures, the infant.

CHAPTER 2

Infant Saints: The Cult of the Holy Innocents

> Then Herod, when he saw that he had been tricked by the wise men, was in a furious rage, and he sent and killed all the male children in Bethlehem and in all that region who were two years old or under, according to the time which he had ascertained from the wise men.[1]
>
> *-Matthew* 2:16

The child martyrs of late antiquity, while never a significant group in terms of size or prestige, presented a clearly defined and compelling image to early Christians. Child martyrs found the strength to defy pagan society, secular authority, and even, at times, their own parents, and provide inspiration to the adults around them. As the object of the hagiographer was to inspire the faithful rather than to record actual events, the multiplication of tales of heroic children indicates that the motif appealed to the Christian community on a level that could not be met by the many stories of adult martyrs. In an era where approximately one third of all children died in the first year of life,[2] grieving parents may have derived some comfort from the thought of God's favor bestowed on children who faced death so bravely; thoughts of the faithful parents who encouraged their children to seek death in the promise of a blessed eternity may also have provided support. Recognizing children as martyrs allowed for the veneration of their relics as well, an important aspect of the cult of the martyrs since the second century.

As has been seen, the cults of child martyrs were carefully presented within a doctrinal framework that included, as basic ingredients, an explicit profession of faith, such as the proclamation *Christianus sum,* and an evocation of the *puer senex* motif to indicate the exceptional nature of the child in question. These characteristics were fairly uniformly applied to children from three to thirteen, despite the decreasing likelihood of verisimilitude with the reduction of age in the subject. Increasingly, the treatment of child saints in the literature of the early Church demonstrated a shift in the conception of childhood from that of pagan antiquity. Just as the weakness of the child martyr validated the grace of God more perfectly than in the adult, so the quality of weakness in the child was transformed into a type of perfection unattainable by adults.

> …let us pose the question of childhood. Let us see if any crime can be found therein, if greed, ambition, guile, rage, and insolence are there. It claims nothing for its own, assumes no honours for itself, knows not how to prefer itself to another, knows no guile, does not wish to and cannot avenge itself. Its pure and simple mind cannot comprehend the meaning of insolence.[3]

In Christian thought, the defining behavioral characteristic of childhood was no longer represented by *infirmitas*, but by a superior state of innocence and virtue. By awarding moral superiority to the innocent child rather than the rational adult, Christianity turned the pagan concept of childhood upside down. If innocent childhood was more pleasing to God than the sinful state of adulthood, then the younger the child, the more perfect and closer to God. It would logically follow that the greatest virtue would be found in newborn infants.

The cult of the Holy Innocents, as the infant victims of Herod's legendary wrath came to be known, represented the most successful adaptation of the theme of the child martyr in the history of the Church. They are considered protomartyrs of the Church because they died in place of Christ. The infants were honored as martyrs from the end of the second century, and their feast was incorporated into calendars by the later fifth century. The Leonine Sacramentary, ca. 485, but claiming to incorporate traditions dating to the mid-4th century, placed the Feast of the Holy Innocents in the month of December, but gave no specific date. The earliest verifiable mention of a feast on a specific date in honor of the Holy Innocents was found in the Calendar of Carthage, ca. 505.[4] Relics of the Innocents were venerated in Jerusalem, Rome, and countless churches throughout the medieval west. In the popular imagination, the Holy Innocents were memorialized in verse, letters, and iconography.

The immense popularity of this cult has obscured several fundamental objections to its legitimacy. By any objective historical measure, the incident itself never took place; neither, however, did many of the martyrdoms commemorated by the faithful. If a massacre did occur, the children were martyred for a religion which did not yet exist. Since the massacre predated the practice of baptism, the children died with the stain of original sin on their souls, so that martyrdom could not earn them a place in heaven. If these objections were overlooked, the scenario would still present the faithful with a group of martyrs who were incapable of even comprehending of their fate, much less willingly accepting death as witnesses to faith. The cult of the Holy Innocents perfectly exemplifies both the substantial difficulty of promoting children as saints and the immense popularity of doing so.

No historical corroboration for the massacre of the Innocents exists. Josephus, the principal source for Herod's reign, failed to mention the slaughter of the Innocents even though he did not hesitate to record numerous other atrocities.attributed to Herod. In the fifth century, Macrobius attributed to Herod the massacre of a group of Syrian children under the age of two, but since he included Herod's own son among the victims, the incident was clearly fictional.[5] The execution of targeted groups of children may have been a motif borrowed from Roman culture; according to Suetonius, the emperor Augustus survived such an incident in his childhood,[6] and Nero ordered the execution of the children of those who conspired against him.[7] The purpose of the Gospel story was undoubtedly to highlight the miraculous survival of such a tragedy by the infant Jesus, rather than to create an indeterminate number of anonymous protomartyrs.

The popular appeal of the cult may be explained in terms of human emotional response to the fate of the helpless infants, and the enthusiasm of the faithful for the relics of martyrs. In the relic trade, the Holy Innocents could function in much the same way as the much later eleven thousand virgins martyred with St. Ursula; since the number of children killed was unknown, a limitless supply of relics was thereby made available to the faithful. While modern estimates of the number of victims, ignoring the fictional nature of the incident, range between six and forty,[8] medieval claims ran into the thousands. From earliest times, however, the popularity of the Holy Innocents depended more upon quality than quantity. Fathers of the Church such as Augustine, Cyprian, Irenaeus, and Peter Chrysologus actively promoted the cult, defending it against doctrinal challenges.

The principal objection raised to veneration of the infants in the early centuries was the problem of whether they, or any babies, were able to demonstrate intent. Martyrs showed the power of their faith, and of God, by deliberately choosing over life. How could an infant, incapable of autonomous speech or movement, make the profession of faith necessary to signify acceptance of martyrdom? "In the case of the infant, where nature itself was still held captive, what will power was present, or what act of decision?"[9] Peter Chrysologus acknowledged this objection to insist that martyrdom was derived from grace, rather than through the merit of any particular action. The child martyrs who insisted on the divine source of their remarkable courage laid the groundwork for the bestowal of sanctity on helpless infants. If the martyrdom of children demonstrated the power of God rather than the qualities of the individual, then even the limitations of infancy could not defeat the Divine plan. In the case of the Holy Innocents, the action of martyrdom and the grace attained through the act became passive and circumstantial.

Rather than raising insurmountable difficulties, the youth of the victims became the principal justification for the cult. "An age not yet fit for battle was fit for the crown," said Cyprian,[10] using the image of the slaughtered toddlers to inspire other Christians to fortitude in the face of the persecutions. Chrysologus noted that "[t]heir tongues have been silent, their eyes have seen nothing, their hands have done nothing."[11] Physical incapacity was transformed into a state of moral innocence. While the infants were unable to profess their faith, they were also unable to commit any sins. Christ in his infancy had not yet preached a doctrine of Christianity to which the infants could profess allegiance; the act of martyrdom, therefore, could only be made legitimate and comprehensible by viewing it as a corporeal rather than a spiritual action. Although they could not comprehend the full import of their actions, and did not volunteer for such a fate, the Innocents died for Christ in a very real way. Through their example, baptism by blood became an acceptable substitute for baptism by spirit.[12]

A controversy similar to the viability of the cult of the Innocents, but with more immediate significance for many Christians, was the question of infant baptism.[13] Infants do not understand the significance of the sacrament of baptism, and must be sponsored by adults who will speak for them, but they do possess bodies capable of undergoing the ritual. The debate over allowing infant baptism was framed on one side by objection to conducting a ritual without the acknowledgement of intent on the part of the subject, and on the other side by the very real concern that the child would not live long enough to participate by choice. The Church was adamant in its assertion that unbaptized children would be excluded from the beatific vision, although it allowed the creation of Limbo to preserve such children from the eternal torments of Hell.[14] Children who died in albis, wearing the white garment associated with baptism, were popularly thought to gain immediate entrance into heaven. Loving parents wished to erase the stain of original sin, and prevent the loss of eternal life along with earthly life, as soon as possible. Since the Holy Innocents did not understand that they suffered for Christ, but their bodies could undergo death in His place, their example bolstered the case for infant baptism.

"As no act came from them, where would guilt come from?"[15] asked Chrysologus. This question marks a crucial development in the popular understanding of martyrdom. Other child martyrs were killed because they actively confessed their faith and steadfastly refused to recant their beliefs. The Holy Innocents, with no faith to confess and no power of speech to express their thoughts, went to a blameless and unjustified death. Unlike the child martyrs whose behavior was notably unchildlike, no hint of the *puer senex* intruded into descriptions of the Innocents, who were instead portrayed realistically as normal, helpless babies.

> The infant smiled at his slayer. The child made fun of the sword. The babe in arms saw, in the place of his nurse, the frightfulness of the man ready to strike. The tender-aged boy so soon to die, and scarcely aware of the light, rejoiced. An infant son looks to every man, not as a foe, but as a parent.[16]

The image of happy, laughing infants reaching out in play toward the men who would viciously kill them was emotionally compelling and more than a bit manipulative. Bereaved parents who had lost infants or children of their own could find in the graphic descriptions of the slaughter of the Holy Innocents a catharsis and a comfort for the grief caused by the untimely death of their own innocent. The suffering of the infants was matched by the agony of their mothers; the children were literally torn from the breasts at which they nursed to be run through with the sword, so that their blood was mingled with their mothers' milk.[17] Just as the Innocents were baptized with their blood, their grieving mothers were baptized with their tears, and so presumably earned a share of God's grace. Presenting the slaughter of the Innocents in such extreme terms may have helped to assuage the suffering of parents who lost children in less gruesome circumstances.

The writings of Paulinus of Nola also suggest that parents who had lost children of their own would find comfort in the cult of the Holy Innocents. Paulinus had lost his only son as an infant, and buried the tiny remains near the tomb of the child martyrs Justus and Pastor.[18] In a hymn to parents who had lost their own eight-year-old child, Paulinus wrote

> You must take consolation from my words, and with hope in the truth revive your spirits. Believe that Celsus, whom you jointly love, is enjoying the milk and honey of the living in the light of heaven. Kindly Abraham has him in his arms and nurtures him, and Lazarus benignly feeds him with water from his finger, or he is in paradise with the children of Bethlehem, whom the wicked Herod struck down out of jealousy, and he is playing in a scented glade, weaving garlands as a reward for the martyrs' glory.[19]

Entry into the afterlife depended upon exemplary conduct in life; the path to heaven was difficult and uncertain. A brief life, ended unexpectedly through accident or illness, might not have allowed sufficient time either to demonstrate merit or prepare for a final judgment. The words of Paulinus not only comforted the parents with the image of their child in Heaven, but also reassured them with realistic references to the necessary care given to young children. Like the Holy Innocents, no special demonstration of faith was necessary for children to enter into their eternal reward; as Paulinus said of Celsus, "Your age was young, but your merits great, your life short in years but powerful in its godliness."[20]

Just as parents who have lost a beloved child may question the concept of a loving God, early writers tried to explain the divine wisdom which would allow babies to suffer such pain in the name of Christ. Chrysologus declared that only Herod could be blamed, since the babies had done nothing, and the infant Jesus had done nothing to provoke the soldiers.[21] Such an argument may have been useful in diffusing parental resentment and self-recrimination, as the Holy Innocents were not only innocent victims, they were also innocent by proxy. The infant Jesus did not merit death any more than the children who died in his place.

Of all of the child martyrs, the Holy Innocents received by far the most attention in patristic writings. Ecclesiastical interest in the cult of the Holy Innocents may have been grounded in the popular appeal of the tiny and helpless victims, but its demonstrable significance is in the amount of theological convolution necessary to justify the authenticity of the cult. In recognizing the qualities of childish innocence and unjust death as equal to conscious spiritual motivation, the Fathers of the Church legitimized a popular understanding of martyrdom that extended to children who died in even more doctrinally questionable circumstances than the Holy Innocents. Ultimately, all such cults demonstrate the pliability of doctrine in the face of popular belief.

In recognition of the sympathy surrounding those who died young, the early Church accorded veneration to certain children who died in religious circumstances. The cult of the child-martyr Agnes inspired the worship of a second young girl of the same age named Emerentiana, whose cult can be traced from the fifth century. Eemrentiana was a catechumen who was stoned to death while praying at the tomb of Agnes, traditionally identified as her foster-sister, two days after her death.[22] Her relics were deposited with those of her more famous associate, and she was honored as a virgin martyr.[23] Although a *passio* attributed to St. Ambrose awarded her a baptism of blood, noting "...there is no doubt that she was baptized in blood, who, for the defense of justice, while confessing to the Lord, steadfastly accepted death,"[24] the justification is problematic. Her death was a result of mob violence rather than a conscious defense of Christian faith, and as a catechumen, she was not yet baptized. Like the Holy Innocents, Emerentiana entered the ranks of the blessed as the result of a violent attack. The attribution of the term *catechumena* established the purity and innocence of her youth.

Sanctity by association was also used to create the boy saint Deutherius, or Eleutherius. Just as Emerentiana was honored because she was killed at the tomb of St. Agnes, Eleutherius died while praying at the tomb of his father, the martyr St. Longinus. While the surroundings were similar, the circumstances were not, for Eleutherius apparently died of natural causes. It is unclear whether he was sanctified for his action of prayer, the location of his death, or his youth, but the *puer senex* motif was evoked by the statement that "the infant showed a man's spirit."[25]

The early Church, in addition to celebrating the courage and faith of children martyred under a variety of circumstances, also extended recognition to the *innocenti* who died of natural causes soon after baptism. These children, honored as confessors, gave little or no indication of pious behavior or good works before death, but were venerated simply because they died young, in a childish state of innocence. Like the catechumen Emerentiana, newly baptized children were often described as *in albis*, wearing the white garment of purity.

Several child confessors of this era came from saintly families. St. Gelasius of Piacenza died in the early fifth century, "in the white innocence of his baptismal robes."[26] One night the child heard his brother praying, and received a dream or vision of the angels singing "Suffer the little children to come unto me, for of such is the kingdom of heaven."[27] Gelasius died soon afterwards. His relics were preserved and venerated in the Church of St. Savin, and translated to a new church of the same name in 1484.[28] Although his cult was justified on the grounds of his innocence and untimely death, Gelasius may have benefited from his family connections as the brother of saints Olympus and Opilius. The cult of St. Lusor of Deols was considered to be of great antiquity in the time of Gregory of Tours.[29] Lusor was the son of a third century Roman senator, Leocadius, who gave the best of his possessions in Gaul to St. Ursinus, first bishop of Bourges. Lusor also died *in albis*, inspiring the tradition that he died as a child.[30] The tomb, which survived into the present century, contains designs of a hunt and a banquet, and nothing of a specifically Christian character.[31] Nothing exists to explain the religious significance of Lusor's death, other than his relationship to a wealthy senator with Christian leanings, and a reputation for having died in the innocence of youth. St. Dentlin of Cleves is similarly worshipped for no other reason than an uneventful yet innocent demise. His veneration is generally explained by the proliferation of saints in his family.

An extreme example of venerating the newly-baptized dead is that of St. Justinianus, who died at the age of four days. A childless pagan couple was converted to Christianity by Martial, Bishop of Limoges, when he promised a cure of their infertility. The couple conceived a child, and set out to inform the Bishop of the miracle. The baby, Justinianus, was born during the journey, and taken to Martial to be baptized, but died on the return trip at the same spot where he had been born. The four-day-old infant was venerated as a saint by the local population, and many posthumous miracles were reported.[32] The death of this child, conceived in order to demonstrate the power of God and effect the conversion of his parents, may seem like a cruel joke, rather than the basis for veneration of a saint. It is not recorded whether the couple remained Christians after the loss of their promised son. Certainly the only miracle in the life of Justinianus was his birth, rather than his death. The rise of the cult may indicate popular sympathy for grieving parents who had lost a child, in the same way as the cult of the Holy Innocents, but this is pure speculation. The only indisputable basis for the cult was the youth, innocence, and untimely death of Justinianus.

Some children may have made the decision to emulate adult saints, rejecting the habits of childhood and embracing a life of pious asceticism. The *vitae* of many saints record the ways in which their subjects precociously demonstrated the piety which was recognized later in life. Athanasius recorded that St. Anthony as a child avoided both the games and the thoughtlessness typical of boys, and refused to listen to children's stories, but wished to stay at home with his parents.[33] Sulpicius Severus reported that St. Martin ran away to a church at the age of ten and tried to become a catechumen without the knowledge of his parents, and spent his boyhood pondering the works of the Church. A youthful wish at the age of twelve to become a hermit in the desert, however, was defeated by "the weakness of his age."[34] St. Simeon Stylites the Younger ascended his first pillar, a training pillar only five feet high, at the tender age of seven. Few such examples are found among the ranks of the child saints because, unlike martyrdom, piety and asceticism did not result in immediate death, but several children earned the reputation of sanctity through this route.

St. Musa, a young girl whose story was told in the *Dialogues* of Gregory the Great, died in the sixth century after receiving a vision. While asleep one night, she dreamt of the Virgin Mary, who showed her a group of little girls in white and told her that she would join them in thirty days if she was very good and did not act like the other children around her. Upon awakening, Musa reformed her errant ways and was obedient to her parents, who were amazed at the change in her behavior. She died at the end of the thirty days.[35] While some might take issue with the contention that behaving politely, rather than acting like a normal child, constitutes holiness worthy of sanctity, Gregory followed the story of Musa with that of a young boy who received no correction from his father, and had a habit of swearing and bad behavior. He also died at a young age, but instead of receiving a comforting vision of heaven, he was dragged off to Hell by demons. Gregory also noted that "Even though we must believe that all baptized children who die in their infancy go to heaven, we should not suppose that all children, once they have learned how to speak, will enter the kingdom of heaven."[36] Gregory's examples combined the pagan view of childhood as weakness with the Christian view of childhood as innocence. The further a child progresses from birth, the greater the likelihood of sin; good intent must be present, and lack of sin is not natural to the state of childhood.

The inclusion of Musa in the ranks of the blessed is based more on her immortalization by Gregory than on any substantial *cultus* centered on her relics.[37] Other children demonstrated greater fortitude. St. Neophytus, the child of pious Christian parents, was an example to all of his schoolmates in the matter of piety. He became a hermit at the age of nine when instructed to do so by a dove with a human voice. At the age of fifteen, he voluntarily presented himself for martyrdom.[38] St. Romana or Calpurnia of Todi was a young girl who became a Christian and was baptized by St. Sylvester without the knowledge of her pagan aristocratic parents. She became a recluse in a cave, and died, worn out by her asceticism, at the age of either 12 or 18.[39] These stories were meant to caution, as well as inspire, children and parents. Children may possess the potential for holiness, but attainment of that state requires conscious effort. These examples, while few and far between, began to emphasize the attributes of a pious life rather than simply a sudden death.

Although the attributes of sanctity were recognized in child confessors as well as child martyrs, the moral fortitude required for attainment of either state severely limited the number of each group, especially with the ending of the persecutions. The more passive route to sanctity pioneered by the champions of the Holy Innocents, however, provided an outlet for the popular urge to venerate children. The cult of the saints, with its emphasis on the efficacy of the blood and bodily remains of its heroes, was viewed with distaste by the ancient world.[40] As Christianity spread throughout Europe in the second half of the first millennium, the legends and relics of the saints met as dispersed by missionaries were met with great enthusiasm, transcending chronological and geographical boundaries. The acceptance of existing child saints and the recognition of new ones by medieval society provide the real beginning of this study.

CHAPTER 3

Translations and Inventions: The Veneration of Child Martyrs in Medieval Europe

T he introduction of the Roman child-martyrs to the religious communities of medieval Europe developed, as with saints' cults in general, through the spread of relics, the promulgation of legends, and inclusion in the liturgy. Many classical cults did not retain popularity in the Middle Ages; The *Golden Legend,* the most widely known collection of medieval saints' legends, dedicates only eight out of two hundred and forty-three entries to child saints.[1] A number of early cults, however, achieved substantial fame in medieval Christendom. Others sustained regional popularity, and several inspired derivative cults of saints with similar names, legends and attributes, but no historical or archaeological evidence for the antiquity claimed by the promoters of the cults. Sufficient ecclesiastical and popular support for the cults of children can be found to assert that the concept of the child saint was accepted and promoted throughout medieval Europe.

The relic trade was perhaps the most important route of transmission for the cults. While Rome largely controlled the spread of relics in the early Middle Ages, sending bones and other objects as gifts for church dedications, the central Middle Ages witnessed a great increase in the widespread trade and theft of relics, pursuits both pious and commercial.[2] Medieval relics found many commercial applications beyond the initial gift or sale; they functioned as "fund-raisers" for churches and monastic communities by attracting pilgrims who would leave donations. Religious construction projects were frequently financed by a tour of the community's relics through the surrounding area, combined with a recitation of the legend of the saint and the miraculous cures produced. The custodians of powerful relics also enjoyed the intangible benefits of prestige and influence conferred by the reputation of the saints.[3] The initial spread of individual cults can be seen as official promotion, while the less regulated diffusion of relics in the central Middle Ages represented acceptance of the cults in the form of popular demand. As Patrick Geary has noted,[4] the transfer of relics from one location to another did not result in the transfer of the regional cultural or religious values associated with the relics in their original setting. Many relics of child saints were undoubtedly traded or acquired for commercial rather than spiritual reasons, with little or no consideration for the identity of the saintly source. Relics of the Holy Innocents, especially, were frequently used to enhance larger collections, such as the "shoulder-bone of one of the Holy Innocents" contained in the relic collection of Peterborough in the twelfth century.[5] An examination of the spread of the cults of child saints, therefore, must consider the legendary and liturgical evidence as well as tracing the movement of relics. The presence of relics in any region does not assure special devotion to the saint.

Medieval Europe was acquainted with the image of the child saint, and specifically the child as martyr, from the advent of Christianity. The areas of Europe which had been under Roman control possessed a tradition of indigenous martyrs which included some children. The cults of Justus of Beauvais and Eulalia of Mérida, both located in relatively well-populated areas, enjoyed sustained veneration in their localities and widespread reputations which encouraged pilgrimage. The cult of Ste. Foy was also ancient in origin, but expanded in the ninth century in part because of its fortuitous location on one of the more heavily-traveled pilgrimage routes to Santiago de Compostela, and in part because her relics were stolen from Agen and installed at Conques.[6] The cults of saints Pancras, Agnes, Cyricus, Vitus and the Holy Innocents achieved a more widespread diffusion through the popularity of their legends and relics. Gregory of Tours mentions shrines to St. Pancras and the boy martyr Celsus, as well as Eulalia of Mérida and two Gallo-Roman saints, the boy Lusor, a girl named Criscentia, and an unnamed girl whose remains were accidentally discovered, incorrupt and buried in a white robe.[7] The latter two cults dated from Roman times, but did not spread beyond their immediate localities.

Minor changes occurred as the legends of the child saints traveled over time and distance along with their relics. The element of youth often became more pronounced than in earlier versions. Several child saints developed a special significance for children, either in local traditions or in more general Christian folklore. The majority, however, functioned as general saints for a particular locality; veneration may have been based upon regional interest in their legends, or the possession of coveted relics.

The Roman child martyrs were the first to achieve widespread fame in early medieval Europe. The cult of the boy martyr Pancras gained great popularity through promulgation of his reputation and his relics. According to Gregory of Tours, Pancras was thought to punish those guilty of perjury. Because Pancras would not perjure himself to deny his faith, he was believed to hate those who swore falsely upon any matter. Gregory recorded the custom of swearing oaths at his tomb in Rome, which was located not far from the city wall.[8] Jacobus de Voragine, author of the thirteenth-century *Golden Legend*, reported that the practice of taking oaths on Pancras' relics was widely practiced in his own time.[9]

The cult of St. Pancras became particularly widespread in the early medieval period as a result of the dispersal of his relics. Gregory the Great, whose devotion to the boy saint was seen in both actions and writings,[10] sent relics of Pancras to England with St. Augustine of Canterbury, who used them to rededicate a pagan temple.[11] It has been suggested that the transfer of Pancras' relics to England was considered appropriate by Gregory because Pancras was a patron of children, and Gregory undertook the conversion of England after seeing English slave-boys in the marketplace.[12] Gregory also sent relics to Saintes for the consecration of an altar by Bishop Palladius.[13] In the seventh century, Pope Vitalian sent relics of Pancras to Oswald of Northumbria, and six other ancient churches, all in the southeast of England, were dedicated to Pancras.[14] The saint's ongoing veneration at Rome is attested to by the numerous repairs to the basilica which housed his relics. His cult was initiated at his tomb in a cemetery on the Via Aurelia; from there his relics were moved to a basilica dedicated to him, S. Crisogono in Trastevere. At the beginning of the sixth century, Pope Symmachus enlarged the basilica over his tomb. His head was later moved to the Lateran Basilica; in the Middle Ages, the relics were dispersed through many cities in France and Italy.[15] In the late tenth century relics of Pancras were sent from Rome to Belgium "not for money, but for love."[16] The unspecified relics were preserved with much devotion, and celebrated daily in the mass.

Pancras was not identified as a child martyr by Gregory of Tours, but Jacobus de Voragine considered the youth of Pancras to be an integral part of his identity as a martyr.

> Pancratius comes from pan, meaning all or the whole, gratus, pleasing, and citius, faster, so the whole more quickly pleasing, because Saint Pancratius was pleasing to God quickly, in his childhood.[17]

The presentation of his story in the *Golden Legend* made Pancras appear even younger than his fourteen years. Diocletian begged Pancras to save himself from a dreadful death. "Because you are still a child, you are easily misled." Pancras replied, in the manner of a *puer senex*, "I may be a child in body but my mind is older."[18] Although technically at the age of *adolescentia*, Pancras was pictured as a vulnerable but miraculously brave *puer*, thus rendering his eventual fate all the more poignant. In sympathy for the predicament of the child, Diocletian promised that if Pancras repented, he would treat him as his own son. While the promise was of fatherly love rather than imperial wealth, attempts at bribery are found in the *passios* of many martyrs. The veneration of St. Pancras as an example of childish faith and bravery has continued into the present. Considered to hold special significance for children in the time of Gregory the Great, Pancras is still one of the patrons of children in the Catholic Church, and is especially so honored in Italy.[19]

Relics of St. Agnes, the young Roman girl martyr, enjoyed similar dispersal and popularity throughout medieval Europe. In addition to her fame in early Christian writings, Agnes was celebrated in medieval works by Aelfric, Flodoard, Hrosvitha of Gandersheim, and several anonymous writers.[20] Agnes was established as a *puella senecta*; Aelfric's *Old English Martyrology* described her as "a child in years, but old in mind."[21] The *Golden Legend* echoed this theme, saying, "Childhood is computed in years, but in her immense wisdom she was old; she was a child in body but already aged in spirit."[22] In Hrosvitha's version, youth erased the qualities of age and wisdom entirely, as the prefect told Agnes, "I know you are in the bloom of your first years, young in nature and tender in age."[23]

Later medieval versions of her legend de-emphasized her youth by concentrating on the threat to her chastity. Agnes came to the attention of the authorities because of her refusal to marry a pagan suitor. This act, as well as the suitor's response, suggests a young woman of marriageable age, rather than an innocent child. In the medieval legend, the jilted suitor initiated an episode of sexual humiliation meant to deprive Agnes of both her virginal chastity and her womanly modesty. He had the young girl cast naked into a brothel, but her hair grew to cover her nudity, and she was miraculously protected from an attempted gang-rape. The *Golden Legend* reflected this tradition, as an angel met her at the brothel and cloaked her nakedness with a shining mantle of radiance. "Thus the brothel became a place of prayer, and anyone who honored the light came out cleaner than he had gone in."[24] The prefect's son attempted to force himself on her and was struck dead; the prefect accused Agnes of using magical arts against his son, but she prayed and he was brought back to life, as a Christian. Agnes survived being thrown into a fire, but died when a dagger was thrust into her throat.

The popularity of the cult of St. Agnes, as attested by the spread of her relics and the breadth of devotional materials, made her perhaps the most popular of all of the child martyrs, but medieval versions of her legend placed little emphasis on her youth, and instead attempted to strengthen her identification with virgin martyrs. Her recorded miracles do not identify her with children in any substantial way.[25]

Medieval legends enhanced the youth of St. Pancras while minimizing this element in the life of St. Agnes, but retained in both the behavior of the *puer senex* by describing miraculously mature behavior for their years. St. Vitus was treated in a similar fashion. In a version of his *passio* which probably dates from the late seventh century,[26] and was popularized in the *Golden Legend*, his age was advanced from seven to twelve years, and his behavior modified accordingly. Although technically younger than Pancras, Vitus was treated as an *adolescentius*. Faced with the Christian resolve of his son, Vitus' father tried to convince him to apostatize his faith by providing him with music and dancing girls.[27] In response, God sent angels who raged about him and emitted a wondrous perfume. The father was then blinded by the will of God. Vitus cured his father, but the embittered pagan desired his son's destruction. Vitus fled with his tutor, Modestus. He was later captured by the emperor Diocletian, who wished his son to be cured of demons. After Vitus performed this miracle, he was cast into prison, and God avenged him by destroying the imperial palace. Diocletian fled, crying, "Woe is me, I've been worsted by one mere child!"[28] Vitus survived the fiery furnace and an attack by a lion; rescued from the rack along with his tutor Modestus and his nurse Crescentia by an angel, they were taken to a riverbank and expired of natural causes. Still, they were counted as martyrs.

St. Vitus became renowned for his role in the cure of St. Vitus' Dance, a nervous disease affecting children,[29] as well as other afflictions involving involuntary movement,[30] and his cult spread throughout Europe along with the dispersal of his relics. Relics of Vitus traveled to St. Denis in the late eighth century,[31] and to Saxony in 836, where they inspired a great devotion to the saint. In 1355, the Emperor Charles IV translated a quantity of relics to Prague. Popular veneration of the virtuous boy saint was widespread throughout Italy.[32] Aside from his patronage of a disease specific to children, Vitus also functioned as a saint with general curative powers not associated with his youth. The elevation of the relics of Vitus at Corbie in 836 by Abbot Hilduin produced a number of miracles involving the cure of children, but many adults were healed as well, and no special affinity was claimed between the child saint and the afflicted children. An eight-year old and a five-year-old boy were cured of paralysis, a girl born with a shriveled right hand was made whole, and a four-year old girl cured of blindness. Three adult women and one man were also cured of blindness, and a woman who had been hunchbacked and deformed since the age of twelve was also healed. Vitus cured other children, including a six-year-old boy with crippled hand, a deaf and mute girl, and a crippled adolescent named Theodoricus.[33] The author of the work was particularly careful to follow established doctrines in reporting the miracles; for instance, the five-year-old boy cured of paralysis was careful to pray first to God and only then to the saint. Numerous other cures, primarily of adults, were also reported. Cures were reported of a man blind since birth; another blind man; a woman with crippled feet; a mute woman; a nobleman named Wigo, weakened and crippled in all parts of his body; and several others cured of unspecified ailments.[34]

The cult of St. Faith was one of the earliest of a child saint to originate in Europe. She was most famous for the ongoing battle for her relics between her native Agen and nearby Conques, but her worship can be traced back as far as the fifth century, when her relics were elevated by Bishop Dulcidius and a basilica erected.[35] She is listed in the *Martyrology* of Jerome, but the only surviving versions of her legend, and most of her fame, stem from the controversy over her relics. The pious theft occurred in 865 or 866, but the action was disputed for some time by Agen, which refused to admit that the relics had been translated.[36] The proliferation of miracles reported by the new custodians of her relics at Conques, however, was apparently persuasive.[37] The version of her legend which survives to the present dates from the tenth century, and tells of a young girl who was first roasted on a brazen bed and then beheaded.[38] She was included in numerous medieval martyrologies. Relics of Ste Foy also traveled to England, where her arm was kept at Glastonbury, and several churches were dedicated to her. The city of Rodez in Spain acquired relics of the child, as did Seligenstadt in Germany, where a monastery was dedicated to her in the eleventh century.[39] Numerous miracles were attributed to the power of the saint. She healed the blind and lame, granted fertility to a woman, cast out demons from a peasant and a child, and raised a mule from the dead.[40] As with the miracles of St. Vitus, children benefited from the intervention of the martyr, but were not the principal recipients of her favor. Only four out of a total of twenty-four miracles claimed were bestowed upon children. While there is nothing to contradict her identity as a child, little surviving evidence attaches any significance to her youth.

Several of the more prominent cults of child martyrs were thus transported to the West in the early Middle Ages and grew steadily in popularity, but appreciation of the saints as children may have diminished.[41] The case of St. Cyricus indicates that such treatment was an indication of ecclesiastical prejudices rather than popular attitudes. The cult of the toddler saint Cyricus and his mother Julitta was widely promoted in Western Europe. His legend, like many others, became embellished with fabulous additions by the early sixth century, concentrating on the power of speech. The simple mimicry of his mother's cry found in the earliest version of the legend, which is not contradictory to the capabilities of a three-year-old, gave way to a miraculously precocious oratorical ability. Asked by the prefect who had taught him to speak, he replied, "You are mad and without reason, asking a child of two years and nine months who has taught him to speak, father or mother, or another; where else could this come from but the Holy Spirit?"[42] The *Golden Legend*, surprisingly, maintained a plausible outlook with regard to his developmental abilities. Cyricus struggled against the prefect's restraint, "crying out in harmony with his mother's voice, `I too am a Christian!'"[43] After biting the governor, his brains were dashed out on the stone steps.

The *Golden Legend* further relates that the bodies of Cyricus and his mother Julitta were ordered "cut up so the Christians would not be able to bury them but the pieces were collected by an angel and buried at night by Christians."[44] Their location was miraculously revealed in the reign of Constantine. Relics of Cyricus were first introduced to the west in the fourth century, when they were brought to France by St. Amator, who became Bishop of Auxerre in 388.[45] Auxerre became a well-known center of the cult, from which relics of the boy and his mother were dispersed throughout France, and through the Norman Conquest, into England as well. The cult was also popular in Cornwall, Wales, and Scotland, where, in a curious conflation of saintly identities, Cyricus' name became confused with that of the sixth-century bishop Curig. The feast days of the two saints were celebrated on June 16th, and the bishop was sometimes portrayed as an infant.[46] This may have been a deliberate substitution by Latin missionaries to restore orthodoxy to the Celtic church. Movement of the relics inspired cults in Spain and Ravenna as well.[47] Despite liturgical and literary promotion of the cult of Cyricus, popular acceptance on the scale accorded to other child saints is not evident. The only recorded miracles attributed to the intervention of the young saint were limited to a ninth-century monastic community.[48]

The cult of the Holy Innocents continued to exert strong appeal throughout the Middle Ages. Both the legend and the relics of the infants were amplified to reflect a widespread popular interest within medieval society, and in fact the possibilities for amplification may have contributed substantially to the growth of the cult. In a telling passage of the *Golden Legend*, Jacobus de Voragine noted that "some of the Holy Innocents' bones have been preserved and are so large that they could not have been two-year-olds. Yet it might be thought that at that time men grew far larger than they do now."[49] Voragine cited St. John Chrysostom, who believed that Herod might have murdered all children over the age of two rather than under. Obviously, bones of many sizes were passed off as relics of the unfortunate children, while the reconciliation of such theological subtleties was left to the minds of scholars.

The popularity of the Holy Innocents is attested to by more than the ready availability of relics. One significant medieval development was the personalization of the cult, to the extent that individual sets of remains acquired names. The church of St. Cecilia, Cologne, claimed the relics of an Innocent named Innocentius;[50] St. Memorius, an Innocent whose relics were translated from the Church of St. Peter's in Rome to the Cathedral of St. Front in Périgueux during the time of Charlemagne, may have acquired his name from an inscription on his tomb, "Memoriae martyris innocentis."[51] St. Sicarius, venerated as a Holy Innocent at the monastery of St.-Pierre-de-Brantôme in Périgord also from the time of Charlemagne, may have acquired his name through a similar misunderstanding. He may have been an "innocent" child whose parents named him after Sicarius, bishop of Laon; the resulting tomb inscription would have led to his veneration as one of the famous infant martyrs.[52] The impulse to personify the supposedly ancient relics with names may imply a heightened sympathy for the sufferings of the infants, and perhaps for their grieving families as well. Most of the Holy Innocents were venerated under the generic title, although those with specific names inspired more focused cults. The local feasts of Sicarius and Memorius were celebrated on May 2 and 26, respectively, rather than on December 29. Local rituals from the seventeenth through the nineteenth centuries invoked Memorius against maladies of the head, including madness and headache. Sicarius had many churches dedicated to him in the region of Périgord, and was invoked for general cures. The celebration of these feasts in spring rather than winter might also suggest a connection with fertility.[53] Relics of the Holy Innocents were also found in Provence, Rome, Padua, Lisbon, Milan, Jerusalem, and of course Bethlehem.[54] Western pilgrims to Bethlehem were able to visit a shrine to the Innocents in the sixth century.[55]

The church of the Holy Innocents at Paris was presented an "entire Innocent, in a grand crystal casket" by Louis XI.[56] In 1465, the lips of one of the Holy Innocents were listed in the relic collection of the cathedral at Canterbury: "'The lips of one of the infants slain by Herod' in that massacre of which no historian, save the author of the Gospel according to St. Matthew, has ever heard."[57]

The liturgical popularity of the Holy Innocents was also widespread. Gregory the Great observed the feast day of the Innocents as a day of mourning. The children were mentioned in the Historia Francorum of Gregory of Tours and the Martyrologium of Bede.[58] Peter Abelard, in a hymn to the Holy Innocents included in the *Hymnarium Paraclithensis*, borrowed from the emotional account of Peter Chrysologus by presenting children laughing at one moment and perishing at swordpoint at the next, while grieving mothers clutched the bloody remains to their breasts.[59] Over the centuries, however, the graphic emphasis on the suffering of the infants declined.[60]

The conflicting imagery found a cultural reflection in popular celebrations of the Feast of the Holy Innocents in England, France and Germany from the thirteenth century. Although the liturgy specified a day of special mourning, December 28th became a day of carnival and reversal of the social order, as children were elevated to positions of clerical importance. Many dioceses elected a boy-bishop, and provided diminutive garments for him and his retinue to wear. Ceremonies became quite elaborate, frequently lasting from Saint Nicholas Day, December 6th, to Childermas on December 28th. In addition to their more ornamental functions, the boy-bishops would be called upon to preach sermons.[61] Girls sometimes participated in analagous ceremonies.[62] The general appeal of such festivities was in the incongruity of seeing children copy the actions of adults. Such activities, like the cult of the Holy Innocents itself, were usually considered harmless because they involved children, but did not always meet with official approval. In England, priests assisted at mass with painted faces, or in masks. Sometimes they dressed as women. Dancing occurred in the choir, and sometimes obscene songs were substituted for prayer. In one particularly enthusiastic celebration, "after the mass ended, everyone ran, jumped, and danced about the church; some stripped themselves naked and were drawn about the streets in a manure cart, and pelted the people with dung."[63] This was the Feast of Fools, associated with the Roman Saturnalia.

The ancient controversy over the qualifications of the Innocents for martyrdom lingered on, as illustrated by the observation in the eleventh-century *Micrologus de ecclesiasticis observationibus*. Noting that less prestige is assigned to the Feast of the Holy Innocents than is accorded to other martyrs, it explains, "though they were crowned with martyrdom, they went at once not into Paradise, but into Limbo."[64] St. Bernard of Clairvaux, a strong defender of the cult (perhaps his only point of agreement with Abelard) declared, "Truly they are martyrs...If you search for the meritorious actions for which these infants were crowned by the hand of God, search also for the crimes for which they were cruelly massacred by Herod."[65]

The *Golden Legend* explored the etymology of the name "Innocenti" and gave three reasons for the attribution. First, they were innocent by life, unable to do ill to anyone. Second, they were innocent by martyrdom, victims of unjust suffering without being guilty of any crime. Third, they were innocent by the effects of death; their martyrdom conferred baptismal innocence and purified them of original sin.[66] The cult of the Innocents, unlike any of the other child martyrs, rested primarily on the concept of childish innocence and the sorrow associated with premature death. These are emotional rather than doctrinal qualifications, ultimately summed up in the statement, "They suffered innocently and through no fault of their own."[67] Amalarius, Bishop of Metz in the ninth century, explained the liturgical significance of the feast of the Holy Innocents by saying, "the author of this office would have us sympathize with the feelings of the pious women who wept and sorrowed at the death of their innocent children."[68]

Pancras, Agnes, Vitus, Faith, Cyricus and the Holy Innocents were the most well-known and influential child martyrs in medieval Europe. All were recognized and promulgated by ecclesiastical authorities through inclusion in martyrologies, liturgical mention, and the dispersal and veneration of relics. Popular interest is more difficult to gauge; in some cases, awareness of the saint's status as a child may have been diminished, but the shrines established by the Church continued to perform their functions. Societal interest in child saints is more strongly indicated by the localized cults of indigenous martyrs, as well as by the creation of spurious cults modeled on the more famous of the cults. While liturgical offices may have been dedicated to the Roman martyrs, and their relics included in more diverse collections, the shrines of lesser child saints were often venerated for their healing powers and became the objects of at least regional worship. Such shrines may have played a more significant role in the daily lives of the local population than the distant shrines of saints glorified in liturgies and martyrologies. In contrast to the examples discussed earlier, several of these child saints were particularly associated with the healing of children.

The cults of Eulalia of Mérida and Justus of Beauvais gained great popularity in the Middle Ages. While they did not attain the success achieved by St. Faith in creating a market for relics, both were so popular that derivative cults were established in neighboring cities. The cult of Eulalia of Barcélona was approved by the Synod of Toledo in 663, but as noted in the Bibliotheca Hagiographica Latina, "Whether she is different from Eulalia of Merida, it is not the place to inquire here."[69] This Eulalia, a young girl of fourteen, presented herself to the authorities for voluntary martyrdom in order to defy the pagan gods. She was placed on a little horse, an instrument of torture, and whipped, torn with iron hooks, and finally, according to differing versions of the legend, either crucified or thrown into the sea.[70] Relics of the martyr were dispersed throughout Spain and into parts of France, in the districts of Guyenne and Languedoc.[71] Whether true martyr or pious clone, in 1106 her corpse was reported to be in an aromatic condition.[72] Since in some versions of her life she was killed by being thrown into the sea, she became the patron of sailors, and was also invoked against drought. In the celebration of her office at Barcélona, children played an important role. Processions in her honor were led by children, and during a celebratory pageant in 1339, the royal children were honored guests.[73]

The more venerable and established Eulalia of Mérida nevertheless remained more popular than her competitor. Perhaps in an attempt to assert her spiritual superiority over the upstart Eulalia of Barcélona, her medieval biographers compiled an even more lurid list of tortures than those inflicted upon her rival. After being stretched on the rack and torn with iron claws, her sides were burned with flaming torches, and she was killed when fire was forced down her throat.[74] Although her relics seem not to have been dispersed beyond the borders of Spain, her fame was much more widespread than that of her rival. Mention of her story by Prudentius, Augustine and Venantius Fortunatus undoubtedly led to the familiarity of such authors as Bede and Aldhelm with her story.[75] Gregory of Tours knew of her cult, and reported on the miraculous occurrences at her tomb. Every year on her feast day, December 10th, three trees in front of the altar covering her relics blossomed in the shape of a dove. The speed with which this miracle occurred would provide a portent for the coming year. People who prayed at the shrine just before the miracle of the blossoms, for the resolution of problems or quarrels, would see that their prayers were answered if fragrant flowers resembling jewels appeared. These flowers also had the ability to cure the sick. [76]

The cult of Eulalia of Mérida, in addition to inspiring the cult of the fictitious Eulalia of Barcélona, was also the catalyst for the creation of a saint with an actual existence. Augustus was a young boy who, from a very early age, had served in the church of St. Eulalia, caring for children. He was of a

pious and innocent temperament, which was seen as pleasing to God. One
night he had a dream, which he later related to the priest, of an elegant
banquet, attended by Señor Jesus and a multitude of angels and saints, all in
white, decorated with gold and jewels. The most majestic of all the men
showed the boy a beautiful garden, and said that the boy would soon join him
there as part of his retinue.[77] Upon awakening from this vision, Augustus
began to prepare for his imminent death. It was soon forthcoming. The night
before the corpse was to be buried, it began to exhibit miraculous signs. A
companion who kept vigil in the crypt to watch the body heard the corpse
call his name. Approaching the body fearfully, he saw the face begin to glow.
The next day, the blessed corpse, henceforth referred to as Saint Augustus,
was interred in the church.[78]

The story of St. Augustus provides an informative example of the
formation of a cult and the popular conception of miracles in the early
Middle Ages. That a child whose entire existence is centered around a church
should have such a dream is not implausible, but that this vision should be
taken as a sign from God demonstrates the atmosphere in which such cults
flourished. The prophetic nature of the dream is similar to the stories of SS.
Musa and Gelasius related by Gregory the Great in the *Dialogues*, but may
also illustrate the power of suggestion. Did Augustus die because he thought
he was going to die? Finally, the posthumous miracles were either a product
of the overworked imagination of a superstitious monk sitting up with the
corpse of a child in his room, perhaps dozing, and hearing his name called, or
the societal fear of a premature burial.

Justus of Beauvais, the child cephalophore, was the object of great
popularity and pious outpourings. His unreliable legend dates in its present
form from the eighth century. The earliest location of the cult may be at
Juste-en-Chaussée, which was at a crossing of two important routes, Vemand
to Beauvais and Amiens to Senlis.[79] The crossroad was considered a site of
supernatural or magical significance in pagan tradition, and was frequently
criticized by churchmen for its use in Christian lore.[80] The diffusion of
Justus' cult through the movement of his relics resulted in a number of
conflicting claims. Beauvais obtained possession of the coveted headless
corpse in 900,[81] and in 924 the monastery of Winchester in England recorded
receiving the head of the martyr from king Aethelstan.[82] During the early
eleventh century, however, the Abbey of Malmedy in Belgium claimed that it
had acquired the body of the martyr "at a good price."[83] The relics of Justus
may have been paired with those of St. Cyricus, also claimed by the
monastery.[84] Auxerre also claimed a relic of the martyr, specifically a
fragment of the head. The Abbey of St. Riquier acquired a certain bone from

the "little body" in 866, and Coira in Switzerland received unspecified relics of the saint in the early eleventh century.[85] Justus may also be the patron of two parishes in Cornwall.[86] St. Justus was lauded for working cures on the blind, the lame, and the feeble.[87] The identity of a nine-year-old child, through whose *corpusculum* God chose to work miracles, was never lost.

In the ninth century, the church of Notre-Dame of Paris advanced the claim that it possessed the relics of a nine-year-old boy named Justin who was beheaded by the Romans when he tried, with his father, to gain the release of his brothers who had confessed to Christianity.[88] Although his story is nearly identical with that of the more ancient St. Justus, with the exception that Justin of Paris was not a cephalophore, his cult failed to achieve the same level of popularity. No disputes over relics are known to have occurred.

The cult of Emerentiana, the foster-sister of Agnes, gained new popularity in the ninth century.[89] At this time, her relics were brought from her basilica in the Ostian cemetery to the church of St. Agnes, and her legend developed more fully.[90] The occasion of her translation was followed by a broad dispersal of her relics, which were claimed by many churches. Her cult gained great popularity in Spain, where she became the principal patroness of the diocese of Tereul. Churches in Spain, Germany and Belgium all claimed to possess relics of the saint.[91] Her martyrdom at her foster-sister's tomb, stoned to death by pagans before she had received baptism, was mentioned in the story of Agnes in the *Golden Legend*.[92]

In addition to the more famous child saints and their derivatives, several others were accorded regional devotion. The relics of SS. Cantius, Cantian, and Cantianilla were moved from the cathedral at Aquileia, which celebrated their martyrdom, to Étampes in the early eleventh century by Robert the Good. They became the principal patrons of the city, and were especially identified with the protection of children. A list of miracles was compiled in 1603. The miraculous cures deal almost exclusively with children, including one case from 1638, which describes a five-year-old girl, paralyzed since birth, who had confounded the doctors of Paris but was cured at the shrine of the three saints when brought there by her mother.[93] This association has lasted into the modern era. Although most of the bones were scattered in 1793 during the French Revolution, some were preserved, and "every year at Étampes on May 31st, a procession of the 'Corps Saints' takes place, to which great numbers of children are brought by their mothers."[94] The cult was also established in Saxony in the fifteenth century, when the church at Hildesheim claimed acquisition of certain relics of the children, including the

heads of SS. Cantius and Cantian, as well as parts of their sister.[95] Étampes, however, claimed the bodies in their entirety.

St. Christina of Bolsena, one of the patron saints of children, whose cult was diffused throughout Italy in the tenth through twelfth centuries, was also appropriated by the French. She became the patron of children in the diocese of Orléans.[96] Her relics also traveled to Belgium. Tuscany claimed a piece of her foot, and both France and Bavaria claimed her entire body.[97] She continued to be honored in her native region as well. A hospital was dedicated to SS. Mary and Christina in 1284 at Bolsena, and a confraternity dedicated to the saints was founded there as well.[98] Most of the miracles attributed to her involved the appearance of visions rather than cures. The visions appeared to both young girls and adults.[99] Agapetus of Praeneste, whose cult was established by at least the fifth century in both Rome and Besançon, was the subject of renewed enthusiasm in the eighth and ninth centuries, when his cult spread to Spain and Germany.[100] Because he was martyred in his youth, he was invoked against colic, digestive ailments, and other illnesses which affect children. He was also considered a patron of oblates, infants, and children, and was prayed to by the mothers of newly born or newly baptized children.[101]

St. Flocel, the child martyr of Autun, inspired a longstanding popular cult in the area which spread throughout the region with the dispersal of his relics over the centuries. The cult was active at Bayeux from the sixth century, as well as at Beaune, Coutances, and Artois.[102] The cult was established in Beaune ca. 965, but it is less clear when the relics arrived in the other areas. Coutances is considered to be the birthplace of the saint, and a cult can definitely be demonstrated in the twelfth century. The arrival of the cult in Artois is the latest, and probably occurred toward the end of the fifteenth century. Relics were translated from Coutances to Beaune in 996, and elevated in 1265. Traditions connected with the saint varied by region. At Autun, in addition to the general range of miracles such as the cure of paralysis and delivery from demons, Flocel was also invoked by childless couples who wished for children.[103] At Artois, he was considered an intercessor for the safe delivery of children, and was also invoked for children who had difficulty in walking.[104] Prayers associated with the office of the saint included a special prayer for children and young people to obtain, through his intercession, the grace of perseverance.[105] He is honored in the liturgy as a "blessed child and martyr" possessing innocence and virtue.[106]

A number of other child saints remained the objects of localized veneration. The reputation of St. Devota remained with her relics at Monaco, of which she is patron saint.[107] The tomb of St. Lusor at Deols was a pilgrimage site from Merovingian times; Gregory of Tours recorded his identity and a number of miracles which occurred at his shrine. "He was the son of Leucadius, [who was] once a senator, and he is said to have migrated fromthis world [while dressed] in the whilte robe [of someone recently baptized.]"[108] The popularity of the cult declined in later centuries, and the church dedicated to him at Deols was later rededicated to St. Stephen.[109] Saint Columba of Sens was venerated in over thirty parishes in France, as well as in Spain, Germany and Italy.[110] Her cult became identified in the Middle Ages with that of SS. Sanctianus, Augustinus and Beata, who were also buried near Sens and had been honored by a church erected in the time of Constantine.[111]

The cult of Celsus, who was martyred with Nazarius, maintained a liturgical and material popularity dating from the discovery of their relics by St. Ambrose at Milan in 395.[112] Gregory of Tours mentioned their cult. Their bodies were undiscovered until a miraculous pear tree grew from their grave. The fruit cured anyone who was sick. The tree was owned by a poor man, who became rich through the miracles worked through the tree. Finally the saints revealed themselves in a vision, ordered the tree cut down and a church built.[113] The association of miraculous tree or plant growth with the location of a saint's relics is a common theme in medieval hagiography, as is the veneration of burial sites. Jacobus de Voragine traced the etymology of the name Celsus from *excelsus*: "Saint Celsus lifted himself above himself, rising above his childhood age by the strength of his spirit."[114] The cult expanded throughout Gaul, and the feast of Celsus and Nazarius was celebrated on July 28 in Autun, Carcassonne, Digne, Gap, Montpellier, and Beaucaire.[115]

The cults of several child saints did not cross the Alps, but remained strong in Italy. The relics of St. Conon and his son were taken to Acerra, where they became principal patrons of the diocese. The translation was commemorated by a new version of their *passio* written in the thirteenth century.[116] The tomb of St. Crescentius attracted pilgrims at Rome until the translation of his relics to Siena in the mid-eleventh century.[117] St. Dominica, one of the young female idol-smashers, was transported to Calabria from Campania by angels; the relics were kept there with great veneration and made no other journeys.[118]

Not all child saints sustained popular devotion. Some, for reasons lost to history, failed to attract sufficient interest to sustain a following. The cult of St. Criscentia had declined into obscurity by Merovingian times. Gregory of Tours related that local clerics discovered a tomb near Paris with the inscription, "Here lies Criscentia, a girl dedicated to God," and assigned her the power of saintly intervention. "But no generation could remember of what value her merit had been and what she had done in this world."[119] Accordingly, her cult was promoted and she became known for cures of toothache and fever. Her tomb was erected by a grateful beneficiary of her intercession. By the later Middle Ages, however, her shrine was no longer visited. Gregory also mentioned the body of an unknown girl in the church of St. Venerandus, whose body was discovered when a section of the vault collapsed from long neglect.

> A girl was visible, lying in the sarcophagus; all her limbs were as intact as if she had been recently taken from this world....the robe that covered her lifeless limbs was as[white as] a lamb and intact, neither mutilated by any decay nor discolored by any blackness, Why say more? She appeared to be so robust that she as thought to be sleeping rather than dead. Because of the shiny whiteness of her silk robe some of us thought that she had died while wearing the white robes [immediately after her baptism.][120]

The remains produced one miracle, restoring the sight of a noble widow, but subsequent miracles failed to materialize.

Other cults also failed to maintain popular support. The various stories of schoolboy saints, such as Ansanus, Pergentinus and Laurentinus, and Justus and Pastor, remained for the most part edifying legends for the faithful. Only the cult of Justus and Pastor exhibited any following in the west. Relics of the pair were translated in the eighth, eleventh, and fifteenth centuries.[121] In 1058, relics were taken from Madrid to Narbonne, but the former church still retained the entire left leg of St. Pastor, with the foot covered with flesh and skin, and toes and toenails attached, as well as one rib and two vertebrae of St. Justus.[122] In the fifteenth century, the relics were translated to a closer proximity to those of St. Eulalia of Mérida.[123] Relics of the other scholar-martyrs failed to attract the attention of medieval Christians. The failure of many cults to achieve prominence or even minor success in the West is probably more closely related to the vagaries of the relic trade than a lack of popular interest in child saints, as can be seen by the additional cults which developed in this period. These cults were modeled on the earlier stories of child martyrs, but were largely fantastic concoctions, rather than elaborations of any historical remnant.

The great church at Constantinople, Hagia Sophia, was known in the Middle Ages not as a tribute to Holy Wisdom, but to a woman named Sophia, or Sapientia, who was the mother of three young daughters, Fides, Spes, and Caritas. According to tradition, the martyrdoms took place in Rome. The legend is paralleled in the Eastern Church, with appropriate Greek names for the daughters: Agape, Chionia, and Irene. Although the individuals never existed, and the legend was not known until the sixth century, the story may have been modeled on the older cult and legend of St. Bassa and her three sons, the pious mother who exhorted her children to a glorious martyrdom.[124] The three girls, aged twelve, ten and nine years, respectively,[125] or eleven, ten and eight,[126] were encouraged in martyrdom by their grieving but steadfast mother. She encouraged the youngest to endure the torments of whips, fire, and branding-irons. The martyrdom of the children was only peripherally caused by their defense of the Christian faith; the Emperor Hadrian, enamored of their purity, wished to adopt them if they would renounce Christ. When they refused, he had them tortured and murdered. Their mother fortunately and inexplicably survived, and so was able to gather up their remains. The origin of this spurious legend, which dates from the sixth century, may have resulted from the misreading of a tomb inscription under the Church of St. Pancras in Rome.[127] While the relics of the children remained largely confined to Rome and the Eastern Church, their story was more widely circulated. Certain relics moved to Gaul and Germany in the time of Charlemagne; the feast of the three children is mentioned in the martyrologies of Usuard and Notger,[128] and Hrosvitha of Gandersheim honored their memory in a play entitled *Sapientia*.[129] In this play, the ages of the three girls were eight, ten, and twelve years, and their behavior combined faithful obedience to their mother's will with the miraculous eloquence of the *puer senex*. Hrosvitha also honored the subjects of the Eastern version of the legend, Agape, Chionia and Hirena, with a separate play, *Dulcitius*. The girls in this version, however, were somewhat older and more autonomous in their actions than their Latin counterparts. Their mother did not witness their execution.[130]

The credibility of this hagiographical motif is stretched even further in the medieval legends of SS. Felicitas and Symphorosa, each of whom was martyred along with their respective sets of seven sons. In both cases, the mothers exhorted their sons to martyrdom, and endured the additional pain of seeing all of their children killed before their eyes. The seven sons of Symphorosa were named Crescens, Julian, Nemesius, Primitivus, Justin, Stacteus, and Eugenius.[131] The seven sons of Felicitas were named Januarius, Felix, Philip, Sylvanus, Alexander, Vitalis, and Martial.[132] While neither set of sons is identified as particularly young, the emotional issue of mothers losing beloved children is similar to the medieval image of the Holy Innocents, while the number of martyrs involved could allow for exploitation of the relics on a similar scale. Noting the proliferation of relics of the sons of St. Felicitas in the Middle Ages, one hagiographer remarked, "Their loss at the French Revolution would have been greatly to be deplored had there not been so many more bodies of the same persons dispersed through the churches of Christendom."[133]

Other child martyrs with claims to an ancient and honorable history also appeared for the first time in the Middle Ages. The boy martyr Goswin, venerated in Germany and Belgium, was recorded for the first time in three martyrologies of the sixteenth century, although his cult may be older. According to his *passio*, he suffered martyrdom in Rome while still a child.[134] The relics of St. Donninus, or Domnin D'Avrilly, were the center of a cult at Puy. He was presented as a ten-year-old boy who suffered martyrdom by being crucified and then beheaded, but all of the elements of his *passio* are fabulous and his cult cannot be dated with certainty.[135] St. Potitus, *dum esset in infantia*,[136] was said to have been martyred in the second century under Antoninus, but the first mention of his name appeared in the ninth century in the *Liber Pontificalis* and a contemporary calendar. By the twelfth century his relics had spread from Apulia to Naples, Capua, Benevento, and Sardinia.[137]

Perhaps more significant than the invention of child martyrs is the attribution of youth to a martyr previously not identified as one. St. Ansanus, known as the first apostle of Siena, became the object of revived interest in the twelfth century; the translation of his relics gave rise to a fanciful life which transformed him into a boy martyr.[138] St. Tarsicius, an acolyte murdered on the Appian Way by pagans while transporting communion wafers, was also characterized as a child in a tradition beginning in the sixth century, although his cult predated this period. His popularity is demonstrated by a long series of relic translations and church dedications from the seventh to the twentieth century.[139] He is the patron saint of altar boys, and one of the two patrons of first communicants, the other is the Blessed Imelda Lambertini, who died in 1333 at the age of eleven.

The attribution of youth to a martyr can play a role of great significance even in cases where little information besides the death itself survives. The relics of St. Gordian, martyred with a companion, Epimachus, in the third century, were preserved in a church in Rome on the Via Latina; while archaeological and liturgical evidence of the cult is plentiful, hagiographical information is scarce. An inscription at his shrine mentions him as a child, and so "It is said that he was a boy, and because of being so young, deserved great glory for shedding his blood for Christ."[140]

No liturgical mention or trace of a cult existed for St. Reparata of Caesaria until a mid-ninth century version of Bede's Martyrology, which identified her only as a virgin.[141] The establishment of her cult, however, led to the development of a legend which enjoyed great popularity.[142] Reparata was a twelve-year-old girl martyred in Caesaria in the third century when she refused to sacrifice to idols. She survived various torments, and finally gave up her spirit in the form of a white dove.[143] Relics of the saint were claimed by Chiesa, as well as by the diocese of Naples, where she is a minor patron. She was honored in Pisa, Lucca, Florence, Naples, and several smaller towns.[144]

The cults of saints Prisca and Restituta, although probably dating from the fourth century, were also amplified with fabulous legends in the early Middle Ages. The relics of St. Restituta, a girl martyr who suffered under Aurelian, were brought to the city of Sora in 1104 by an angel to grace the new cathedral. A fanciful *vita* was concocted soon afterwards by Gregory, Bishop of Terracina, involving the survival of many hideous tortures by the saint.[145] Popular devotion is attested to by the cures performed at her shrine, which involved the cure of blind, crippled, and possessed people.[146] The cult of St. Prisca, a virgin martyr of thirteen with an ancient cult in Rome, also acquired a fabulous *passio* which included the taunting of demons, and the young girl's survival of both wild beasts and flames before her eventual saintly demise. Her relics circulated in Gaul and Belgium as well as Rome, but no significant new shrines emerged.[147]

Through various means and in many areas, the image of the child saint was preserved and promoted in medieval Europe. Official promotion was usually strong; popular acceptance varied among individual cults but on the whole remained steady. As with the legends of many saints, elements of the fabulous increased in the later *vitae* of the child martyrs. A further new element entered into the legends of some child saints in this period. In several instances the children were suspected by their persecutors of being magicians rather than saints, and of practicing magical arts. This accusation was made against both male and female saints; Flocel, Vitus, Justus of Beauvais, Agnes, and Potitus were all accused of being magicians, although each protested that the power came from God rather than from demons.[148]

The earliest appearance of this charge is from the *vita* of St. Agnes by Ambrose, and may reflect pagan incomprehension of Christianity. The charge may indicate an attempt to reduce the beliefs of the Christians into something more understandable to the Romans, and also occurs in the legends of adult martyrs. Children were not usually portrayed as practitioners of magic, although they were sometimes utilized as acolytes in religious rituals.[149] In the ancient world, children were often utilized in magical or religious rituals such as divination because their sexual purity rendered them more susceptible to spiritual messages. Witches were suspected of killing young boys to use in their ceremonies.[150] Although the purity of children often dictated their roles in such rituals, the marginality of their social status prevented full inclusion.[151] The image of the child magician may be a medieval addition to several of the legends. The child as magician is also seen in the *Dulcitius* of Hrosvitha, where the three girls Agape, Chionia and Hirena are denounced as witches by the prefect.[152] Curiously, unlike *Sapientia* and similar narratives, their virtue was never recognized by their executioners. The theme of the child witch may also receive a faint echo in the *Sapientia*, when Hadrian exhorts the youngest child, Karitas, to worship "Great Diana."[153] Popular practices associated with the cult of the saints tapped into popular conceptions of magic, which utilized children as virginal conduits of supernatural power.

The effect of an idea upon an individual, group, or society is impossible to measure and frequently difficult even to gauge. Many individuals in the Middle Ages were strongly affected by the legends of the saints; others less so and some perhaps not at all. Children and adults were healed by child saints just as they were by adult saints. In some cases, children were seen as the most efficacious agents for the healing of children. Legends and relics of the child martyrs were widespread and popular. Some individuals took these legends to heart. For all of their visibility in the Middle Ages, however, the child martyrs of the early Church were by no means the only types of child saint known to medieval society. While the majority of the cults of child martyrs, with the exception of those few promoted by Rome, remained limited in scope to their regions of origin in France, Italy, and Spain, other areas less affected by Roman culture and Christianity began to develop their own concepts of the child saint. The continuing elevation of the child as an object of popular piety throughout the medieval period, as seen in the generation and development of truly medieval cults, illustrates both the importance of the child in society, and often the perverse nuances of popular mentality as well.

CHAPTER 4

Martyrdom and Murder: Child Saints of the Early Middle Ages

The acceptance of Christianity in early medieval Europe provided continuity and change in family relations and attitudes toward children. Within the Celtic and Germanic cultures of pre-Christian Europe, "barbarian children grew up in an atmosphere of benign neglect."[1] The classical origins of Christianity instilled its teachings with an emphasis on socialization and social structure that altered Germanic customs in many ways.[2] Specific to children, the Christian emphasis on moral development introduced the concept of investing resources in children through formal education and increased parental concern for their salvation. The inclusion of children in Christian rituals such as baptism provided a more formal role for children in religious practice, while missionary disapproval of pagan superstitions profoundly affected practices meant to ensure child health and safety.[3]

Harsh material conditions, endemic violence, and a generally low rate of survival may have acted to elevate the value of children in this society in contrast to the outlook of classical antiquity, and discourage systematic infanticide even before its prohibition by the Church.[4] Centuries after Tacitus' observations on the childrearing customs of Germania, aristocratic women in Frankish society depended on the survival of their children to ensure their own position within marriage.[5] The importance of children to the upper class can also be seen in the plethora of statutes relating to the question of legitimacy of offspring, especially with regard to the inheritance of property and titles.[6] The adverse material conditions of precarious life expectancy and short labor supply may have created a situation in which children's lives were valued at all levels of society.[7] While the clerical prohibition of infanticide probably faced no great societal opposition, denunciations of the practices of abortion and overlaying in the penitential literature of this period indicate that general societal attitudes did not always hold true on an individual level.[8] Caesarius of Arles, whose works were influential throughout the Carolingian period, also cautioned women against the use of abortificants.[9]

Moving beyond the basic question of life and death for infants, the historical sources exhibit many instances of love for children, as well as the recognition of children as developmentally distinct from adults in behavior. Infant mortality was high, but archaeological and documentary evidence from Anglo-Saxon England indicates that children, even the sick and weak, received considerable care from their parents.[10] In the mid-ninth century, Dhuoda, a Carolingian noblewoman, was separated from her two sons through a dispute with her husband, and composed a manual of instruction addressed to her elder son in which she stated, "The sweetness of my great love for you and my desire for your beauty have made me all but forget my own situation."[11] Her love for her absent son was the motivation for her writing.

> I am well aware that most mothers rejoice that they are with their children in this world, but I, Dhuoda, am far away from you, my son William. For this reason I am anxious and filled with longing to do something for you.[12]

The attention given to the raising of children exhibits awareness that children progress through developmental stages, and sensitivity to the limitations of the young mind, both intellectually and emotionally. Dhuoda mentioned on several occasions that she was writing for a child rather than an adult, but that her younger son, who was taken from her by her husband as an infant, was not yet of an age to read or comprehend her message.[13]

> The knowledge in this little book is partly derived from several other books, but my loving intent has been to refashion their content in a manner appropriate to your age.[14]

The writing of the manual was consistent with one of the principal duties of the mother, the training or education of her children in the early years of their lives, and Dhuoda's advice recalled the hagiographical motif of the *puer senex*. Citing the examples of Samuel and David, who acted as judges "even as boys in the flower of youth," she reminded William that wisdom was not a corollary of age, but rather the gift of God.[15] She also showed that she understood the physical as well as the moral requirements of raising young children.

I have seen fit to address myself to you, who are only a boy, in the childish terms appropriate to my own understanding. I have done so as if you were unable to eat solid food, but could take in only something like milk...I who am but a child myself have given you milk rather than solid food, for you are also a little one in Christ.[16]

Love for children was often expressed within the context of grief. As early as the sixth century, epitaphs record parental love for their deceased children and care for their eventual resurrection.[17] The epitaph of Charlemagne's infant daughter Adelaide states that "the heart of her mother is wounded with sorrow from afar,"[18] and the nun Rictrude mourned the death of her youngest daughter on Holy Innocents Day, "when Holy Church recalls the Massacre of the Innocents and the misery of their bereft mothers."[19] Gregory of Tours reported that an epidemic of dysentery

attacked young children first of all and to them it was fatal: and so we lost our little ones, who were so dear to us and sweet, whom we had cherished in our bosoms and dandled in our arms, whom we had fed and nurtured with such loving care. As I write I wipe away my tears and I repeat once more the words of Job the blessed: "The Lord gave, and the Lord hath taken away..."[20]

Religious education was especially considered the province of women, so that the introduction of Christianity has been viewed as enhancing the mother-child bond.[21] The withdrawal into monastic life, however, with the occasional abandonment of children, would not have occurred without Christian influence; while some children accompanied their mothers into the cloister, children below the age of seven were generally excluded. The religious vocation could also deprive the family of the father's presence through monastic vows. Finally, the practice of oblation removed children from their parents and placed them in a religious community at an early age. Many young boys crossed the thresholds of monasteries and as oblates, and the monks became responsible for their care and training.[22] Most children became oblates between the ages of five and seven, as *infantia* gave way to *pueritia* and moral instruction could begin. Bede was entrusted to the monastic life by his family at the age of seven, and spent his life in a cloistered existence.[23] Orderic Vitalis was ten years old when he was placed in the Norman monastery of Saint-Evroul by his father, and Hermann of Tournai entered the monastery of Saint-Martin as a newborn infant.[24] The institution of oblation was the prerogative of the father, or of the mother if the father had died.[25] Guibert of Nogent was promised to God by his family, if he should live, as his mother struggled in childbirth; his father died while he was an infant, and Guibert later praised God for the death, because if his father had lived, he would not have followed through on the vow.[26]

The problems associated with oblation led to its decline by the end of the twelfth century. Parental choice of the religious vocation for an infant or young child meant that the child may have no calling to the religious life. While authors such as Bede and Guibert of Nogent were happy with their fate, others asked to be released from their vows because they had not made the choice of their own free will. As early as the ninth century, St. Benedict required that the child profess approval of the parental decision.[27] The Cistercian order, which supplanted the Benedictine order in popularity in the twelfth century, prohibited the reception of boys until the age of fifteen, and later raised the threshold to eighteen, and at least some of the Benedictines followed suit.[28]

Religious communities were also concerned with the training and education of children. St. Benedict and other clerics generally cautioned against corporal punishment of children as "such strong measures can…make children worse than before, and not improve them.[29] In contrast to the abbot who remarked that the boys under his charge were constantly misbehaving, even though "we never give over beating them day and night," St. Anselm in the eleventh-century compared raising a child to planting a tree, and condemned the use of harsh methods as inappropriate for very young children. While "bread and all kinds of solid food" were good for older children, an infant who was fed such food rather than milk "would be strangled rather than strengthened."[30] Anselm, like Dhuoda, saw a parallel between the physical and moral nourishment of children. Moral perfection or adult standards of behavior were not expected of young children. Medieval penitential literature frequently exhibited a compassionate recognition of the frailties of childhood. In the *Penitential of Columban*, ca. 600, youth afforded some protection against the full penalty for the sins of masturbation and bestiality. "If anyone practices masturbation or sins with a beast, he shall do penance for two years if he is not in orders, but if he is in orders or has a vow, he shall do penance for three years unless his [tender] age protects him."[31] *The Penitential of Cummean*, ca. 650, which circulated in various forms through the early ninth century,[32] contained an entire section devoted to the "misdemeanors of boys." The rules exhibit both an awareness of the behavior to be expected from groups of boys, and a scale of punishment based upon the age of the perpetrator, as well as intent and the frequency with which the offense was committed.

> 10.9 A small boy misused by an older one, if he is ten years of age, shall fast for a week; if he consented, for twenty days.

10.21 Small boys who strike one another shall do penance for seven days; but if [they are] older, for twenty days; if [they are] adolescents, they shall do penance for forty days.[33]

The Church influenced early medieval society to hold expectations of childish behavior similar to those of classical antiquity, as morally imperfect and unformed, modified by the precarious position of human life in their new environment. Assimilated into a society in which the Church played a substantial role in the education and upbringing of children, images of children as holy figures provided patterns for the development of new forms of sanctity in children.

Classical values did not always transcend the geographical and chronological translations of the cult of the saints. Indigenous saints recognized after the fifth century often resembled their counterparts of late antiquity only superficially. The child martyrs whose relics traveled from Rome to the churches of Europe were, by and large, the beneficiaries of ecclesiastical promotion who met with varying degrees of popular acceptance. Child saints of the early Middle Ages, in contrast, were usually promoted through popular veneration, gaining official approbation only after the establishment of a local cult. Saints of this type generally achieved only local fame, and saw a limited circulation of relics. The regional appeal of these child saints, their cults, and their legends expressed societal needs and preferences through the creation of objects of veneration far more clearly than did the imported and adapted models of late antiquity.

Medieval society expressed a great interest in the concept of sanctity from the early period of missionary activity, and was quick to accord this recognition to many individuals. As Christianity spread throughout Western and Northern Europe, its proponents substituted Christian practices for existing religious beliefs. Pagan shrines became Christian chapels, sacraments such as baptism and communion were promoted as bestowing supernatural protection on recipients, and sacred sites such as trees, wells, and death sites were subsumed into Christian lore. The cult of the saints was integral to this process, as their legends showed then bestowing the miraculous cures and other benefits of religious magic on their followers.

As Christianity in medieval Europe did not face the challenge of persecution by an organized state, but was instead generally adopted by rulers at the outset of conversion, the concept of martyrdom did not achieve the preeminence it had held in the time of the persecutions. Martyrdom, never common, became less so as conversion spread throughout the secular power structure, Most saints were honored for piety, asceticism and miracles. Secular and spiritual prestige frequently mingled, as disproportionately large number of the blessed came from royal or noble households. Martyrdom was still recognized as a path to sanctity, but martyrs of this era met their fate at the hands of marauding Huns, Vikings, or even schismatic Christians in a purely warlike setting, and so became more simply conceived as death of a Christian at the hands of a non-Christian rather than active defense of ideology.

When life rather than death is viewed as the crucial factor in demonstrating sanctity, children are at a distinct disadvantage. To be recognized as a confessor, a child must actively emulate piety and asceticism in noticeable form, and then die within months or years. While child mortality was still very high, death through illness or by mischance was largely unforeseen and accidental, and appears not to have been visited upon any pious children of this era. Instead, the creation of child saints remained confined to the realm of martyrdom. The broader definition of martyrdom, combined with localized and popular recognition of cults, resulted in the creation of saints that allowed the modified survival of pre-Christian practices. The new image of martyrdom was accepted by the Church most strongly and consistently in the cases of child saints. While the child martyrs of the persecutions almost invariably demonstrated understanding and acceptance of their death for Christ, the less sophisticated society of the Franks and the Anglo-Saxons increasingly translated the act of martyrdom into one of outward form rather than inward faith. Physical death rather than spiritual triumph became the principal attribute of martyrdom, and consequently the focus of attention in the legends of various saints of this period. While this pattern of martyrdom was not confined to child saints, it is seen most clearly in such cases, as adult victims often played an active role in the spread of Christianity, whether as missionaries, monks, or members of a royal family.

Several children met death in a way reminiscent of the classical model. St. Livin, missionary to Flanders in the mid-seventh century, baptized a young boy named Brice, or Britius, along with his mother Craphaildis. All three were martyred by pagans in 659.[34] The relics were translated to Ghent in 1007.[35] While this scenario is quite similar to earlier stories of missionary clerics who engaged in baptismal activity before martyrdom, no claim was made that the child made an active choice in either his baptism or his death. This was a clear deviation from the *puer senex* model established by the earlier child martyrs.

The cults of several child saints were the byproducts of barbarian invasions. The persecutors, either Huns or Vikings, were pagan, but they did not murder Christians on ideological grounds, rather in the course of raids or attacks. Adalric, an acolyte in the monastery of Besue in the diocese of Langres, was tortured and killed along with seven monks during a Viking raid, which probably occurred in the later eighth century. While his age is not specified, he is identified as a boy. The eight victims became the object of a local cult.[36] The religious vocation of Adalric and his companions augmented the basic criterion of a Christian murdered by a pagan, but the raiders undoubtedly targeted the monastery for material rather than spiritual reasons.

The cult of St. Donoald or Dinault, centered at Milly in Beauvais, exhibits a similar pattern. A healing well located in the village was known for its healing properties, especially the cure of epilepsy, and continued to be visited by pilgrims even after the removal of Donoald's relics to the monastery of St. Lucien in Burgundy in 1442. The legend associated with the shrine relates that, in the fifth century, marauding Huns attacked the village, and encountered a boy seated by a fountain. Asked his religion, he confessed his adherence to the Christian faith, and in token of understanding the consequences of his admission, voluntarily inclined his little head to receive the blow of the sword.[37] While the cult was certainly in existence before the twelfth century, when the personnel of the local church was expanded to care for the relics, the legend may be no more than a pious fiction meant to justify the use of a popular and probably lucrative healing well.

The Huns are also credited with the martyrdom of St. Memorius and his companions at Troyes in 451; the companions are identified in legend as seven or twelve innocent boys, baptized by St. Lupus to meet and repel the invading forces of Attila.[38] The identification of the victims as boys may indicate societal recognition of the special purity of children. While the story is undoubtedly fabulous, and is not mentioned in the *vita* of Lupus, the relics of the supposed martyrs were accorded longstanding local veneration. They were preserved in the Abbey of Saint Martin en Aires under the title of *Reliques des Saints Innocents*,[39] and were venerated into the modern period.

The conflict between Orthodox and heretical Christians provided the basis for the development of the cult of Saint Gaudins in fifth-century Gaul; the Visigoths, in addition to being invaders, were Arian Christians. Gaudins, a thirteen-year-old shepherd boy of the Haute-Garonne region, was beheaded by the Arian Visigoths in a wave of persecutions. His legend relates that he carried his severed head to his father in Mas-Saint-Pierre, now Saint-Gaudens, and they walked into the church together. The heretics who had killed the boy could not enter the church, but faithful Christians could.[40] The cult of St. Gaudins was popular throughout the Middle Ages, with numerous miracles occurring at the tomb.

In these cases, the identity of the pagan enemy varies with the time period and the locality, but the child victims seem, more than anything else, to have been in the wrong place at the wrong time. These martyrs were not killed as a result of their faith, but as a result of their presence in a place of attack. Nor were the victims, whether child or adult, the steadfast and eloquent champions of Christianity venerated by the early Church. These cases more accurately represent a clash of societies and cultures, with a religious context inserted into the legend to evoke the more classical concept of martyrdom.

The political and social structure that produced the early martyrs was most closely duplicated in the Middle Ages by Moslem rule in Spain. The presence of a dominant Moslem community after 711 produced one of the few areas in the medieval West where the political and social conditions approximated the Roman formula of a martyred Christian minority. Very few martyrs were executed, however, as the Umayyad government's attitude toward Christians was one of toleration rather than prosecution. Many Christian inhabitants of Al-Andalus refused to consider the Moslems to be pagans, since they worshipped the same God as the Christians. Religious conflict under the Umayyads was generally limited to the most fanatical segment of the Christian population, who often had difficulty in finding a Moslem who would persecute them.[41] The Martyrs of Córdoba deliberately courted death by "publicly blaspheming Mohammed and disparaging Islam…It was clear to everyone, even Eulogius, that the martyrs of Córdoba were not martyrs of the ancient Roman cast."[42] All child martyrs in Moslem Spain are found in or around Córdoba, and similarly deviate from the classical model.

The idea of the child martyr was well-established in medieval Spain from the time of the persecutions, as demonstrated by the cults of SS. Justus and Pastor, and the child martyr Eulalia. The cults and legends of child martyrs in the period of Moslem rule, dating from the ninth and tenth centuries, show strong adherence to the earlier models. They are adolescents rather than young children, and great emphasis is placed on their spirited defense of the Christian faith. The most famous was the boy martyr, Pelagius, or Pelayo, whose memory was promoted throughout the Christian west by Hrosvitha of Gandersheim. Another boy martyr, Sanció, was the object of more localized veneration. Although issues of faith are emphasized in both accounts, cultural conflicts are clearly evident. The virgin martyrs Flora and Maria, slain in Cordoba in 851 and are sometimes identified as young girls, but their *passios* do not place any notable emphasis on their youth.[43]

Sancló was a youth brought up in the royal court who converted to Christianity, proclaimed his new faith, and was martyred *in adolescentis*, embracing death without hesitation.[44] Although the outline of his story is simple, it recalls the tensions between parents and children exhibited in *passio* of the earlier martyrs. No historical record of such a member of the ruling family survives outside the realm of hagiography, but his story may have gained popularity among the disgruntled Christian minority by introducing the image of apostasy into the formidable stronghold of Moslem rule.

Saint Pelayo, or Pelagius, is one of the very few male saints honored as a virgin martyr. Pelayo was a boy of thirteen killed in 925 after refusing to convert to Islam.[45] In the process of upholding his faith, he rejected not only the religion of the Moslem rulers, but the cultural practices found most objectionable by the Christian community. The reputation of Moslems for embracing a diversity of carnal pleasures was already well established by the tenth century.[46] Pelayo was sent to the court of Caliph Abd al-Rahman at the age of ten to serve as a hostage in place of his uncle, who was a bishop in the Church. As the boy grew, he became remarkable for his handsome appearance and pleasing ways. At the age of thirteen, he was offered a wealth of treasures and benefits if he would proffer his favors to the Caliph.[47] Pelayo responded by calling the Caliph a dog, proclaiming that he would not renounce his Christian faith, and also that he did not wish to be used in an effeminate manner. The spurned Caliph had the boy slowly dismembered, the amputation of his limbs preceding the final act of decapitation. Pelayo is considered by the Church a martyr to both faith and chastity.[48]

The rapidity with which the cult of St. Pelayo spread in tenth-century Spain and abroad provides a measure of Christian hostility to the Moslem presence. In Córdoba, his body was placed in the Church of St. Genesius, and the severed head in the basilica of St. Cyprian. In 967, the body was translated to León, and in 985 to Oviedo, and the cult continued to spread throughout Spain, where he is venerated to the present day.[49] The story of Pelayo, renamed Pelagius, was compelling enough to find a wider audience in a region outside the sphere of Moslem influence. Around 968, Hrosvitha of Gandersheim honored the youth with a poem recounting his ordeal.[50] Although the poem was separated from the event by four decades, Hrosvitha claimed to write from an eyewitness account. "The details of this were supplied to me by an inhabitant of the town where the saint was put to death. This truthful stranger assured me that he had not only seen Pelagius, whom he described as the most beautiful of men, face to face, but had been a witness to his end."[51]

This "truthful" version, which described how Pelagius miraculously survived being catapulted onto the rocky sea-coast at Granada only to be laid low by decapitation, demonstrates how a saint's legend was transported from one region to another and altered in the retelling. Pelagius became a young man of eighteen rather than a boy of thirteen, and was sent as a hostage in place of his noble father rather than his uncle the bishop. Most tellingly, the request to convert to Islam was omitted, and the only demands that Abd al-Rahman made on him were sexual. Hrosvitha's account of the martyrdom, albeit strikingly different from the Andalusian version, was roughly contemporary. She could not have been familiar with the other version, and probably learned of Pelagius as she said, from a Spanish visitor. The extent of her interest is indicated by the fact that he was one of the very few contemporary saints she chose to write about. Veneration of Pelagius in Hrosvitha's version of the story reflects the later adaptation of the concept of martyrdom to the act of a pagan killing a Christian. With no request that the boy renounce Christianity, defense of the Christian faith was removed as a justification for bestowing the title of martyr.[52] The older Pelagius, advanced in age from thirteen to eighteen, still qualified as a martyr to chastity, but lost his childish vulnerability. Rather than passively accepting his fate, as did the younger Pelayo, he punched the caliph in the face for his offensive suggestion.[53]

The innocence of the child martyrs found a new and more outward manifestation during the period of conversion. Several cults were explicitly tied to the act of baptism, and may have been connected with missionary attempts to introduce baptism as a widespread practice. Pagan parents were wary of submitting their children to this ritual, especially in a time of high mortality for children. Of the three children of King Edwin baptized along with him, two "were snatched from life while still wearing their white baptismal robes."[54] Samson, the son of Chilperic, was ordered baptized during a severe illness. "This was done, the ceremony being performed by the Bishop himself, but Samson died before completing his fifth year."[55] Another son of Chilperic was baptized during an epidemic, but "wasted away before the onslaught of the disease and finally died."[56] The mystery surrounding this ritual may have given rise to "a superstition that to baptize the child was to attract an early death...There are strong hints that baptism may have been seen in the light of a sacrifice, and that baptism, pagan rites of infant dedication and donation, and death may have been subtly interwoven in a difficult and ambiguous pattern."[57] Baptism figures prominently in the stories of Memorius and his companions, as well as St. Brice, although the justification for sanctity ultimately depended on the murder of Christians by pagans. The importance of baptism in the spiritual life and afterlife of children was even more strongly reflected in the promotion of cults of child saints who died of natural causes and were venerated as confessors. The cults of St. Dentlin at Cleves and St. Rumwald in Kent represent examples of this tendency, first seen in the cult of St. Lusor at Bourges.

St. Dentlin, venerated at Rees in the Duchy of Cleves from the seventh century, died, like Lusor, *in albis*[58] in early childhood. The term is supposed to signify the wearing of baptismal garments, although it was also used to convey a general state of innocence and purity rather than a garment for a specific ceremony. The young girl of unknown origin, mentioned by Gregory of Tours, caused similar speculation of death in a state of innocence. "Because of the shiny whiteness of her silk robe some of us thought that she had died while wearing the white robes [immediately after her baptism]."[59] It is likely that many such instances of localized veneration on similar grounds have been lost to the historical and hagiographical record.

Dentlin, like many early medieval saints, was more than just an individual who died in the right way at the right time. He was the son of saints Mauger and Waldetrud, who were also the parents of saints Landric, Aldetrud and Madelberta. Although it has been postulated that "he is probably only venerated because his father, mother, aunt, brother and sister are numbered with the saints,"[60] his cult was unquestionably popular, and numerous miracles were reported at his tomb. Cults to the child existed at Mons and Emmerich, and he was considered the patron saint of Rees.[61] A portion of his relics were kept in the church at Rees which bears his name, and the rest were preserved with those of his father in the church of St. Vincent de Soignies.[62] Although connection with a saintly and therefore well-known family undoubtedly played a significant role in the initial acceptance of the cult, its survival into the twentieth century indicates a greater popularity for the child himself.

The sacrament of baptism played a central role in the legend of St. Rumwald, although unlike Dentlin, his sanctity was accompanied by far more impressive manifestations of divine favor. Rumwald was an infant who was miraculously given the gift of speech. He used this power to request his own baptism, then preached a brief sermon, and died peacefully at the age of three days, around the year 650.[63] Family connections played a role in Rumwald's case as well; his mother, Cyneburga, was the daughter of Penda, the great pagan king of Mercia, and also became a saint. His father was Alchfrid, son of King Oswy of Northumbria. Rumwald is considered to be a hagiographical curiosity, and his existence is probably legendary. Bede records the marriage of his parents, Alchfrid son of Oswiu, and (later Saint) Cyneburga, daughter of Penda, but does not mention a child.[64] The date of Rumwald's death is based on the claim that he was the grandson of Penda. The earliest surviving notice of the saint is found in an eleventh century manuscript, although the cult may be older, and the most detailed account of Rumwald's brief life, including the text of his sermon, is contained in the *Nova Legenda Angliae*.[65]

The legend of Rumwald may have reflected the importance attached to the conversion of the royal families of Anglo-Saxon England, especially the family of Penda, but the central theme of his brief life, illustrated in the sermon preached by the infant, is the importance of baptism as a sacrament and a ritual. His first miraculous declaration at birth, the phrase *Christianus sum* repeated three times,[66] evoked the utterances of early child martyrs such as Hilarion and Cyricus. Rumwald then requested to be baptized, chose his sponsors, pointed out the stone which would serve as a font, and finally gave instructions for the disposition of his body after death.[67] The relics, in accordance with the wishes of the loquacious infant, were first buried at King's Sutton, where they remained for a year. They were then translated to Brackley for two years, and finally to Buckingham,[68] where Rumwald's wish that they remain "for all time" was eventually foiled by the anticlerical depradations of the Reformation. Cults survived at all three locations, in addition to various other locales as far away as Wessex. Colchester and Bonnington, in Kent, preserved churches dedicated to Rumwald, but those at Lincoln and Boxley were demolished. Churches also existed at Cann and Pentridge in Dorsetshire, and Ruboldswyke in Sussex and Romualdkirl in the North Riding of Yorkshire are disputed, but probable.[69]

The memory of little Saint Rumwand survived in a surprising array of folk customs, indicating that the popular appeal of the saint went far deeper than official promotion of the sacrament of baptism. Rumwald became the patron saint of the fishermen of Folkestone, although it is not remembered why, and the town was the center of the traditional rumbal feast. The fishermen held the old custom of rumbal night, in which each man sold the eight best whitings from his boat, and used the money for a feast on Christmas Eve. The fish were called rumbal whitings.[70] Brackley, which tradition held to have played temporary host to the diminutive relics, preserved a healing well, and a mineral spring known as Saint Romualdes well could also be found in the hamlet of Astrop, near Sutton.[71] Six pre-Conquest monasteries in Mercia and Wessex bore his name, and although the last liturgical mention of Rumwald occurred in the eleventh century, in the Bosworth psalter and litany of Winchester, Hollingham in Sussex was known in the thirteenth century as the City of St. Rumwald.[72] The church to St. Rumwald, now demolished, at Boxley, Kent preserved the tradition of youthful innocence and baptismal purity by maintaining a small statue of the saint, "which only those could lift who had never sinned in thought or deed."[73] The pious tradition fell victim to the justice of the Reformation, however, when it was revealed that the priests were able to control the movement of the figure with levers, and the shrine was destroyed.

The creation and veneration of child martyrs and confessors in the age of conversion reveals an appreciation for the state of childhood as well as a significant departure in practice and understanding from the concept of martyrdom established by the early Christian church. On the surface, each cult reflects the idea that sanctity results from the death of a Christian at the hands of non-Christians, or death in a religious context, as in the pure state of baptism. Just as medieval legends of early Christian child martyrs showed pagans attributing magical powers to holy children, many of these cults reveal a connection with pre-Christian religious or magical practices through the association of the cults with healing wells or sacred groves. The spread of Christianity in early medieval Europe is well known for incorporating pagan practices into Christian ritual, and for promoting Christianity as a superior form of magic; Bede and his contemporaries mention numerous examples of syncretism, such as the substitution of Christian churches and relics in the location of pagan temples and altars, or pagans adopting Christian customs such as baptism or communion for the power they expect to derive from the ritual. The cult of the saints, foremost the veneration of relics, was adopted in early medieval Europe with notable enthusiasm; the promotion of children as saints points to a similar role for children in pre-Christian practices that was translated into early medieval Christian society. The cults of medieval child murder victims venerated as saints provide an even stronger set of examples.

CHAPTER 5

Murder as Martyrdom: Child Victims of Violent Crime

Of this, that they feign for themselves that dead persons of whatever sort are saints. [1]
—*Indiculus superstitionum et paganiarum*, 8th c.

The practice of according sanctity through martyrdom to individuals who were murdered for personal or political reasons may stand as the most original and significant contribution of early medieval society to popular religion. Modern researchers in hagiology regularly point out the existence of saints who should not be considered saints in terms of doctrinal belief; the popular appeal of these cults, however, is beyond dispute. One classic study of Anglo-Saxon royal saints begins by noting that "murder by fellow Christians for secular motives may seem to us an improbable qualification for sanctity."[2] Within this dubious category, child saints occupy a position of prominence.

The majority of adult saints recognized in the sixth through tenth centuries demonstrated a religious vocation in their lives as monks, nuns, priests and bishops. Many were also members of royal households who assumed positions of leadership in the secular Church or within monastic communities. A number of secular rulers also achieved sanctity. Most died in battle against various pagan adversaries-Edmund against the Vikings, Oswald and Edwin against Penda of Mercia-and thus could be accorded a nominally Christian demise, although Ethelbert of Hereford was assassinated for purely political reasons. While some child martyrs of this period were accorded veneration because they were killed by pagans, others were awarded the title of martyrdom simply for being killed, often by relatives, and usually for political reasons. Most were of royal or noble blood; public veneration of a murdered member of a ruling family may reflect the relative visibility of noble children in any medieval community, and the importance of inheritance within the noble family to reduce the bloodshed of disputed succession. Viewed within the context of the social function of the cult of the saints in the transition from paganism to Christianity, the preponderance of children within this group suggests particular significance accorded to children within the realm of religion and magical belief.

Murder victims can be venerated as saints only through an imperfect popular understanding of the concept of martyrdom. This was first seen with the cult of the Holy Innocents, innocent victims who died unjustly and through no fault of their own. Further simplification of martyrdom to an unjust death allowed the title to be applied to any death by violence, either murderous or accidental.[3] Christian martyrs died violently, before their time, in defense of a cause they should not have been killed for. So, too, did many medieval figures regarded as saints, and for exactly the same reason. The violent death of a child was seen as a particular tragedy since the life cut short was especially brief.[4] Both family and community mourned the death of a child, and an unjust death was doubly mourned. As Barbara Hanawalt noted in regard to a later group of child martyrs, the ritual murder victims, "People in the Middle Ages did sentimentalize and venerate childhood, but in the way that they knew best-they made saints out of them."

The most fully developed legends of medieval child-martyrs of this type, and the greatest number of cases, can be found in Anglo-Saxon England. All legends revolve around issues of succession to political power and treacherous betrayal, and thus involve male saints. The legends range from the largely fantastic lives of saints in the sixth and seventh century to the historically verifiable life and death of Edward Martyr. Although all subjects predate the Conquest, their legends generally survive in post-Conquest versions. In most cases, pre-Conquest cults can be confirmed.[5]

An entry in the Anglo-Saxon Chronicle for the year 640 records that "Ermenred begot two sons, who were afterwards martyred by Thunor."[6] The names of the children were not recorded, nor was their existence mentioned by Bede. According to hagiographical tradition, their names were Ethelred and Ethelbert, and they died in 670. They were the sons of Ermenred, son of Eadbald, son of St. Ethelbert of Kent. Their age at death is not stated, but they are consistently characterized as young, or small. The only surviving mention of their cult is found in works dating from after the Norman Conquest, [7] but there is evidence that a version was in existence in the early eighth century.[8] According to their legend, their father died when they were of tender age, and the throne of Kent passed to their uncle Erconbert and later his son Egbert. Egbert did not intend to relinquish the throne to his cousins.[9] Although he loved the boys for their blameless lives,[10] Egbert was persuaded by his councillor Thunor to have them murdered.[11] Thunor killed the boys and buried them under the king's seat in the great hall of the royal residence at Eastry. That night, a bright light appeared over the palace and shone until the bodies were discovered. Egbert refused to take blame for the crime, although he did accept responsibility, and awarded a parcel of land as *wergild* to their sister, St. Ermenburga. This land became the foundation of Minster-in Thanet. Thunor protested at the value of the settlement and was swallowed up by the ground.[12]

While this story of political intrigue lacks any religious context except the establishment of a religious community in expiation of the deed, it shows that the boys were recognized as martyrs. William of Malmesbury placed blame for the crime on Thunor's manipulation of Egbert as a good-natured but weak-willed king. Thunor, arguing that the young princes must die, interpreted Egbert's feeble opposition as assent, and killed the two boys.[13] The light illuminating the resting place of the bodies provides the only miraculous occurrence associated with the incident. The cult of the two young princes continued for centuries, and their relics were translated some years after the death of Edward Martyr in the late tenth century.[14]

The legend of St. Kenelm, which was promoted by Bishop Oswald of Worcester, is similar to that of the two princes. Kenelm or Cenelm was the son of Cenwulf (796-821), who was succeeded by Coelwulf, a distant relative. Cenwulf also had a daughter, Cwenthryth or Quendreda.[15] Kenelm was probably the historical Cynehelm, a prince who acted as signatory of a number of charters from 803-811. He died at a young age, probably in his twenties but hardly as a child, some time between 811 and 819.[16] Quendreda was also an historical personage much removed from her legendary persona. She was the daughter of Coenwulf and had a distinguished career as abbess of Southminster in Kent, and possibly Winchecombe Abbey as well.[17] At his death, Kenelm was buried at Winchecombe, and legends attributing sanctity and miraculous powers began to crystallize in a recognizable form by the late tenth century. Around 975, calendars began to list *Cynelmi martyris,* or *sancti Kynelmi martyris.*[18]

The fanciful story of Kenelm's murder, which was popularly recognized as martyrdom, can be found in manuscript form from the eleventh century.[19] Kenelm was portrayed as a seven-year-old boy who was killed at the behest of his evil older sister Quendreda. According to most versions, Quendreda's lover Askbert, who was also the boy's guardian, agreed to perform the treacherous deed, although William of Malmesbury blamed Quendreda for the crime and did not mention Askbert.[20] Askbert lured Kenelm into the woods on the pretext of a hunt, but the normally trusting child divined his impending murder. This gift of prophecy was soon followed by a more substantial miracle; a stick which Kenelm thrust into the ground blossomed into an ash-tree. This tree later became the site of popular veneration.[21]

Askbert beheaded the child and hid the body in a thicket, but Kenelm's ability to work miracles was not limited to his immediate surroundings. A miraculous dove appeared in Rome and dropped a document at the feet of the Pope while he was celebrating mass. The message, written in English, was incomprehensible to the Pope and his entourage until a group of English pilgrims was located. All present then discovered that "In Clento cou bathe Kenelm kynebearn lith under thorne havedes bereaved. [In Clent the cow pasture, Kenelm, the king's child, lieth under a thorn, bereft of his head.]"[22] The search party sent by the Pope to find the body of the murdered child was guided to its hiding place by a pillar of light. The body was removed to Winchecombe Abbey, but the location of the original burial also remained a popular pilgrimage site, and a chapel was built at that spot.[23] The chapel was destroyed during the Reformation, but a modern chapel located on Clent Hill is believed to mark the spot of the murder and burial. A stained-glass window in this chapel is dedicated to the child victims of the First World War.[24] The *vita*, compiled in the eleventh century, makes little attempt to place the death in the context of martyrdom. Kenelm was the young victim of political assassination, a form of unjust death. The only religious element of the legend was the involvement of the Pope in detection of the crime. The detail that Kenelm was said to be singing a hymn at the moment the knife sliced through his neck may have been intended to portray a pious Christian outlook and a willing acceptance of his fate, but is still a far cry from the classical concept of martyrdom.

The ninth-century prince Wistan or Wigstan was also venerated as a martyr following his murder in 849. Wistan was the grandson of Witlaf, king of Mercia, and heir to the throne since his father had died. While still a child, Wistan was murdered by his cousin Bithfour, the son of his uncle Bertulf who had seized the throne because of the opportunity afforded by Wistan's youth.[25] Although the events indicate a political assassination, the eleventh-century legend infused the murder with religious overtones. The murderer, Bithfour, became the boy's godfather as well as his cousin,[26] and Wistan was slain not because of his claim to the throne, but because he opposed his mother's marriage to his cousin and godfather on the grounds that such a union would be incestuous. Wistan's murder therefore assumed a religious context: as a good Christian upholding the laws of the Church on incest,

Wistan was foully murdered. A twelfth-century account in the *Worcester Chronicle* further distanced Wistan's murder from political motives by claiming that he declined to be king for religions reasons.[27] William of Malmesbury did not recount the details of the crime, but attributed Wistan's saintliness to his innocence: *Nihil in Deo puritate tua innocentius, qua invitatus internus arbiter te honorificaverit.*[28] The body, buried at a spot which came to be known as Wistanstow,[29] was revealed by a pillar of light which shone over the area for thirty days. After their discovery, the remains were taken to Repton Abbey in Derbyshire, but the place of his burial continued to receive visitations as well. Thomas of Marlborough in the later twelfth century reported the miracle of "hair" growing on the ground at Wistanstow where the child's blood had run out; the phenomenon was subsequently verified by a factfinding commission sent by Baldwin, Archbishop of Canterbury.[30]

The widespread promotion of Wistan's cult can be dated from 1019 when Aelfwald, Abbot of Evesham, asked King Cnut for the relics of Wistan. Evesham became the center of the cult from that time on. The *vita* and *miracula* of St. Wistan were recorded by Thomas, Prior of Evesham,[31] and seem to be part of a general revival of cults of this type which no doubt proved both popular and lucrative. Evidence for the popularity of Wistn's cult, in the form of church dedications and place-names, indicates that his veneration was confined to the region of his murder and interment.[32]

Edward the Martyr, for whom the most historically verifiable data survives, was killed in 978[33] at the command of his stepmother Elfrida so that her own son could inherit the throne. The authenticity of the events surrounding the murder of Edward and the subsequent establishment of his cult are fairly certain. He succeeded to the throne in 975 at the age of thirteen, and was killed three years later at Corfe Castle in Dorsetshire.[34] Edward was stabbed in the lungs by an accomplice of his stepmother while accepting a cup which she held out to him, but was actually killed during his attempted escape. He slipped from his saddle, but his foot was caught in the stirrup, and he was dragged through the woods.[35] Edward's body was hidden in a marsh and revealed by a pillar of light, as with all of his holy predecessors.

His cult enjoyed almost immediate popularity. As the Anglo-Saxon Chronicle notes for the year, "His earthly kinsmen would not avenge him, but his heavenly Lord has greatly avenged him."[36] The cult was promoted by St. Dunstan, and Aethelraed first ordered the general observation of the festival thirty years later.[37] The allegations of the stepmother's involvement first appeared in writing over a century later, in a life of St. Dunstan.[38]

Hagiographical tradition surrounding the cult held that "[Edward] gave a bright example of piety and purity of life, and by his sweet disposition gained the hearts of the people,"[39] but the historical Edward, was noted for his violent temper. "Long after he had passed into veneration as a saint it was remembered that his outbursts of rage had alarmed all who knew him, and especially the members of his own household."[40] Various relics were dispersed across the countryside. Originally buried at Wareham, Dorsetshire, his body was found incorrupt after three years and translated to the monastery at Shaftesbury, Dorsetshire. Most of the relics were kept at Wareham, but his lungs went to Edwardstow, Dorsetshire, in 1001, and the knife used to stab him was preserved at the church in Faversham, Hampshire, until the Reformation.[41]

The murder of St. Edward, and the atonement by his stepmother, who entered a nunnery, spurred a revival of interest in the cults or earlier royal child martyrs. The relics of Ethelred and Ethelbricht were translated thirteen or fourteen years after Edward's death. St. Wistan's relics became the object of ecclesiastical interest within a half-century of Edward's murder. The cult of St. Kenelm may also have received renewed interest. The chronicles of St. Werburgh's Abbey record that Prince Edward entered Chester on St. Kenelm's day, indicating that the feast was already popular; of course, this coincidence could have been highlighted or invented in light of the similarity of the two stories, including the method of execution.[42] The body of St. Kenelm was supposedly discovered in 1815 during an excavation of the foundations of the Abbey church at Faversham, with a knife at his side.[43]

The cults of murdered Anglo-Saxon saints, whether adult or child, have been characterized as an "unparalleled tradition" in hagiography,[44] but an examination of the cults of child saints venerated elsewhere in Europe reveals many similarities. The fabulous story of St. Melor bears a strong resemblance to the legends of Kenelm and Wistan, and is also connected to the cult of Edward at Amesbury. The legend of Melor, or Mylor, is variously set in the fifth, sixth, and eighth centuries; the legend itself probably dates from the eleventh,[45] although the cult is older than the manuscript version of the legend.[46] The cult originated in Brittany and later spread to England and Cornwall.[47] Details such as the identity of the family members involved and the place names differ, but all versions of the legend concern a family quarrel over power. Melor was the son of the Duke of Cornouaille in Brittany.[48] When Melor was seven, his father was killed by his brother who wished to seize the throne. Melor's life was spared by his uncle at the request of the clergy, but his right hand and left foot were cut off, thus effectively eliminating as a potential rival and rendering him unfit to be king. This double mutilation made Melor practically unfit for mounted battle, and also violated the ancient precepts of sacral kingship. The supernatural qualities associated with early medieval royalty depended upon physical perfection. "They had to be without physical blemish; the loss of an eye or limb rendered them unable to perform their mystical functions."[49]

The mutilated Melor was fitted with a silver hand and brazen foot and confined to a monastery. After seven years passed, Melor reached the ago of fourteen and began to work miracles. His artificial limbs came to life and functioned as though natural, and he worked other miracles as well, such as calling forth a fountain from the earth by throwing a stone on the ground. These miraculous abilities were not ascribed to any qualities of piety demonstrated by Melor, but instead demonstrated divine compensation for the injustice suffered at the hands of his uncle. The uncle, hearing of these events, bribed Melor's guardian to behead him. At the execution of this monstrous crime, angels appeared with lights to guard the body until the deed was discovered. The assassins brought Melor's head to his uncle as proof that they had carried out his command. During the journey, the head spoke to the assassins and produced a fountain to quench their thirst. When the uncle touched the head, he died. Finally, wild white bulls were used to carry the body to its grave.[50]

The translation of the relics to England at some point in the tenth century or later inspired a change in the identity of the family to that of the dukes of Cornwall. The relics were probably translated to Amesbury in England between 910913,[51] although a twelfth-century life of Melor claimed that the relics were acquired later.[52] In 979, Queen Elfrida founded a Benedictine monastery dedicated to SS. Mary and Melorus in Amesbury, Wiltshire, in token of remorse for the murder of her stepson Edward the Martyr.[53] The Abbey was also a site of religious significance in pre-Christian times,[54] but the largesse of the remorseful queen may have been suggested by the prior location of the relics at the site. Various other sites in Brittany and Cornwall contain dedications to the boy prince.[55] King Aethelstan seems to have collected relics of the Breton saint, and distributed them to churches as a sign of his royal favor.[56]

The legend of Melor is the most folkloric of the murdered princes, and even William of Malmesbury put uncertain value on the story.[57] The cult of Melor at the monastery of Amesbury, Wiltshire, did not generate a high income, and William, who lived only thirty miles away, said very little about it. He knew of the presence of St. Melor, but was ignorant of the *vita*.[58] Like the other murdered princes, the secret crime of the aristocracy was revealed to the local villagers through miraculous means. The church dedicated to

Melor at Lanmeur, which claimed his relics into the present era, contains a holy well;[59] the prevalence of miraculous fountains created by Melor in his legend suggest the existence of additional sites now lost.[60] In the legend, Melor appears at seven and again at fourteen, significant divisions in the Ages of Man. Melor's miraculous recovery of the use of his limbs at fourteen, a possible beginning of the age of adulthood, may symbolize the worthiness for the kingship his uncle sought to deprive him of.

While the legend of St. Melor straddles the border between the folkloric and the fantastic, the legends of other child saints murdered by family members reflect typical secular power struggles swathed in a coat of religion. Saint Gerulph of Flanders was the son of a noble of Merendrée, probably an adolescent, killed circa 746 by a relative who was also his godfather. The motive for the crime was the vast estate to which the boy was heir, and a journey from Tronchiennes to Merendrée provided the opportunity for the crime. As the young victim of a violent death, many miracles were reported at his tomb at Merendrée.[61]

Recognition of the miraculous powers of Gerulph's relics precipitated a translation of his body to Tronchiennes around 915.[62] A legendary *passio* was composed at that time, which ignored the secular motives for the murder, and attributed the murder of Geruph to the jealousy felt by his godfather for his exemplary piety. The journey resulting in his death was to receive the sacrament of confirmation at the monastery of Mont-Blandin. The relative, acting as sponsor to the ceremony, felt such violent jealousy for the boy's piety that he conceived the idea of murder. On the return journey, he attacked the boy, still *in albis*, the white of his confirmation robes, near Ghent and left him for dead. Gerulph lived long enough to pardon his attacker, and incidentally to bequeath his relics and his patrimony to the monastery at Tronchiennes.[63] Popular belief continued to credit the relics of Gerulph with miracles into the fifteenth century.[64] Unfortunately, in the sixteenth century most of the relics fell prey to the ire of the Calvinists, although the head was preserved at Tronchiennes, where it was invoked against fever.

Two sixth-century cults in Brittany preserve nothing more substantial than the memory of a murder. The Parish of Saint Geran contains a small chapel dedicated to two princes known only as the *Saints Dredenau*. According to local legend, the saints were two young princes, brothers who were slain by an ambitious uncle. He threw their bodies into a marsh to conceal the crime, but the site was revealed by a white sow that appeared and guarded the spot until the villagers discovered the bodies. No clue to the identity of the princes exists; it has been suggested that they were the sons of

Modred, the royal children murdered ca. 538547 by Constantine of Cornwall, as recorded by Gildas.[65] The chapel has survived to the modern period, and contains crude statues meant to represent the saints, said to be youthful figures.[66] An inscription in the chapel attests that the saints fought to the death for the law of God, but the details of their accomplishments have been lost.

The legend of Saint Tremorus, or Tremeur, also said to originate in sixth-century Brittany, contains little more of substance. Tremorus was the young or infant son of St. Triphina, and was put to death at a young age by his wicked stepfather, Conmore, at the monastery of Rhuys in Carhaux.[67] He became the patron saint of the region, and while the relics were lost after 965, the cult continued in popularity. He was invoked for the recovery of sores and wounds; a sixteenth-century statue portrays him as a cephalophore, which may be a preservation of ancient tradition, or a later confusion of legendary elements.[68]

Similarly shaky doctrinal ground is trodden by the *vita* of Saints Peter and Audolet, young nephews of St. Lambert of Maastricht, killed with him in the first decade of the eighth century for reasons unclear. The later *vita* assigns the act of murder to soldiers of Alpaide, the concubine of Pippin of Heristal; in this version, the pair was killed in defense of their uncle, who had expressed disapproval of Pippin's adulterous relationship with his concubine.[69] The religious motivation for the death of these young men was peripheral; it is possible that their uncle was engaged in the ongoing struggle of the clergy to modify the libidinous behavior of the early medieval aristocracy through the regulation of sexual partners.[70]

Accidental death was less commonly venerated than murder. The only extant example of such a case is the cult of Saint Tyfei of Pembrokeshire, in Wales, attributed to the early sixth century. Tyfei was a young child [*infans*] killed when he interfered in a quarrel between two men over the actions of a herd of swine. A man named Tutuc found a herd of swine in his field, accosted the swineherd, and in the heat of the argument threatened him with his javelin. Tyfei rushed between the two men, and the javelin pierced and killed him.[71] When Tutuc discovered that the child he had killed was the son of a banished prince, and the nephew of the archbishop, Saint Teilo, he presented himself before the archbishop for penance. Through the intervention of the king, Tutuc received as his punishment a blood fine and the reduction of himself and all his progeny into perpetual servitude. The relics of the little boy were preserved in the church at Pennally, Pembrokeshire, a nearby church was dedicated to him, and he became the patron saint of the region.[72] While the popular veneration of the child can be explained as a result of his aristocratic connections, accidental death is rarely an attribute of sanctity. It is possible that the legend masked a political assassination, since Tyfei came from an influential family, but his father was out of favor at the time.

Young murder victims who were honored as martyrs on both a popular and official level represented the innocence of youth as well as the tragedy of an unjust death. All were members of royalty or nobility, and legitimate heirs to power. Popular veneration may have symbolized recognition of the need for stability among rulers, as well as a protest against unjust usurpation. Clerical promotion of such cults may have been intended to curb such violent activities among the nobility, and bring its members more closely under the behavioral edicts of the Church. The significance of childish innocence, however, can be seen by two similar cults in which the succession to power was not an issue because the objects of veneration were female.

Saint Reginswinde or Reginsidis of Lauffen, who died circa 840 at the age of seven, was the daughter of the margrave of Lauffen-on-Neckar. Although the exercise of aristocratic power contributed indirectly to her death, her murder was more a crime of passion than the result of a calculated power struggle. Reginswinde was born to Ernest and his wife Frideburga, and in the manner of the nobility, entrusted to the care of a nurse. When the nurse's brother was whipped to death by the margrave for the crime of horse-stealing, she abducted the child, slit her throat, and threw her into the Neckar. The body was found three days later, and placed in the cemetery of the church. Almost immediately, a number of miracles occurred in the vicinity, and Hubert, Bishop of Wurzburg, received a vision to elevate the relics of the child and build a new church for them.[73]

Although the legend in its present form was probably developed in the twelfth century,[74] there is abundant evidence for the rapid development of a popular cult around the body of the murdered girl. By 850, the name of Reginsidis was already recorded in a martyrology of Richenau, and in the tenth century she was honored at Essen. Her name was included in a mid-eleventh century litany in Tegernsee, Bavaria, and in a version of the Martyrology of Cologne which dates from the early thirteenth century, so her reputation spread beyond the immediate locality, and interest in her cult was sustained for several centuries.[75] She was also the patron saint of a number of churches in the Diocese of Wurzburg, including a parish church consecrated to her, located on the riverbank at the site of the discovery of her body. At least some of her relics were kept at the church; in 1521 they were enclosed in a golden reliquary, but this was melted down in 1534. The relics were translated to a box of tin, and were lost after 1547 in the confusion of the

Reformation. A sarcophagus which had contained some of her relics, dating from 1227 on the occasion of her translation and canonization, survived and was moved to the chapel (now Protestant) in 1880.[76]

Another example of the popular veneration of victims of violent crime is provided by the legend of saint Tanca, a young girl killed violently in an attempted rape by a family servant. After the crime, the body was interred in a manner imitative of the treatment of other martyrs. The cult, which is said to date from the early seventh century, originated in the village of Lhuitre, which possessed the relics. Lhuitre became the center of popular pilgrimage, and various relics, including the head, eventually migrated to Troyes, Anges, and other locations. A pun on the name Tanche-*etanché,* meaning staunched or watertight-has led to her name being invoked against hemorrhage, and against urinary incontinence in children.[77] Since no historical documents verify her existence, nothing can be known of her class affiliation beyond the tradition that she was attacked by a servant. Her legend may have been invented to justify local customs regarding childrearing and healing,[78] but the association remains a curious one.

Examined individually, these cults are often labeled hagiographical curiosities; taken together, they indicate strong currents of popular belief in the quality of sanctity derived from youth and innocence at the time of death, gathered under the umbrella of medieval Christianity, but certainly derived from other than canonical sources. While political or ecclesiastical ends may have been served by the official promotion of all of these cults, none could have existed without substantial popular sympathy for the child victims. That so many dubious cults received ecclesiastical promotion may in part be attributed to societal attitudes, shared by the Church, of lenience and tolerance where children were concerned. Many children in medieval society certainly died before their time, some no doubt violently, without inspiring cults in their honor. In the veneration of children who were so honored, however, we can see the societal reaction to such a tragedy, especially the impulse to honor the dead in a way which was generally condemned by clerics as pagan superstition. The unusual strength of these cults may be due to the innocence of their subjects. Popular enthusiasm for the veneration of slain children may also derive from the pre-Christian association of children and the violently dead with magical practices.

Christina Hole notes that "ghosts of the dead, particularly those who died violently, have been a part of folk-belief since earliest times."[79]

It was commonly believed that suicides, murder victims, men killed in battle - in short, all those who died before their time - could unleash enormous powers of

destruction at the moment of their death and for some time afterwards...The spirits
of those who die young or who die a violent death can turn into vengeful demons.[80]

The power concentrated in the earthly remains of the violently dead could be
used for positive as well as negative purposes. In the ancient world, the blood
of executed criminals could be used in spells, and was especially efficacious
in curing epilepsy.[81] The early martyrs, who could also be considered
executed criminals, were considered to provide miraculous cures through
their blood, bones, and other relics. Jews accused the early Christians of
sorcery using magical power derived from conjuring the spirit of Christ, who
"had died a violent criminal's death,"[82] and much of pagan society looked
askance at the early Christian obsession with "bits of the dead."[83] In the
ancient world, spells which were said at the tomb of the victim of a violent
death were believed to be strengthened through the power represented by
such an individual.[84] This type of magical ritual resembles in outward
appearance the medieval practice of supplication at the tomb of a saint, just
as the medieval martyrs resemble their classical counterparts in outward form
rather than spiritual intent.

Popular practices associated with the cult of the saints were
enthusiastically incorporated into Anglo-Saxon and Germanic culture. Cults
of child martyrs and other royal murder victims may preserve the most
doctrinally palatable remnants of the medieval propensity to venerate the
victims of unjust death as martyrs. Only scattered references to spontaneous
cults suppressed by the clergy survive to indicate a more widespread
practice. A family quarrel among two branches of the viscounts of Comborne
began with a quarrel over inheritance between uncle and nephew. The
nephew publicly violated his uncle's wife on the wall of the disputed manor,
and was later killed by his uncle in revenge. Local sympathy was on the side
of the murdered youth, a young man of nineteen. Marc Bloch, who recounts
the story, notes that "the tragic end, the wrongs which the victim had
suffered, and above all his youth, so moved the people that for several days
offerings were laid on his temporary grave at the spot where he was killed, as
if it were the shrine of a martyr."[85] In the early twelfth century, Guibert of
Nogent complained of the rise of a popular cult around the remains of a
young man of low birth, who had died on Good Friday.[86] Offerings and
candles were brought to his tomb by the local villagers, who were either
unaware of or undisturbed by the cult's doctrinal deficiencies. Caesarius of
Heisterbach recounted the story of a young cleric unjustly accused of
adultery and burned at the stake. "He died, and his bones were buried in the
open field. At his tomb lights were often seen and miracles were
wrought...later a church was built over his tomb."[87] William of Newburgh

reported that in 1190, a former crusader named John who had later turned to crime was killed in Hampton by an associate who robbed him and cast his body outside the town. "The murderer fled when the corpse was recognized, but the belief spread rapidly that John was a martyr; miracles were worked at his grave and pilgrims flocked thither well laden with offerings, to the great satisfaction of the presiding priests, until the bishop came, and, after examining into the affair, put a stop to the absurd cult."[88] Pope Alexander III condemned the ignorant people who, "following the ways of the pagans and deceived by the fraud of the evil one, venerated as a saint a man who had been killed while intoxicated," and prohibited his worship "even though miracles were worked through him."[89]

Guinefort, the dog saint of thirteenth-century France immortalized by Stephen of Bourbon in his own time and Jean-Claude Schmitt in the twentieth century, was also the object of popular sympathy for suffering an unjust death. Guinefort was a dog who protected the infant son of his master from being bitten by a rat, and was killed by the father who walked into the nursery and saw the bloodstained dog standing over the baby's cradle. The body of the dog was thrown outside, but it was retrieved by the local populace. The father soon realized his mistake and erected a shrine to the dog in atonement, which was visited by the villagers [90] Such cases were tolerated by the local clergy, possibly, as H. C. Lea suggests, for financial reasons, but were suppressed by higher authorities. Stephen of Bourbon used the mechanisms of the Inquisition to suppress the cult of Guinefort on the grounds of superstition rather than heresy.[91] Vauchez notes that several individuals of this period killed for secular reasons generated popular cults, including Simon de Montfort and Thomas of Lancaster, as well as Margaret of Roskilde, murdered by her husband, and St. Nantvin, a German pilgrim falsely accused of pederasty and murdered by an angry mob, and that this phenomenon is found predominantly in England and the German-speaking regions of Europe, to the exclusion of the Mediterranean world.[92]

The murder or premature death of a child was thought in the ancient world to give access to magical powers similar to those attained through supplication of the saints. Wiedmann notes that "the ghost of a child who had died prematurely might be invoked to haunt an enemy."[93] Medieval beliefs concerning the magical power of children can be seen in the penitentials; Burchard of Worms condemned the superstition that children who died unbaptized, or mothers who died in childbirth, must be transfixed with a stake or they would injure many after death.[94] From classical antiquity through the early modern period, witches were believed to use the bodies of babies and children in magical rituals, and were prosecuted on such charges.[95] The counterpart to the witch, the midwife, was seen as having the greatest opportunity for traffic in the bodies of babies, and individuals were brought up on charges. In the early fifteenth century, Perrette, a Parisian midwife, was arrested as a participant in a plot to procure the body of a stillborn infant for a nobleman; the fat was said to cure leprosy.[96] The blood of a child younger than two was also thought to cure leprosy.[97] The bones of babies were also said to have magical or healing properties, as demonstrated by the midwife who taught people to cure illness with a magical ritual utilizing the bone of an unbaptized infant.[98] Brine from the umbilical cord of an infant was listed as an ingredient in a recipe for a magical candle; the supposed effect of the candle is unclear.[99] One recipe containing the fat of children specified that the donor must be strangled at night.[100]

The quality of purity dictated the role of children, especially young boys, in Greek and Roman religious rituals.[101] Young boys pure in body were considered to have a gift for prophecy.[102] According to Pliny, the urine of a chaste boy could be utilized as a magical charm.[103] Thorndike notes that "the story of having sacrificed a pure boy for purposes of magic or divination was a stock charge."[104] The power of magic was enhanced by the purity of children, but also made them vulnerable to its effects, creating societal fears for their safety.[105] Youth and purity, qualities found in all child saints and stressed in the cults of murdered children, was viewed as a potent combination for magical as well as spiritual purposes. Magical lore from antiquity was studied by a few individuals in the Middle Ages but was certainly unknown on a popular scale; popular medieval magical beliefs may be unrelated to the classical tradition but exhibit similar characteristics.[106] A number of medieval figures recounted experiments performed with boys. John of Salisbury related many instances of belief in magic and fortunetelling in twelfth-century society, including a childhood experience in which he and another boy were recruited by a priest to foretell the future by gazing into reflecting surfaces. This practice reflected the ancient belief that spirits would appear to a pure boy.[107] A treatise attributed to Michael Scot included the urine of a boy as an ingredient in alchemical charms.[108] William of Auvergne, Bishop of Paris from 1228 to 1249, warned of magicians who would even commit murder to achieve their aims.[109] The general population was doubtless unaware of specific magical practices derived from antiquity, but may have held a similar concept of the power of childish innocence.

Jonathan Sumption attributes the popular propensity to venerate royal murder victims to "ignorant people" spontaneously creating heroes,[110] but fails to explain what qualities of infants or children would be considered heroic. These cults, instead, represented the popular propensity to seek the benefits of magic through the legitimately sanctioned channel of religion. The choice of the Church to suppress such cults when directed at adults, while allowing, and even promoting, cults to children, may have been influenced by cultural appreciation of the innocence of children. The popular appeal of child saints may be found in folklore.

The inclusion of folkloric elements in the practice of medieval Christianity is found in many forms, and has frequently allowed the "survival of pagan practices" to come to the notice of the historian.[111] From at least the time that Gregory the Great instructed Bishop Mellitus to destroy the pagan idols of the Anglo-Saxons, but to leave the temples and turn them into churches, with relics of the saints,[112] a certain amount of syncretism of Christian with pagan beliefs was a part of popular religious practice, and the cult of the saints was at the forefront of this phenomenon. Through such practices, the survival of non-Christian beliefs in European peasant society continued into the modern period.[113] In trying to suppress pagan practices directed at children, Aelfric admonished mothers against drawing their infants through the earth at crossroads, and also warned against seeking out wells, stones, and trees. The worship of wells, trees and stones, as well as "drawing children through the earth" and other forms of sorcery, was also forbidden in a law of Canute.[114] The healing ritual for children associated with the cult of St. Guinefort included the practice of drawing a child between two trees in a sacred grove.[115]

The cults of child murder victims venerated as martyrs were popular in origin rather than officially promoted by the ecclesiastical hierarchy. Although the wave of renewed popularity of some of their cults seen in England in the late tenth and early eleventh centuries following the murder of Edward was due in part to the efforts of several churchmen, this may have been more effect than cause of popular sympathy. The legends of these saints reflect this popular background by exhibiting elements far more folkloric than hagiographical. In many of the stories, the saints created magical fountains and trees, which later become objects of veneration and miraculous cures. The appearance of a column of light or some similar motif was a frequent precursor to discovery of the holy remains. The site of the death and secret burial, usually in a wooded area, was often accorded as much honor as the relics in the local church. In addition, the accordance of sanctity was based not on any qualities which murder victims possessed, but rather on the circumstances of the death alone. These children were magical rather than holy.

The attachment of magical or religious significance to fountains and trees has long been recognized as a survival of pre-Christian practice.[116] St.

Kenelm's Ash, an unusually large and ancient tree located near the chapel believed to mark the site of Kenelm's murder was believed to be the tree he created just before his death.[117] St. Melor, as well, created a tree from a staff stuck in the ground; this was one of the miracles wrought by the severed head as it was carried back to the evil uncle. The miraculous or magical growth of trees and plants is a common motif in European folklore, and especially stories about children. Tyrolean legend recounts the story of a poor idiot boy, who lived alone in the forest and was unable to speak, except for the words, "Ave, Maria." After his death, a lily grew from his grave, with the words, "Ave, Maria," on the petals. In a striking resemblance to the Crocus story of classical mythology, Celtic legend attributes the origin of the daisy to the death of an innocent infant. The peasants of Brittany believed that children who died before the age of seven went straight to heaven because of their piety, and were changed into flowers.[118]

The association of saints with sacred fountains and healing wells was often used to legitimize popularly recognized pre-Christian sites.[119] The well of St. Melor at the church of St. Mabe, Cornwall, which was considered to have been created at the command of the saint's severed head, was used for centuries by local mothers, who gave the water to their children to make them strong.[120] Melor was credited with other healing powers over children, as well. A ruined chapel near Lanmeur was the site of an annual ceremony on the last Sunday in September; children were taken to the chapel to make them walk early, and to recover from teething.[121]

Although the legends of Kenelm and Rumwald do not mention the miraculous creation of a water source, two holy wells were associated with Kenelm and two with Rumwald. Kenelm's holy wells were located at Clent Hills and at Winchecome, the sites of his murder and later interment.[122] The well at Winchecombe was said to have sprung up from the spot where the body was laid before burial. Rumwald was the patron of holy wells at Brackney and King's Sutton.[123] Churches in both areas claimed to have been temporary resting-places for his relics before their removal to Buckingham, and these claims could conceivably have been attempts to retain the magical benefits of the saint after losing his relics to a more powerful establishment.

The legend of Rumwald presents the motif of an infant speaking precociously. While this may be viewed as a graphic variant of the *puer senex* motif, in which the child behaves in a way miraculously beyond the capabilities of his years, the quality of precocious speech may also have magical or prophetic connotations.[124] Saints and magicians both demonstrated their powers by granting babies the ability to speak. In the apocryphal Acts of Peter, Simon Magus caused a baby to speak.[125] Saint

Goar, directed by a bishop to perform a miracle, caused a three-day-old infant who had been abandoned at birth to speak and name his father; the child did so and named the bishop.[126] Renaissance thought held that children who spoke at the age of two months or had discretion beyond their years were influenced by the stars and were subject to supernatural influences. Such infants were destined to die young.[127] St. Rumwald, who shared this fate, was venerated for his miraculous speaking ability as well as the general purity of his post-baptismal infant state.

The most common element in the legends of murdered children is the appearance of a column of light or some similar sign at the site of furtive burial. This is a standard hagiographical motif, and may indicate a natural death in a remote place, or simple neglect of a saint's tomb, as well as a murder.[128] Columns of light also illuminated saints at prayer, or at death.[129] Certain elements of Norse folklore, however, shed some light on the possible broader significance of this phenomenon. In the Nordic tradition, the ghost of a murdered child, called a *myling,* was associated with the appearance of lights, specifically fire or flame.[130] Children and adults buried in the forest were thought to call to people from the body's hiding place. This phenomenon applied whether the death was the result of murder or an accident.[131] The typology of a murdered child carried to the forest and hidden was a common theme in Nordic tradition as well.[132] Further, spirits of the dead children were sometimes thought to appear as pigs.[133] The guardian spirit which appeared at the burial site of the SS. Dredenau was in the form of a white sow, and St. Tyfei met his death in the vicinity of a herd of pigs. Finally, Nordic folklore believed that dead children appear at seven-year intervals, and that children who die before the age of seven do not begin to haunt until that time is reached.[134] Kenelm was murdered at the age of seven; Melor was mutilated at the same age, and began to work miracles at the age of fourteen, the end of the next seven-year interval.

Veneration of the murder site, as well as the location of the relics, substantiates the popular nature of these cults. Kenelm, Melor and Wistan were murdered in the forest, and chapels were erected to commemorate the sites of their martyrdoms. A church dedicated to Reginsidis was built at the site on the riverbank where her body was discovered. The church at Llandyfeisant dedicated to St. Tyfei is believed to mark the site of his martyrdom,[135] and a church was erected near the holy fountain which marked the site of St. Donoald's murder. The attribution of miraculous healing powers to the ground that received the blood of the violently slain can be found in a Christian context as far back as the death of King Oswald.

For at the place where he was killed fighting for his country against the heathen, sick men and beasts are healed to this day. Many people took away the very dust from the place where his body fell, and put it in water, from which sick folk who drank it received great benefit. This practice became so popular that, as the earth was gradually removed, a pit was left in which a man could stand....Many miracles are reported as having occurred at this spot, by means of the earth taken from it...[136]

More exotic memorials than chapels marked the murder sites of St. Wistan and St. Melor. The "hair" which supposedly grew at the discovery site of St. Wistan's corpse has been mentioned above; a similar phenomenon occurred in Brittany associated with the death of St. Melor. A small indentation in the ground, where the grass did not grow and it was said that snow would melt on contact, was known as "Saint Melor's bed." Local tradition, recorded in the early twentieth century, preserved the legend of Melor's flight from his assassins. The flight was called a "passion" by the villagers. The bed was thought to be a place where Melor rested from his pursuers and prayed for help. Local mothers still brought their children to the spot, and laid them in the bed, believing that it would give then the qualities of bravery and strength.[137]

Manifestations of superstition in medieval culture were frequently condemned by medieval clerics as survivals of paganism, and connected with magical practices and beliefs.[138] The establishment of popular cults around the remains of young murdered boys may in part echo both the magical traditions of medieval European society and the magical legacy of the classical world. It may be impossible to determine how closely one tradition influences the other. Few sources exist for documenting medieval magical beliefs, and the role of children in has not yet been sufficiently explored.[139] The cults of child saints may provide some evidence for the connection between popular religion, folklore, and magic. Characteristics of these cults were frequently similar despite variances of time and place. The stories of these marginal individuals were also marginal in doctrinal justification. During this era, the quality of innocence coupled with an untimely death produced cults which were sources of popular veneration and magical healing. The stricter standards of a later age would require further adaptations of the idea of the child saint in order to satisfy both ecclesiastical and popular concepts of sanctity.

CHAPTER 6

The Pious Infant: Child Confessors
of the High Middle Ages

The societal and cultural developments differentiating the high Middle Ages from earlier centuries produced a number of changes in concepts of childhood and religion, with an accompanying alteration of the role of the child saint in popular worship. The intellectual revival and increasing sophistication of medieval society in the twelfth century, combined with an increase in population, promoted cultural interest in the parent-child relationship. A rise in the worship of the Virgin Mary was accompanied by increasingly domestic depictions of her role as the mother of God; worship of the infant Jesus, with iconographic emphasis placed upon his human qualities, also expanded throughout this period. The Virgin Mary was depicted in scenes of pregnancy and devoted motherhood holding, nursing, and playing with her baby. Jesus was shown laughing, eating, and playing.[1] In contrast to the young Jesus of the Infancy Gospels as an immature being with supernatural powers, descriptions from the twelfth century began to emphasize his similarity to other children, while acknowledging his beauty and charm. Cistercians, such as Aelred of Rievaulx and Bernard of Clairvaux, were especially influential in this respect. The Cistercians and other reformed order did not admit child oblates, and thus monks of this era may have been more familiar with the emotions of family life than if they had been raised in a cloister. The Christ child was meant to appear both human and innocently pure. In the mid-twelfth century, Aelred composed a work on "Jesus at the Age of Twelve."[2] The purity of childhood, as exemplified by the infant Jesus, was promoted by Bernard as a behavioral model for faithful Christians.[3] The boy that Anthony of Padua was seen hugging in his chamber was actually the child Jesus. Women, too, experienced visions of Jesus as an infant or a child, often caring for him as they would a real child. St. Ida of Louvain once gave the infant Jesus a bath, in tepid water, with the help of St. Elizabeth, mother of John the Baptist.[4]

The increasing religious emphasis upon childish purity was often at odds with the naturalistic observations of childhood found in pedagogical literature of the period. Authors such as Bartholomeus Anglicus produced descriptions of behavior in children which, while unarguably naturalistic, did little to promote the child as a creature of superior morality.

> The hot humor that dominates [boys] makes them restless and fickle. They tend to eat too much and are susceptible to various diseases in consequence. They think only of the present...and care nothing for the future; they love games and vanities but refuse to attend to gain and utility...They want what is hurtful and contrary to them...[Girls] take short steps, and in mind...they tend to be haughty, are prone to wrath, tenacious in hate, merciful, jealous, impatient of labor, docile, tricky, bitter, and "headlong in lust."[5]

In the mid-thirteenth century, Vincent of Beauvais produced a treatise on child care derived from the Moslem physician Avicenna, which addressed issues of health and education. Ramon Llull composed the *Doctrina pueril,* which was quickly translated from Catalan into French and Latin for an interested lay audience. These three authors are the most well-known of a tradition of literature dating from the twelfth century.[6] Theological opinion reflected a more realistic view of children by positing that the capacity for sin increased during each of the stages of childhood; virtually nonexistent in *infantia* the impulse for sin developed at age seven, the beginning of *pueritia,* and increased dramatically with the onset of *adolescentia* at age fourteen.[7] Secular literature concerned with the problem of education during these stages of life was preoccupied not so much with the development of the soul as with the formation of personality and temperament. These qualities were shaped by both heredity and environment. Astrological configurations which dictated the balance of the four humours were also considered.[8]

These works reflected the concept of childhood seen in the pedagogical literature of classical antiquity, as a state of weakness and imperfection which needed much care and attention to properly develop. Philippe of Navarre noted in the thirteenth century that "Childhood is the foundation of life, and on good foundations one can raise great and good buildings."[9] Parents were expected to lavish greater attention and a greater share of resources on their offspring than were those of an earlier era; religious training, though, occupied a smaller percentage of the educational experience. The literature on childhood expressed a variety of spiritual and secular factors of concern to parents which contributed to the moral development of the child. Childhood and society encountered increasing elements of secularization. By the end of the twelfth century, liturgical practices recognized the changing view of children by excluding them from communion, confession, and extreme unction on the grounds that they were too young to understand or appreciate the holy sacraments.[10]

At the same time, the power of the Church, and particularly the papacy, was exerting a considerable influence upon popular religious practice and the cult of the saints. Papal control over the recognition of saints, embodied in the formal canonization process which developed during the late twelfth and thirteenth centuries, introduced new sets of criteria to the formation of saints' cults.[11] While the formation of popular cults did not entirely disappear, their number was drastically reduced. The cults of popular saints were limited in appeal, and usually confined to a small area. These saints, whether male or female, adults or children, generally shared the characteristic of having suffered a horribly violent and undeserved death.[12] The formal canonization process, consisting of a request for canonization, a preliminary inquiry and a final hearing, required postulants for the saint's cause with ties to the ecclesiastical bureaucracy. Thus candidates for sanctity, both successful and unsuccessful, became increasingly associated with established religious orders and subjected to increasingly stringent criteria for the recognition of divine favor.[13]

The necessity of legitimizing popular devotion to a particular saint through formal ecclesiastical channels created a new set of spiritual criteria. Although miraculous abilities were still recognized as a part of the canonization process, and in fact expected on the popular level, an increasing emphasis was placed upon piety and good works.[14] The full significance of this shift may be more literary than behavioral, as *vitae* were composed with the criteria for canonization increasingly in mind,[15] but some changes reflected the increasing societal interest in the state of childhood, as well as the trend toward realistic portrayal of children's behavior. Saints such as Catherine of Siena and Anthony of Padua supposedly practiced piety, asceticism and charity from an early age; Catherine was said to have exhorted her little playmates to follow her example and flagellate themselves.[16] The cleric Guibert of Nogent described the distaste he felt for the games of war practiced by other children, and his intense desire to continue upon an ecclesiastical career.[17] Such activity was considered worthy of report not only because it fit the criteria of pious behavior, but because it was unusual in contrast to the thoughtlessness and selfishness of normal children. The motif of the *puer senex* was thus reinstated in the hagiographical tradition, but in a more comprehensive and naturalistic manner than in late antiquity, since examples of behavior in childhood tended to encompass a greater range of instances and experiences than the earlier formulaic invocations of the motif.[18]

The altered priorities and increasingly stringent criteria attached to the recognition of sanctity acted to reduce the number of saints created during this period, but also carried a special difficulty for children which excluded them almost entirely from the ranks of the blessed. Children were not considered to possess the moral capacity of adults, and since the formal recognition of sanctity required evidence of active piety, did not meet ecclesiastical standards. Although many adult saints were described behaving piously as children in their *vitae*, no children died after exhibiting similar noteworthy behavior. More pragmatic concerns also contributed to the exclusion of children. The ecclesiastical affiliations so important to the promotion of saints during the canonization process were generally not available to children. The practice of monastic oblation had been discouraged by a number of factors, including the Gregorian Reform movement, a growth in population which increased the ranks of adult recruits, and a shift in religious outlook which stressed the importance of free choice in the acceptance of monastic vows. The number of children involved in monastic life declined steadily throughout the eleventh and twelfth centuries, and children virtually disappeared from religious establishments by 1300.[19] An increased societal emphasis on the importance of marriage and life in the secular world may have also contributed to the factors which limited the participation of children in religious life.[20]

Ecclesiastical expectations of saintly behavior in turn raised the expectations of society. Children were less readily seen as holy figures, despite their innocence and purity. The legends of earlier child saints underwent modification in this period to accentuate the pious qualities of the subjects over the circumstances of violent death. In the mid-eleventh century, elements of religious behavior were added to the story of the murder of St. Kenelm. A twelfth-century version of the Edward legend, *De Infantia Sancti Edmundi*, emphasized the precocious piety of the youthful murder victim. Compositions dating from the pontificate of Innocent III show even a greater concern for religious themes. A *vita* of St. Wistan dating from the late twelfth or early thirteenth century depicted him as a martyred innocent who, for religious reasons, refused to accept the throne at his father's death.[21] Such additions were meant to stress the pious nature and habitual religious practices of the young saints, but these embroideries did not erase the secular nature of the murders. In the few cases of cult formation for child saints found in this period, similar hagiographical techniques were utilized to justify the existence of the cult on both popular and ecclesiastical levels.

Despite the obstacles to the recognition of children as saints in the high Middle Ages, a number of cults did manage to form. These saints fell into two broad categories. The first group conformed to the ecclesiastical model for canonization and stressed piety, zeal and asceticism and consisted of children who exhibited such characteristics and died of natural causes. The second group was comprised of murder victims whose stories were augmented with elements of religious significance. The latter cases declined in the thirteenth century, but neither group was sizeable to begin with. Practitioners of precocious piety numbered no more than eight, and rehabilitated murder victims only three. The legends of some child saints are so sketchy that it is impossible to assert with any assurance that the pious acts were actually performed. In some cases, the tradition may have been constructed in order to justify popular veneration, and some children in the former category may in fact belong to the latter group. Their legends obscure the actual events. Only four children, three of whom were technically adolescents at the age of death, were promoted through the formal canonization process; several never achieved greater than local fame, and little information on their lives or cults survives.

Child saints after the year 1000 straddled the transitional period between locally-sponsored veneration of saints and the increasing power of papal control. As marginal images of sanctity, child saints were more likely than adults to be locally venerated, and less likely to attract papal attention. Thus, violent death was still a path to sanctity. Increasing popular acceptance of the newer behavioral criteria, however, increasingly dictated the modification of their legends in order to emphasize the spiritual qualities of the victims.[22] In a further demonstration of the growing popular interest in extreme religious devotion, several children adopted such behavior, and died prematurely in adolescence as a result of their excesses of piety.

A prototype of the pious infant is found in the case of the eleventh-century Nicholas Peregrinus. Honored in both the Western and Eastern churches, he was born in Greece in 1075 of a humble peasant family, and was raised near the monastery of St. Luke at Stira.[23] His *vita* records that he was virtuous and pious from infancy. One day at the age of eight, while tending his mother's sheep, he began to cry *Kyrie eleison*. He repeated the cry throughout the day and night. His distraught mother thought that he had gone mad, and sought to subdue him, but when he had not ceased in his behavior by the age of twelve, she threw him out of the house. This began for

St. Nicholas a period of wanderings which lasted until his death in Trani at the age of nineteen. He was first taken in by the neighboring monks, but his sanity was questioned here as well, and he embraced a hermitic existence on a mountaintop. Here he was visited by the angel of the Lord, who brought him across the sea to Lombardy, and told him that he would find great glory there. He had by this time acquired a follower, a monk named George, who was attracted by the "angelic fervor and purity shown by this miraculous boy."[24] Nicholas traveled across Italy, crying *Kyrie eleison* and collecting a large following, composed principally of young boys, who also took up the cry. He worked many miraculous cures, and cast out demons. Eventually he made his way to Trani, as foretold by the angel, where he died surrounded by an adoring crowd. The proliferation of miracles at his tomb, which were almost exclusively cures of women and children, led to his canonization by Pope Urban II in 1098.[25] The translation of his relics inspired further miraculous cures, and he was venerated into the seventeenth century.

The rapid canonization of Nicholas was based on societal recognition of the qualities which the papacy intended to promote in candidates for sanctity; papal intervention in such matters in the eleventh century was by no means widespread or uniform. Public acceptance of Nicholas as a saint, however, was not so easily subject to papal decree. Throughout his career, popular opinion was divided on the question of whether he was holy or insane. While the account of his early years before his arrival in Italy is less reliable than the record of his later wanderings, the ambivalence engendered by his flamboyant behavior demonstrates the difficulty of imposing models of sanctity from above.[26] Ultimately, though, his appeal was sufficiently widespread to attain for him a substantial cult and almost immediate official recognition after his death, in recognition of his youthful precocity.

Rose of Viterbo, who died in 1251 at the age of 17, was, like Nicholas, too old to be considered a child at her death, but exhibited signs of miraculous devotion at a similarly young age. Both Innocent IV and the author of her *vita* identified her as *puella* rather than *virgo*, indicating that her youth was a determining factor of her sanctity.[27] She achieved her greatest fame through her gift of prophecy, which she combined with political commentary. She was said to have predicted the death of Frederick II, and at the age of seven, preached against the submission of Gregory IX to Frederick. She was given over to the tutelage of the Franciscans as a child, and some of her early miracles reflect their influence. When she ate bread as a little child, the birds flocked around her to pick up the crumbs. She was also much given to piety and asceticism, and abhorred the vanities of worldly existence. From her earliest years she expressed a desire to align herself with the Franciscans, and became a tertiary in the Order of St. Francis before her untimely demise.

Rose of Viterbo was portrayed in her *vita* as a *puella senecta,* "in her youth possessing the wisdom of the aged,"[28] whose actions contradicted the typical activities of children, but her life was more directly related to that of normal children than was the *puer senex* of an earlier era. One of her miracles involved the miraculous repair of a water jug accidentally broken by another little girl, in order to spare the child from the wrath of her parents.

> When this Virgin, who was supported by the grace of omnipotent God, in childhood would go to the well with the other girls with jugs to draw water, and the jug of one of the other girls, which she was carrying, fell and broke into many pieces, being called by her parents, just as the girl answered falsely...the Blessed Rose hurried to the spot where the broken jug was, and brought together the bits and pieces, and through the merits of this Virgin, as the omnipotent power of God was demonstrated through her, so that all the pieces which were scattered and divided were replaced in their proper place, and it was no longer broken. And she gave this jug back to the girl whole and sound...[29]

Although Rose was set apart from the other children by her virtuous and unchildlike conduct, she shared their values and understood their behavior. Her popularity during her lifetime, as well as her posthumous reputation and eventual canonization were much advanced by the efforts of the Franciscans. The majority of her posthumous cures seem to have been directed at children and women.[30] She favored the latter group with, among other benefits, the restoration of beloved husbands and children to life, and was also invoked in cases of difficult pregnancy. Effort was also made by the author of the vita to appeal to the tradition of child saints and the childhood of other saints. Rose, in her infancy, was compared to John the Baptist, who worshipped Jesus while still in the womb, and to St. Nicholas, who stood upright in his baptismal font, and refused to nurse on fast days. A similarity to St. Agnes was also invoked. While this served to link Rose with other examples of the *puer senex* motif, it also reflected the growing interest of contemporary hagiographers in the state of infancy.

The canonization process for Rose of Viterbo was instituted soon after her death, in 1252 by Innocent IV.[31] Lists of posthumous miracles were compiled, her *vita* was composed, and her body examined and found to be miraculously incorrupt. The process was not, however, successfully concluded until 1457 by Pope Callixtus III. A pivotal ingredient in the official success of her cult, if not its popular appeal, was her affiliation with an established religious order.

The Blessed Peter of Luxembourg, who died in 1387 at the age of seventeen,[32] accumulated a reputation for piety which was perhaps the greatest and most extensively documented of the saintly youths of the era. An anonymously authored *vita* appeared one year and three months after his death,[33] and the process of beatification, attempted four times before its successful completion in 1527, was first begun in 1389.[34] Both the life and death of Peter of Luxembourg were noteworthy in his own time, and the popular veneration of his remains began soon after his death.

Peter was born on July 20, 1369. His father, Count Guy of Luxembourg, died in 1371, and his mother, Mathilda of Châtillon, died in 1373. He was educated by his aunt, Giovanna of Châtillon. His professional career began at the age of eight, when he was appointed a canon in the cathedral of Paris by the Avignonese Pope Clement VII in 1378. Clement was a strong patron of the child, naming him a canon of Cambrai in 1382. Peter became Bishop of Metz in 1384, at the age of fourteen, and in the same year cardinal deacon of the church of St. George in Velabro.[35] At this point, Peter's career stalled, caught in the battle between Rome and Avignon; this controversy also affected the first four attempts at beatification in 1389, 1390, 1433 and 1435. In contrast to Rose of Viterbo and other saints with affiliations to mendicant orders, Peter was aligned with the secular clergy, but his cause was promoted by political patronage; papal investigation into claims of Peter's sanctity was solicited in 1389 by Pierre d'Ailly, in the name of Charles VI.[36] Despite numerous investigations, and the odor of sanctity exuded by his corpse,[37] Peter was never formally canonized.

The remarkable piety of Peter's childhood was recorded in testimony at Avignon, and followed the pattern found in the lives of other churchmen, as well as some child saints. This "most noble and devoted *puerulum*"[38] practiced none of the sins of youth, but instead remained at his studies. He evinced an aversion to the comforts of the flesh. He was the only one of the children attending church who joined in the recitation of the mass instead of running around in play. Peter's chastity, asceticism and studious nature set him blessedly apart from normal boys. He was portrayed as a *puer senex*, "and although counted as a child in years, yet his mind showed the immense wisdom of old age."[39] Most children would not have wanted to emulate Peter. He was known to recite hundreds of prayers at a time, and would regularly flagellate himself to the point of grievous bodily harm.

Popular devotion to Peter was strong and sustained; he was considered both a saint and a thaumaturge, and was declared patron of Avignon in 1432.[40] Hundreds of miraculous cures were recorded by ecclesiastical investigators to have been achieved through his intercession.[41] His cult was also strong in the dioceses of Metz, Paris, Verdun, and Luxembourg. The relics preserved at Paris were displayed in 1597, but dispersed in 1793, during the revolution. The remaining relics were maintained at the church of St. Didier in Avignon.[42]

The influence of the Dominicans combined with the power of a noble Bolognese family to promote one of the most poignant examples of child sanctity in history, the blessed Imelda Lambertini, who died in 1333 at the age of eleven. Imelda was a child much given over to pious acts from earliest memory, and, like Peter, exhibited none of the characteristic defects of childhood. "She was neither insolent, nor silly, nor immodest, but exhibited maturity, which is rare in childhood, and universally admired."[43] At the age of nine she entered a Dominican convent in Val de Pietra, giving up the comforts of her father's house. She distinguished herself not only by her delight in prayer, but by her fervent desire to experience first communion. Although the custom of the region and time was to reserve this sacrament until the age of twelve, an exception was made for Imelda. After receiving the wafer on her lips for the first time, she died at the altar.

The actual cause of death, as well as its precise timing, may be open to question. Imelda's legend reflects the growing fervor over the sacrament of communion, the vogue for childish piety demonstrated by cults such as that of Rose of Viterbo, and sympathy for a premature death. What is certain is that a young girl belonging to a noble family died while in a convent, and the Dominican sisters inserted her life into the martyrology of the establishment. "The death of sister Imelda who surrendered herself to heaven by accepting Holy Communion."[44] The nuns also composed an antiphon in her honor, and her cult was sustained both through popular interest and the interest of the order. A translation of Imelda's teeth to the church of St. Sigismund in Bologna occurred in 1582, with the bones following at a later date. They were still preserved in that location into the present

The cult of the Blessed Imelda remained, however, limited in popularity for many centuries. Evidence for the process of beatification was not collected until the eighteenth century, under the pontificate of Benedict XIV (1740-58). Pope Benedict, born Prospero Lorenzo Lambertini "of noble but impoverished parentage,"[45] had a keen interest in the cult of the saints but may have been guilty of personal bias in the case of Imelda. He included Imelda in his classic treatise *De servorum Dei beatificatione et beatorum Canonization*, but despite his efforts at promotion, her sanctity was not officially confirmed until 1826, by Leo XII.[46]

The Dominican order also promoted the cult of Blessed Fina of San Gimignano, who died in 1253 at the age of fifteen.[47] Her life, recorded in the early fourteenth century by the Dominican Giovanni del Coppo,[48] was brief, but intensely religious. At age ten, she was struck by an illness which left her with little movement. Her mother died soon afterwards. Fina exhibited remarkable devotion to the cult of the Passion of Jesus, to the Virgin Mary, and to Saint Gregory the Great, on whose feast day she died after announcing her imminent death.[49] The cult developed at once, beginning with the odor of sanctity which enveloped the *corpusculum*.[50] Numerous miracles were reported at her tomb. She became the patron of her native town, and was venerated as an example of patience in adversity.[51] Although her *vita* was composed by a member of the Dominican order, Fina was unaffiliated with the order, and the promotion of her cult may have been local rather than institutional.

Imelda Lambertini and Fina of San Gimignano were children who were credited with intense piety, and then died young. Their cults were promoted by a powerful religious organization. Detailed contemporary inquiry into their lives, such as was conducted for Rose of Viterbo and Peter of Luxembourg, did not take place. It is therefore impossible to state with any certainty that these were anything other than "constructed" saints, whose *vitae* reflected contemporary ideals of spiritual perfection, but not necessarily the actual behavior of young girls. These cults may represent nothing more than the veneration of young and innocent death in a highly disguised form.

Other cults of child saints present an even more ambiguous picture. The blessed Achas of Thourout died at a young age in the year 1220, after having given signs of extraordinary piety. No *vita* was generated to elaborate on this theme, however, and his cult remained limited to the area surrounding Thourout in Flanders.[52] It is therefore impossible to separate actual behavior worthy of sainthood from the popular sympathy surrounding an untimely death.

The city of Venice harbored the cult of the blessed child Contessa or Comitissa, of the noble family of Teleapetra, who died in 1308 at the age of thirteen. She lived a simple life dedicated to God, to the apparent consternation of her parents. Forbidden one day to go to mass, she miraculously walked across water, and dying soon afterwards, was buried with honor and venerated for her piety.[53] In 1354, her relics were placed in the church of St. John, near the altar of the child martyr St. Vitus. Her legend was preserved in the eighteenth century after the cult had been in existence for some four hundred years. The body, which was elevated in 1702, was found to be incorrupt.[54]

The blessed Agnes of Bavaria, who died in 1352 at the age of seven, also clashed with parental authority over devotion to religious ideals. The daughter of Ludwig IV von Wittelsbach, Agnes was sent at the age of four to the Klarissenkloster St. Jakob in Munich to be educated. She soon expressed a desire to remain within the religious life, "so that she could grow up in holy innocence among the holy virgins,"[55] but it was not to be. Her father, who wanted to use her for marriage alliances, tried to remove her from the cloister at the age of seven. Ulcerous sores appeared all over her body, and, as she requested of God, she died.

The life and death of Agnes were presented as undeniably holy. Like Imelda Lambertini, she showed a great devotion to the Eucharist.[56] Her desire to escape marriage and remain in the convent, a normal reaction for a child of seven who had known no other life, turned her death into a miracle from God meant to preserve her virginity. The sores on her body were considered by some to be stigmata, although the appearance was described as more like pestilence. When her tomb was opened in 1375, the body was found to be incorrupt. Her beatification was approved in 1705, on the basis of the existing cult.[57] As in the cases of Fina and Imelda, all that can be ascertained with certainty is that behind the walls of a convent, a child of important parents died at a young age. Like Contessa and many other saints of the twelfth, thirteenth and fourteenth centuries, Agnes clashed with her parents over her superior piety. Such stories may have been intended, in part, to caution parents against discouraging religious vocation in their children.

The move to attribute lives of unusual piety to popularly venerated children can be seen also in the cases of child saints which more clearly reflect the earlier medieval theme of secular murder and, in particular, domestic violence. The cults of Lié of Savins, Reinildis of Reisenbeck, and Panacea of Novara, originated in the murder of children by family members, but were enlarged by the addition of more acceptable hagiographical elements. The cults of Lié and Reinildis remained localized, and acquired relatively few hagiographical embellishments, but that of Panacea achieved greater fame.

Saint Lié, or Laetus, who died in 1169, was the product of popular canonization and was, like his predecessor St. Pelagius, a male martyr to chastity. Lié was a young boy of great beauty, whose attractiveness moved a member of his own family to attempt acts of unnatural lust. He died resisting these base advances, and his relics were preserved for veneration at the church of Savins.[58]

The legend of Reinildis[59] recounts that she was killed in 1262 by her mother, at the instigation of her stepfather, who wished to take control of her father's inheritance. While the theme and the circumstances clearly reflect patterns of popular veneration of murder victims found in the early medieval period, the cult managed to sustain itself into the modern period. The legend was composed in the eighteenth century, although it may have been retrieved from an earlier oral form. The basic story was enhanced with hagiographical motifs found in other *vitae* of the region, perhaps in order to justify the validity of the cult. Archaeological evidence for the cult is based on an epitaph dating from the late thirteenth or early fourteenth century preserved in the parish church of Reisenbeck, in the diocese of Munster; excavations at the church in 1809 at the site found no trace of bones, relics, or a tomb.[60] Because of the uncertain date of the *vita*, the presence or absence of pious behavior in the girl who became worshipped as a saint cannot be determined.

The legend of Panacea of Novara, who died in 1383 at the age of fifteen, is little more than a variant of the Cinderella story without a happy ending. The murderous villain was, of course, the wicked stepmother. Panacea was born at Quarona, in Valseria, in 1368, to Lorenzo de' Muzzi and Maria de' Gambini. Her mother died when she was three, and her father married a widow with daughters of her own. Panacea was regularly abused by the stepmother and her daughters, and was beaten so severely by them that her father once found her unconscious under the straw in a stable.[61]

Panacea was finally killed by her stepmother in a violent rage when she was gathering firewood and the sheep that she was supposed to have been tending returned alone to the sheepfold. On her return, she was beaten repeatedly by her stepmother with various objects, and finally stabbed to death with a spindle. Panacea's excuse, as preserved in the legend, was that she had lingered on the hilltop to pray. Whether this was a genuine element of the story, or added later to provide an admittedly slim religious basis for veneration, Panacea was praised for her piety. The anger of the stepmother, directed against the "innocent and pious girl" recalls the ancient theme of violent death visited upon an innocent child.[62]

The cult was promoted by the Bishop of Novara, who took a personal interest in the case and the blessed remains, although popular sympathy for the violently murdered child undoubtedly helped to establish the cult. According to the legend, the body of the child became heavier than lead, and could not be moved until the arrival of the bishop.[63] Under his direction, it was placed in a cart, and conducted to Quarona. Miracles followed the translation of the remains, and recognition of the sanctity of the child increased. Her tomb became a popular pilgrimage site, and she was invoked as an aid against epilepsy. In 1409, two chapels were built in her honor at Novara.[64] Her case was reviewed in 1593 by Clement VIII, and her cult was officially confirmed in 1867 by Pope Pius IX.[65]

The cults of Reinildis and Panacea were not anomalies in the annals of hagiography for this period; several other cases of innocent death avenged through popular veneration also occurred. Radegund of Augsburg, a servant girl torn apart by wolves in the thirteenth century at whose tomb myriad cures were recognized, was venerated as a holy virgin and linked with devotion to St. Ursula.[66] Her age is not known; she is usually referred to as a girl, but this may reflect her lowly status as a servant rather than her age. Margaret of Louvain was killed by robbers along with her employer and his wife, who were innkeepers. Her legend stated that she was vowed to perpetual virginity and had intended to embrace the religious life.[67] Like Radegund, her age is unknown and she may have been either a girl or a young woman. St. Belina was a twelfth-century peasant girl of Troyes who died resisting a rape attempt by a local noble and was honored as a virgin martyr.[68] The theme of rape suggests that she was not a child; however, this story closely parallels the modern saga of St. Maria Goretti, who was raped and murdered at the age of twelve. The legend of each bestowed a reputation for piety but the factual elements of their stories more closely conform to the practice of popular veneration of violent death common to the early medieval period. At most, such legends illustrate the continuing difficult faced by the medieval papacy in exerting control over popular manifestations of religious impulses.

Pietization of the legends of murder victims was not limited to children in this period. In most of the cases cited by Vauchez of victims of violent death popularly venerated as saints, a religious element was present. Several victims were clerics killed for secular reasons: Honoré de Thénezay was killed by two servants whose honesty he had questioned, and Buonmercato de Ferrare was unjustly accused of murder and lynched. Nantvin of Germany was a pilgrim unjustly accused of pederasty by a group of villagers and burnt alive. Others, such as Radegund of Augsburg, the serving-girl killed and eaten by wolves, were endowed with a reputation for pious and charitable works before their untimely end. Adult political figures such as Simon de Montfort and Thomas of Lancaster, if not overtly religious during life, were venerated for dying in defense of a just cause.[69]

Papal control of the canonization process, although slow to spread to every isolated village, was beginning to have an effect on popular thought and practice. The growth of urban society and the power of the religious orders facilitated the spread of the newer standards of sanctity. Urban cults of child saints more closely reflected papal priorities, and achieved more lasting and widespread fame. Popular worship of murdered children declined in favor of emphasis on pious behavior. In a clear indication of the desired spiritual direction of this era, attempts to satisfy the Church through the addition of spiritual motivation to secular murders suggest that the side of orthodoxy was gaining the upper hand.

Official promotion of saints' cults increased from the eleventh to the fifteenth century, and exerted significant pressure on popular concepts of sanctity. But popular concepts were changing as well. The growing urbanization and sophistication of lay society, as well as popular recognition of adult saints whose behavior conformed to spiritual standards of piety and zeal, combined to alter the manifestations of sanctity seen in medieval society. Such conditions, coupled with the increasingly realistic portrayal of children's behavior, excluded children from the one avenue to sanctity left open to them in the early Middle Ages: that of being murdered. By the thirteenth century, children had to be good, as well.

Some children, such as Rose of Viterbo and Peter of Luxembourg, clearly rose to the challenge. Although these saints died in adolescence rather than childhood, all established patterns of saintly behavior well before puberty. The extremity of asceticism practiced in the cases of Peter of Luxembourg, Nicholas Peregrinus and Rose of Viterbo probably contributed directly to their deaths, while Fina's faith developed after a serious illness and the death of her mother. The cases of the younger "pious infants," Imelda Lambertini, Contessa, and Agnes of Bavaria, may have been due to natural causes, and in the cases of Imelda and Agnes, credited to divine intervention rather than to any ongoing behavior on their part.

The impact of these child saints on other children remains difficult to gauge. Children were the principal followers of Nicholas Peregrinus in the eleventh century, indicating the susceptibility of children to religious messages, and especially those promulgated by another child. In the great religious revival that swept northern Italy in 1233, boys and girls were eager participants; the preaching of Brother Benedict of Parma drew great crowds of enthusiastic children.

> He went about with his horn, preaching and praising God in the churches and the open places; and a great multitude of children followed him, oft-times with branches of trees and lighted tapers.[70]

The Children's Crusade of 1212 consisted of two groups of children, one from northern France and one from the Rhineland, each headed by a child. The children were to recapture Jerusalem through the power of purity and innocence. Although the father of the German leader, Nicholas, was hanged after the failure of the crusade for having encouraged his son in such disastrous folly, the ultimate motivation for the large numbers of children involved must have been derived from societal concepts which promoted such ideas of childhood. The majority of children who embarked upon the crusade did not persevere. The rest came to an ignominious end; they either died on the journey or were sold into slavery to Moslems. Their memory, however, was honored by those who promoted pious children as saints. The Church proclaimed the crusaders "new Innocents," and a "Church of the Innocents" was erected in their memory by Gregory IX on the island of San Pietro near Sardinia.[71]

As Jean André observed in the fourteenth century, one must find in saints faith and good works, otherwise one ought to venerate as saints those infants who die after baptism, which would be absurd.[72] The child saints venerated in the high Middle Ages represented the natural development of such popular concepts. The impulse to venerate the innocent victim, especially the child victim, was not entirely eradicated in this era. That the earlier legacy of diverse expectations and understandings continued to present challenges to the intrepid hagiographer is amply demonstrated by the development of yet another model of childish piety in this period, the ritual murder victim. Although dealt with separately because of the nature of the historiography surrounding them, these cases were contemporary to the cults discussed in this chapter, and were shaped by the same cultural trends. The little children who were venerated because it was thought that they were murdered by Jews can be seen as a continuation of the earlier trend to worship victims of violent death, but on more doctrinally acceptable grounds.

Sacred Passions: William of Norwich and the Origins of the Ritual Murder Accusation

The elevated standards of popular piety and increased papal control of the canonization process seen after the 11th century were, in general, effective in curtailing the growth of dubious cults, with one noteworthy exception. The child "martyr" who was in reality a victim of violent crime was excluded from the formal canonization process, but re-emerged in the mid-twelfth century in a form that would become infamous in later history - the ritual murder victim. Despite repeated disavowals by the papacy and other authorities, cults to nearly thirty children considered victims of ritual murder at the hands of Jews were established between 1150 and 1600.

This problematic group of saints presents a compelling example of the tension between popular patterns of worship and the growing ecclesiastical emphasis on conventional expressions of piety. The basic premise of the ritual murder charge was that Christian children were killed by Jews, usually around the time of the convergent feasts of Easter and Passover, because they were Christian. One scholar has defined ritual murder as "the killing of a human, not merely from motives of religious hatred, but in such a way that the form of the killing is at least partly determined by ideas allegedly or actually important in the religion of the killer or the victims."[1] Ritual murder, also known as the "blood libel," refers to the murder of a Christian by a Jew, or group of Jews, in a manner meant to mock the passion of Christ. In its original manifestation, the victim was tortured and crucified. As the legend developed, the murders were explained by the supposed demand for innocent Christian blood in secret Jewish magical rituals. Christian blood was claimed to be an ingredient of Passover matzoh, and the charge of ritual murder was often combined with desecration of the Eucharistic Host for subversive magical purposes. The crime of ritual murder was described as a communal act, of which the entire Jewish community was aware, even if only a few individuals directly participated in the torture and murder. Cults dedicated to the alleged victims were clearly popular in that none of the subjects were canonized in the Middle Ages, nor were their feasts incorporated into general calendars of the Church.[2] Simon of Trent, who died in 1475, was the first ritual murder victim to be canonized, in 1588, by Pope Sixtus V. Most ritual murder victims achieved only regional popularity, and their cults have since sunk into purposeful obscurity.

The line between popular enthusiasm and ecclesiastical disapproval was eroded by the enthusiasm with which such cults were promoted by local clerics. In many cases, the patronage of the local abbot or bishop was the motivating force behind the advancement of the cult and the punishment of Jews suspected of involvement. Lay acceptance of the ritual murder victim as an object of veneration varied by region. In England, where the charge originated, initial resistance was only gradually overcome by arguments and miracles. Elsewhere, the concept was more readily accepted. As the idea of ritual murder of children gained credence throughout European society in concert with growing animosity toward the Jewish population,[3] the forces of ecclesiastical manipulation and popular devotion converged. Vauchez treats the ritual murder victims as a subset of popular canonization, in particular as a combination of the valorization of childhood as an age of innocence and perfection, and virulent cultural anti-Semitism; in general, these cults earned the unwavering disapproval of the papacy and other highly placed ecclesiastics.[4]

The number of historically verifiable ritual murder charges, conservatively estimated to be in excess of one hundred and fifty,[5] far exceeds the number of religious cults venerating the alleged victims. This may reflect papal disapproval of such charges, but also testifies to broader societal concerns and fears concerning children. All individuals identified as ritual murder victims in the Middle Ages, and all who inspired religious cults in the Middle Ages and later, were children. At the center of each charge was the pure body of an innocent child, unjustly slain. Most were young boys ranging in age from two to twelve years old. Without exception, the young victims were seen to embody the quality of innocence, of being slain without sin, and of suffering martyrdom on behalf of, if not actually in defense of, the

Christian faith. The motif became so popular that Chaucer's *Prioress's Tale* provided a fictionalized account of a "litel clergeon, seven yeer of age" who suffered a brutally violent death at the hands of the Jews in his town.[6] Chaucer repeatedly describes the boy as an innocent, and attaches the holy qualities of martyrdom and virginity to the child.[7] Hagiographical and literary sources imbue the ritual murder victims with many of the qualities attributed to the child martyrs of the early Church, but the historical outlines of their stories more closely parallel the child murder victims of the early Middle Ages. The shifting contours of popular piety in this era, already evident in the twelfth-century emergence of the cults of pious infants, may also have been instrumental in influencing the presentation of the ritual murder victims as true martyrs to the faith rather than as victims of random violence.

The literature on the history of ritual murder charges is voluminous. Scholarly discussion of the charge originated with the 1759 report of Cardinal Ganganelli (later Clement XIV) who was sent to Poland by the Inquisition to investigate such charges,[8] and has continued to the present. Recent scholarship has provided an extensive analysis of the role of the Jew as "other" in medieval society, and pointed to specific historical factors such as the identification of Jews with the practice of magic and sorcery, which was frequently thought to involve the blood of young children,[9] or the involvement of Jews in the medieval slave-trade, which may have given rise to charges, and perhaps actual instances, of child-stealing.[10] Other historians, inspired by the proliferation of scholarship on medieval childhood, have focused on the role of the child-victim and societal responses to the violent death of a child.[11] All interpret the development of the cults as evidence that medieval society viewed the murder of a child as an especially serious crime, and that the elevation of murder victim to the status of sainthood, albeit popular, was a manifestation of societal love for children. One study postulates, without providing specific evidence, a correlation between ritual murder accusations and affection for children at various periods in Western history.[12]

Study of these saints and their cults, however, has focused primarily on the group viewed as responsible for inflicting the martyrdom, and on whether or not the crime occurred in reality, rather than how medieval communities viewed, and venerated, the child saints and their stories.[13] Unremarked within this voluminous discourse is the historical precedent of the early medieval child martyr as an innocent victim of secular crime. The ritual murder victims present a unique case in the annals of hagiography in that little attention has been paid to the saints themselves; rather, scholarship has focused on the group judged responsible for the martyrdom. The combined forces of heightened popular religiosity and aggrandizement of papal power in legitimizing popular cults have already been seen to affect the recognition of child saints in this era. An innocent child, unjustly slain, was no longer sufficient in and of itself to inspire formal veneration for martyrdom. A religious context must be provided for the death. In a religiously cohesive Christendom, earlier enemies such as Vikings, Huns, and Moslems had long disappeared, and no new invading hordes threatened. Jews were a powerless minority population with no legal, political or military power. As non-Christians, however, they were the only identifiable societal group that could be charged with murder of Christians on ideological grounds. The cusp of popular devotion represented by veneration of this group of saints resisted the recognition of martyrdom without an element of religious conflict, as can be seen in the origin of the charge.

In 1144, in Norwich, England, a twelve-year-old boy named William disappeared a few days before Easter and was later found dead in nearby Thorpe Wood. His body was buried in the forest, and his mother and uncle accused the local Jewish community of his murder. At the time, little action was taken to investigate the crime beyond calling in representatives of the Jewish community for questioning. The accusation was discounted by the sheriff, the Jews were dismissed without being charged, and popular opinion largely ignored the incident. Within a month, however, rumors of miracles and popular visitations to the dead child in the woods prompted the monks of Norwich to disinter the body and move it into the Monks' Cemetery.[14] In 1150, the body was moved from the cemetery into the chapter-house, whence in 1151 into the cathedral church, and finally in 1154 a fourth and final translation within the church to the Chapel of the Martyrs. Each translation reflected an increase in the popularity of the cult, and in turn fed the demand for a new translation and further honors.

The *Life and Miracles of William of Norwich* was written by Thomas of Monmouth, a monk who arrived at Norwich Priory some time between 1147 and 1150,[15] when he experienced a series of visions culminating in political agitatiom for the translation of the body from the churchyard to the chapter-house, and soon after into the Cathedral proper. From the start, Thomas was a strong proponent of William's cult, going so far as to incur the wrath of the prior in his excessive devotion to the relics of the little victim. In this role, Thomas holds the dubious distinction of introducing the ritual murder accusation to history by claiming, not only that William had been murdered by Jews, but that the child had been crucified in imitation of Christ.[16]

Much scholarly attention has been paid to the origin of the medieval ritual murder accusation. The most influential work on the origins of the blood libel remains Cecil Roth, who traces the source to a curious incident in fifth century Syria recorded by the historian Socrates Scholasticus. In 415 or 416, during the feast of Purim, a group of intoxicated Jews supposedly tied a Christian child to a cross and tortured him until he died.[17] Thomas of Monmouth does not mention this incident, and it is not certain that he had knowledge of the reference.[18] Other scholarship points to the story, first mentioned by Posidonius, and repeated (and refuted) by Josephus in *Against Apion* that every seven years, the Jews captured a young Greek, fattened him up, and then killed and ate him as an expression of their undying enmity against the Greeks.[19] Thomas instead credits a contemporary source, one Theobald of Cambridge, a converted Jew who became a monk, with the previously unsuspected revelation that

> In the ancient writings of his fathers it was written that the Jews, without the shedding of human blood, could neither obtain their freedom, nor could the ever return to their fatherland. Hence it was laid down by them in ancient times that every year they must sacrifice a Christian in some part of the world to the Most High God in scorn and contempt of Christ, so that they might avenge their sufferings on Him.[20]

No prior written record of this or any similar accusation has been found in medieval writings, nor has the existence of Theobald been verified by any independent source, but this highly suspect information triggered numerous cults and even more persecutions across Europe.[21] On what basis, and to what purpose, did Thomas make this assertion?

The rabid anti-Semitism of the medieval period provides at best only a partial justification to such an unprecedented charge. The first book of the *Life and Miracles*, recounting the *passio* of little William, was written around 1150, relatively soon after the event, and Thomas was familiar with descriptions of the crime and the accusations made. He did not claim that William's relatives made any mention of crucifixion at the time, only that they charged the Jews with the slaying. The body lay exposed in the woods for several days before it was found, and lay in the ground at least a month before it was examined by the monks of Thomas' order, making it difficult to identify marks of crucifixion on the body.[22]

In laying out the charge of ritual murder as the basis for martyrdom, Thomas appeared to break new hagiographical ground, but actually relied on long-accepted practices for popular veneration then under attack by the growing assertion of Papal control over the legitimization of localized cults. In naming the Jews as murderers and providing ritual murder as the motive, Thomas may not have intended to endanger the Jews of Norwich, and in fact no Jews were punished for the crime. The claim attributed to Theobald was listed merely as the "fifth argument" in a list of seven reasons set forth by Thomas to convince skeptics that William was slain by Jews,[23] which were part of a broader attack against those who mocked the "poor ragged little lad" as unworthy of sanctity, and his miracles as fictitious.[24] At no point did the accusation of ritual murder become the central point of the case for sanctity, although Thomas apparently saw establishing the guilt of the Jews as crucial to William's cause. It is to the accusation of the Jews, rather than the methods they supposedly used, that we must look in determining the intent of Thomas of Monmouth.

The editors of the *Life* advise the reader to separate the parts of the story relevant to Willliam the saint from those describing William the murdered child.[25] The body was found in the woods with marks of violence upon his body and assumed to be murdered. Veneration by a portion of the community occurred almost immediately, and at first was unconnected with any charge against Jews. Although Thomas states that the Jews of Norwich were suspected from the beginning, the first serious action was taken five years after the crime, when several members of the Jewish community became involved in a property dispute with a local nobleman, Simon de Nodariis, and brought a lawsuit against him. He retaliated by murdering the Jew Eleazor, and excused his action by insisting that the Jewish community's involvement in the murder of William be investigated and punished[26].

The Prior of St. Pancras, in Lewes, who was present at the synod of April 1144 when Godwin Sturt denounced the Jews for the crime, was among the first to recognize the potential value of the incident. Hearing that a child was buried in the woods, he asked permission to acquire the body of the "holy boy."

> But when he could not prevail in obtaining his request, it is said that he answered that if he had been so fortunate as to get him at St. Pancras, no sum of money would have induced him to allow of his being taken away elsewhere, but that he would have kept him with the utmost diligence as a most precious treasure, that he should have been exalted worthily according to his desserts and have become famous by conspicuous veneration and worship. Which words of the prior so affected the mind of Bishop Eborard that they became an incentive to his veneration and served to increase his devotion to the holy boy.[27]

Following this pronouncement, the body of William of Norwich was taken from its grave in the woods and translated to the monks' cemetery at Norwich Cathedral. Six years later, Thomas persuaded Prior Elias of Norwich that translation of the relics into the chapter house would prevent the body from being stolen.[28]

The Prior of St. Pancras may well have had in mind the popularity of earlier cults to young boys murdered in the woods, such as Edward, Kenelm, and Melor, but although the popular understanding of martyrdom as unjust death had not disappeared from English society by the twelfth century, papal attempts to regulate the veneration of saints had made some progress. Early attempts to promote William's worship were met with the objection, "Not the suffering but the cause of suffering makes the martyr."[29] It was in this atmosphere that Thomas constructed his narrative of William's life and death. In order to satisfy heightened societal expectations of saintly behavior, Thomas presented to his readers the life of a child who had exhibited prior merit and had undergone martyrdom rather than murder. Meeting such criteria necessitated, in addition to proving his death to be an actual martyrdom, the reconstruction of a life which, like those of the child martyrs of previous centuries, had not been particularly noteworthy until the subject was killed.

The *Life* authored by Thomas of Monmouth marshals evidence to convince readers that William met his death at Jewish hands, but also claims that he was destined for a life of pious fame from the moment of conception. His mother, Elviva, experienced a prophetic dream of a fish before she was aware of her pregnancy. The dream revealed a fish called a luce, which "had twelve fins on each side, and they were red and as it were dabbled with blood."[30] She tried to pick it up and hold it closely, but it grew so that she could not hold it, and flew through the clouds into heaven. Elviva's father, a priest, interpreted the dream to mean that she would "bring forth a son who shall attain to the highest honor in the earth, and after being raised above the clouds shall be exalted exceedingly in heaven...[and] when they son shall have attained to twelve years, then he shall be raised to the pitch of glory."[31]

Prophetic dreams of greatness by the mothers yet-unborn of saints are often found it Celtic tradition.[32] Once born, William continued to distinguish himself in the manner found in the *vitae* of many saints. He performed a miracle while still an infant; on the feast of his weaning, his touch shattered the iron bonds of a man doing penance. The local priest, who was present, gathered up the pieces of iron and preserved them in the church at Haveringland, although the relics did not make a later appearance in William's story.[33] William was a pious child, fasting on three days of the week before the age of seven, and taking great delight in attendance at church.[34]

As William grew, he continued to excel in spirituality. Apprenticed to a skinner at the age of eight, he moved to Norwich and distinguished himself as the best of all the apprentices. He also began to associate with the Jews of the town, who sought him out because he was so young that they could bargain with him for cheaper rates. When William was twelve, his aunt's husband, Godwin the priest, discouraged his association with the Jews. For a time he complied, but since he was destined through the will of God to become a martyr at their hands, their interest was also dictated by divine predestination. They lured the boy away from his family by offering him a fictitious job in the kitchen of a prominent cleric.[35] William's mother had vague misgivings, but accepted three shillings for her inconvenience. When the body was found several weeks later, William's aunt reported to her husband that at the time of the boy's disappearance, she dreamt that she was standing in the market place and was seized by Jews, who tore off her right leg. She now connected this image with the murder of her nephew.[36] Upon leaving his mother's house, William was supposedly taken, not to the cleric's household, but to the home of a certain Jew, where he was tortured, crucified, and finally killed on Wednesday, March 22nd. His body was taken out of the city by two Jews and disposed of in the woods. On Good Friday, a miraculous shaft of light appeared over the remains. The body was discovered on Holy Saturday, and was visited by crowds of people on Easter Sunday before its burial in the woods where it was found.[37]

While Thomas presented his narrative with the assumption that the Jews were guilty of the crime, the early miracles worked by William's remains exhibited much in common with earlier Anglo-Saxon legends of children mordered for political reasons. This may reflect the initial popular appeal of the cult inspired by the identity of the victim rather than the perpetrators of the crime. The body, hidden in the woods, was revealed by a miraculous column of light, which "blazed in the eyes of many people who were in various places thereabouts...What else did the divine grace wish to signify to His faithful ones herein but that it was His pleasure to declare, by an evident token to all, how great was his merit whom He was so glorifying by signs form heaven?"[38] Miraculous pillars of light had marked the murdered bodies of Kenelm, Ethelred and Ethelbert, Wistan, and Edward, and the decapitated body of Melor was guarded by angels with lights. The light illuminating William's body was formed in the shape of a ladder reaching from heaven, with one ray at the child's feet, and another at his head. In 1168, a chapel was built in the woods where the body was first buried. The site attracted pilgrims and produced miracles although the body had been removed to Norwich in 1144.[39] A holy well was also discovered by Bothilda, the wife of the monks' cook, at the site of the forest burial, although no spring was located there.[40] The body itself was said to be incorrupt when first found in the woods, when dug up from its forest burial and translated to the monks' churchyard, and when brought into the church a month after William was killed. The remains exuded a fragrant odor at each translation.[41] A rose bush, planted at the little martyr's grave, miraculously bloomed in the winter "as a testimony to the act of his martyrdom,"[42] much as St. Kenelm's Ash flourished in an earlier century.

The language used to describe the young victim relied heavily on images of the earlier child martyrs of the Church. Calling for justice from the Bishop, the boy's uncle Godwin proclaimed that "a certain boy-a very little boy-and a harmless innocent, too-was treated in the most horrible manner in Passion Week [and] was found in the wood."[43] In one of the numerous passages defending the legitimacy of William's cult against its detractors, Thomas of Monmouth asserted that

> [T]he blessed William's innocence preserved his boyhood and...the purity of his virginity exalted it; and by the certain marks of his wounds, whoever may have inflicted them, he is proved as it were by sure arguments to have been indeed slain, and who can believe that, young as he was and innocent, he can have deserved death, since no previous fault was known?[44]

Even if the citizens of Norwich failed to recognize the role of the Jews in the crime, William deserved popular worship on the same grounds used to justify other child saints of dubious doctrinal merit, including the Holy Innocents themselves.

Thomas awarded William "the ornament of the triple stole: for he dyed with the rosy blood of martyrdom the two stoles of innocence and virginity which he already had, that he might claim for himself the third stole."[45] During the translation of the body from the monks' cemetery to the chapter-house, William appeared to Thomas is a vision and instructed that "a little resting-place be made ready for me in the Chapter House, because there for a little while, as a boy among the boys, I desire to rest."[46] Fixing blame upon the Jews was but one element in the case for veneration of the holy boy, and in its own time, perhaps the least important.

Public criticism of the cult, including the disapproval of the local clergy, fell into three categories, all reported and refuted by Thomas. The first objection indicates that papal attempts at centralization and standardization of the canonization process, and at imposing papal control over questionable local cults, were largely successful. Some said that it was "presumptuous to maintain so confidently that which the church universal does not accept and to account that holy which is not holy."[47] A similar criticism leveled at the cult noted that "it is rash to venerate so extravagantly him of whom, as they say, it is uncertain yet whether he be glorified."[48] The second objection revived early criticisms of the Holy Innocents and other child martyrs, that a young child who died unexpectedly had not accumulated enough good works to qualify for sanctity. Drawing an obvious parallel to a certain carpenter's son, Thomas mocked those who, "because they had known him as a poor ragged little lad picking up a precarious livelihood at his tanner's business, think scorn of him; and so can by no means believe that such an one, with no previous merits, should have attained to such an eminent excellence."[49] As refutation, Thomas provided examples of the exaltation of the humble, and reminded his readers of other boys chosen by God for the glory of martyrdom, specifically Pancras, Pantaleon, Celsus, and the Holy Innocents, "whom no previous merits distinguished in life, but only the grace of God glorified."[50] It is possible that the initial episodes of childhood piety and miraculous power included in the Life were intended to bolster William's reputation against such objections.

The third criticism of the cult was the most potentially damaging. Thomas admitted that

> ...there are some too who, though they saw with their own eyes that he, whatever he was, was cruelly murdered, or heard of it with their ears, or read of it in this present record, yet say: "we are indeed certain of his death, but we are entirely uncertain and doubtful by whom and why, and how he was killed. So we neither presume to call him a saint nor a martyr. And since it is not the pain but the cause that makes the martyr, if it be proved that he was killed in punishment by Jews or anyone else, who could confidently believe that this lad courted death for Christ's sake, or bore it patiently for Christ's sake when it was inflicted on him?"[51]

Thomas believed devotedly in the sanctity of the boy martyr, and the miraculous abilities of his relics. His stake in William's reputation was personal as well as institutional; he himself had committed a pious theft of two of the child's teeth during a translation of the body, and employed them in a number of miraculous cures.[52] As late as the tenth century, and even into the eleventh, the violent death of a child and the discovery of a corpse in the woods would have been sufficient motivation for popular veneration, but by the twelfth century this practice was open to question. *Martirem pena non facit sed causa* was a formidable objection, and so Thomas was obliged to make the case that William had died, not only young and violently, and at the hands of non-Christians, but in a Christian manner for the sake of Christ. By amplifying what may have been the actual suspicions of family members that the Jewish community was responsible for William's death, Thomas can be credited with creation of the ritual murder accusation in medieval Europe.

Blaming the Jews of Norwich for William's murder served the purpose of promoting his cult, and in fact provided the only opportunity for legitimizing his identity as a martyr. If a true martyr must be a Christian killed by non-Christians, then the Jews of Norwich were the only available candidates. Ample demonstrations of Thomas's anti-Semitism can be found in his repeated association of the Jews who killed William with the Jews who killed Christ, but this circumstance alone was not strong enough to sustain popular support for the cult; any evidence of more widespread anti-Semitism in the Norwich community is contradicted by the relative indifference of the general population to the murder charge, as well as the support of the Jews by the sheriff. The innocence of the victim, a recurring theme in the legends of child martyrs from the Holy Innocents to early medieval murder or accident victims, was also considered insufficient grounds for veneration. Thomas claimed repeatedly that William's murder was not a random crime, but that the child had been targeted as a victim precisely because of his "unusual innocence."[53]

> And again, if they say that his is against him that no previous merits gave any evidence of his deserving sanctification, I point to the Innocents of two years old and under, whom no previous merit distinguished in life, but only the grace of God glorified.[54]

Books I and II of the *Life* make clear that popular objections to William's cult were directed more at the religious shortcomings of the child than the supposed manner of his death. Thomas credits the early miracles, such as the delivery of a young woman from the torments of an incubus, with reviving "the memory of the blessed martyr William...for it had gradually been waning, yea in the hearts of all it had almost entirely died out."[55]

Continued indifference to the cult of the young martyr made it necessary for Thomas to create a scenario that would demolish all objections to William's saintly status. Accordingly, the particulars of the ritual murder charge outlined the gruesome steps in the young boy's crucifixion. Thomas reconstructed the fateful final days of the boy martyr through the testimony of three witnesses: a Christian servant in the Jewish household where he was allegedly slain, William's young cousin who followed him to the house, and Aelward Ded, who saw two Jews in the forest carrying a sack. Their evidence did not surface until five years after the murder, around the time that Thomas received three visions advocating the translation of William's relics into the Chapter House. According to this new evidence, William was lured to the house of the Jew Eleazor, where he was at first lulled into a false sense of security, then seized and tightly bound. Various instruments of torture were applied to his innocent form. He was scourged, a teazle was thrust into his mouth, his head was shaved, and thorns run into his tender skin. His body suffered so many cuts that he was doused with boiling water to staunch the bleeding. Finally, he was nailed to a crucifix and allowed to die. The Jews resolved to dispose of the body by leaving him in the woods rather than dumping him into the cesspool beneath the house, in the hope of avoiding detection. Two Jews placed his body in a sack and carried it into the forest, where they suspended it from the trunk of a tree.

Evidence of the crime was sparse. The only witness who saw William in the house, a Christian servant, claimed that she saw a boy tied up in a room just before Easter. Her testimony was elicited half a decade after the event. Aelward Ded claimed that he saw two Jews in the woods carrying a heavy sack, and that by brushing against the sack he determined that it held a dead body, but he too provided this testimony five years after the murder, on his deathbed. He claimed he had been sworn to secrecy by the corrupt Sheriff of Norwich, who schemed to protect the Jews.[56] A body left exposed in the woods for days would normally attract the attention of predators; this in fact was the fate of Eleazor, whose house was the alleged scene of the crime, and who was later murdered by a Christian, Simon de Nodariis, who owed him money.

> The Jew who with wicked hands had enticed a Christian into his house and killed him, when he had killed him had had flung him into a wood, and there had exposed him to the dogs and the birds-this same man was enticed out of his own house, was killed by the hands of Christians in a wood, and exactly the same way was left in the open air and exposed to be torn to pieces by dogs and birds.[57]

William's body had lain exposed in the woods for an indeterminate amount of time before its burial, translation, reburial, and retranslation, at which point it was examined for evidence of his demise. It was judged miraculously incorrupt a month after death, clearly exhibiting the marks of crucifixion on the head, hands, and feet, but was not damaged by the pecks of crows or the ravages of dogs. An early visitor to the body in the woods reported that the carrion-eaters who alighted on the body were miraculously unable to do their work, "but kept falling off him on this side and on that."[58] All signs of mutilation, therefore, must have been made before death rather than afterwards, and supported the charge of murder by crucifixion.

Despite its regrettable and sustained impact on European society, the ritual murder charge was not the principal focus of Thomas of Monmouth's story. It was the means to an end. The first two books of the *Life* include the charge of ritual murder among many supposed justifications for veneration of William; the remaining five books consist of miracle lists attributed to the martyr's glory, and contain no further references to the Jews. No Jews were ever tried or punished for playing a role in the death of William, despite Thomas' published identification of the very house where the murder took place.[59] Although Eleazor, the owner of the house, was brutally killed and his murderer escaped punishment, the cause was a recent dispute over a debt, not a murder from the distant past. The passage in the *Life* purporting to narrate the trial and exoneration of Simon de Nodariis is labeled by Thomas as "imaginary."[60] Similar lack of action against the Jews in other English towns that produced ritual murder victims for veneration provides further evidence that creating martyrs, and not persecuting Jews, was the principal goal.

The cults of ritual murder victims, once established in the popular imagination, functioned no differently than those of more conventional saints in terms of miracles, excitement, pilgrimage, and revenues. The translation of Williams's body from his forest grave to the chapter cemetery was accompanied by "crowds of people that were pressing in desiring to kiss the bier, and if possible to rush forward to see the body."[61] Thus honored, William performed miraculous cures of men, women, boys, girls, babies, pigs, oxen, and a falcon. He rewarded those who honored him, but punished those who did not give him the respect that was his due. Prior Elias, who never fully accepted the adulation of the martyr, and had forbidden Thomas from adorning the shrine with carpet and candles, died prematurely as a result of the saint's disfavor, "for perhaps they may say in their hears that the martyr William punished-and justly punished-by the vengeance of his wrath the insult offered to him by the hardened Prior. For it is said by many that the martyr threatened him, and that his death followed thereupon."[62] Prior Richard, who succeeded Elias, saw to it that the young martyr received proper veneration by returning his carpet and candles.[63] Godwin, the boy's uncle, who had kept the teazle found in William's mouth and used it to effect miraculous cures in exchange for payment, tried to extort the price of a hen from a poor women. She called upon Saint William and was cured, but Godwin suffered the loss of his entire flock of chickens.[64]

In just over a year, the cult outgrew surroundings; "...so great a crowd began to assemble daily at the tomb of Saint William, who still lay in the Chapter-house, that the brotherhood of monks who abode in the cloister could no longer put up with the daily pressure of so great a multitude."[65] Here, as the result of additional miracles, "he began to be waited upon by unwontedly large crowds," and so as to institute better crowd control, his relics were moved to the chapel of the Holy Martyrs.[66] In his new place of honor, the miracles continued unabated. "Every day the fame and wonder of the holy martyr continued to grow, and many came thronging to him, even from remote districts....marvel followed upon marvel...Were I to relate everything as it happened my book would be so long as to engender disgust."[67] The third, fourth, fifth and sixth books of the Life and Miracles detail the cures, curses, and other miracles wrought by the holy martyr between the first translation in 1150 and the fourth translation in 1154. At that time, the martyr ceased his interventions for a period, but in 1155, "the power of the holy martyr seemed to renew itself, and shone forth with a greater multitude of signs than before."[68] The miracles of Book VII were performed between 1155 and 1172, at which time Thomas completed his work and composed the prologue of the book. By this time, the fame of the young martyr was such that a second ritual murder victim, Harold of Gloucester, had been discovered in 1168 and was gaining his own hallowed reputation; neighboring Bury St. Edmunds would soon follow in 1181 with the martyrdom of little St. Robert. The charge would proliferate in England and abroad for several centuries, but no Jews were arrested or executed on the charge of ritual murder in England until the death of little Hugh of Lincoln in 1255. Other accusations of ritual murder occurred, without the formation of cults, until the expulsion of the Jews in 1290. Similar charges on the Continent, however, proved deadly to the Jews from their inception.

In 1389, the guild of St. William at King's Lynn was founded "of young scholars…to maintain and keep an image of St. William standing in a tabernacle in the church of St. Margaret of Lynn."[69] One of the first medieval organizations formed entirely of young members to have a religious purpose, the guild helped its members, young scholars, by providing assistance to members in need and funeral masses in times of bereavement. It met thrice each year, held an annual festival on the Feast of Relics, and provided six tapers for the church on festival days. By this time, over two centuries after the establishment of William's cult and a century after the expulsion of the Jews from England, popular memory may have erased the circumstances under which William was awarded veneration. His memory inspired other boys to good works, but like the cult itself, his guild functioned no differently than other such confraternities in the adult world.

CHAPTER 8

Holy Innocents and Sacrificial Lambs: Child Saints and Ritual Murder

The popular veneration of William of Norwich following the charge of ritual murder led to an almost immediate expansion of similar cults in England, France, Spain, Italy, and Germany. Over time, the nature of the charge developed from crucifixion into a more formulaic set of actions, such as draining the blood of the little victim to be used for magical rituals. Some charges of ritual murder resulted in the torture and execution of Jews, but did not generate a cult to the victim, and in some cases Jews were persecuted without the body of a victim to provide the basis for a crime.

It is impossible to state with any certainty the number of cults to alleged ritual murder victims formed between the twelfth and the sixteenth centuries. In 1902, the *Jewish Encyclopedia* listed one hundred twenty-two instances of the blood accusation in Europe, of which forty-seven occurred before 1500, but the list is incomplete and does not differentiate between cases that resulted in popular cults to the victims, and those that did not.[1] In general, the Papacy discounted the allegation of ritual murder and strongly discouraged the formation of such cults until the canonization of Simon of Trent, who died in 1475, in 1588. Scattered references to ritual murder victims of whom little or nothing is known indicate the popular appeal of the murdered children as objects of veneration, and suggest that the details of many individual cults have been lost to history. Even with the imperfect information that has survived, it can be stated that the ritual murder victims compose the largest set of child saints after the child martyrs of late antiquity.

After the establishment of William's cult at Norwich, the blood libel accusation next surfaced in Gloucester in 1168. The body of a boy was found, brutally disfigured, with "scars of fire, thorns fixed on his head, and liquid wax poured into the eyes and face,"[2] after it had been thrown in the Severn River. The history of the Monastery of St. Peter at Gloucester briefly mentions the death and discovery of Harold of Gloucester under the year 1168, but there is no evidence of a formal *vita.* The monks may have borrowed ideas from the popularity of William of Norwich, but without the type of detailed information provided by Thomas of Monmouth in the initial case, it is unclear whether the Jews were immediately suspected, or even how seriously they were suspected at the time. No mention was made of the boy's family, or of their reaction; the only indication that the community knew the identity of the corpse is that he was called Harold, and had probably disappeared on February 21, at which time he was "said to have been carried away secretly by Jews, in the opinion of many."[3] A large assemblage of Jews had taken place in Gloucester on March 16, ostensibly to celebrate a circumcision, and the body was found soon afterward, but "[i]t is true that no Christian was present, or saw or heard the deed, nor have we found that anything was betrayed by any Jew."[4]

Harold's body was discovered on March 17th, but his feast was sometimes celebrated on the 25th of March. This may be a later development meant to synchronize the alleged crime with Passion Week as the strict association of ritual murder with Easter and Passover developed over time. This requirement sometimes proved awkward to champions of local cults when bodies were discovered weeks or months after Easter. In Harold's case, no explanation was provided for the considerable lapse of time between the abduction and the murder, and the hesitancy of the chronicler in stating the chronology of the crime has been noted by one historian.[5] As with William, the childish innocence of the victim was central to recognition of the martyrdom. "It was clear that they had made him a glorious martyr to Christ, being slain without sin."[6] No individuals were punished for the crime, so it is questionable whether the good people of Gloucester truly believed the ritual murder charge, or simply wanted another saint to worship. The enshrinement of the martyr in the Church "near the altar of St. Edmund the Archbishop, and of St. Edmund, king and confessor, on the north side"[7] and the accompanying miracles, may have been the true goal of the community.

Robert of Bury St. Edmunds, whose cult was established following the discovery of his body in 1181, was also said to have been secretly murdered by a Jew, although there is no mention of anyone being tried or punished for the crime. The only surviving information on the saint is a brief mention by Jocelyn of Brakelond. "It was at this time also that the saintly boy Robert was martyred and was buried in our church: many signs and wonders were performed among the people, as I have recorded elsewhere."[8] The life of Robert mentioned by Jocelin has, sadly, not survived. The date of the child's death is unknown;[9] the discovery of his body occurred on June 10th, but his feast was established as March 25, the feast day of William of Norwich.[10] This may have been intended to provide a more direct connection with the ritual murder charge than the discovery of the body in June could support. No further mention of the crime or punishment of perpetrators has survived in existing records, and the church that housed the child's remains is today only a ruin. André Vauchez also includes Herbert of Huntington, killed in 1180, among the ritual murder victims, but the *Chronicle of Melrose*, which mentions his death just after the entry on the murder of Robert, does not indicate that he was killed by Jews.[11]

In 1244, an unnamed baby became the center of a cult in London. The body was found in the cemetery of St. Benet, with marks on his body judged to be Hebrew words. The justification for veneration offered by Matthew Paris provides an indication of the popular enthusiasm for ritual murder victims.

> And because it was discovered that Jews had formerly perpetrated such villainies, and that the holy crucified bodies had been ceremoniously received in the church, and miracles had broken forth, although the stigmata of the five wounds in the hands and feet and side did not appear on the said little body, nevertheless the canons of Saint Paul's seized it and solemnly buried it near the high altar.[12]

Nothing was known of the anonymous infant before the discovery of his body, but the ritual murder charge provided a quick and easy path to veneration. Public willingness to worship a holy innocent resulted in the imputation of a ritual murder without even the pretense of physical evidence or previous piety of the victim.

The death of Hugh of Lincoln in 1255 marked the first case in England to result in the execution of Jews for the crime of ritual murder, and the last cult formed in England prior to the expulsion of the Jews in 1290. In an atmosphere of increasing hostility toward the Jews, cults of ritual murder victims grew in popularity. The shrine of William of Norwich was prospering; offerings at the shrine increased throughout the thirteenth century and in 1277 reached the level of £21 3 s. 4d.[13] Relics of rutial murder victims were prized possessions. One contemporary relic collection included relics of William of Norwich and Robert of Bury St. Edmunds.[14] Popular interest in such cases was thus at its height when the body of an eight-year-old boy named Hugh was found in a well in or near the city of Lincoln

The principal sources for the story of Hugh of Lincoln, the *Chronica Majora* of Matthew Paris and the anonymous *Burton Chronicle*, provide conflicting accounts of the discovery of the body. The *Burton Chronicle* does not specify a location, but notes the Christ-like suffering of the child.[15] Matthew Paris, generally regarded as the less reliable of the two accounts, claimed that the body was found in a well near the house of the Jew Copin. The murderers threw the body into a well after the river and the earth rejected it.[16] Hugh's death may have been accidental; popular ballads recorded the tradition that Hugh was playing ball, and one scholar has surmised that he was running after a ball when he fell into a well or cesspool,[17] much as children today are cautioned not to chase balls into busy streets. The location of the well, if it existed, is uncertain, and may not have been located near the home of a Jew.[18] As with earlier cults, no evidence connected the body with the Jews in order to prove the charge of ritual murder, but in an interesting coincidence, the *vita* of William of Norwich described the Jews contemplating hiding his body in a cesspool, but reject this solution because the crime would be too easily discovered.[19]

The legend that developed after the discovery of the body was that the child was kidnapped by the Jews of Lincoln and held for a period of time before being crucified and, according to Matthew Paris, eviscerated for magical purposes.[20] Popular suspicions were confirmed by the gathering of Jews from across England under the pretext of celebrating a wedding. The resting-place of the young victim was revealed by a heavenly light and a miraculous fragrance.[21] Although the date of the disappearance and death, late July to late August, could not be manipulated to connect it even remotely with the feasts of Easter and Passover, torture of the Jew Copin produced sufficient confirmation to establish the veracity of the cult. Copin, or Joppin, the Jew at whose house Hugh was supposedly killed, was hanged in Norwich, while numerous other Jews (Matthew Paris gives the number as 91) were imprisoned in London. Both the Franciscans and the Dominicans were said to have attempted to secure their release. Eighteen Jews were later executed for the crime by Henry III, and the rest were eventually set free.[22] Unarguably the most famous of the English examples, besides its immortalization by Chaucer in The Canterbury Tales,[23] the legend spawned a number of popular ballads in England, France, Scotland, and even a version sung on the streets of New York City in the late nineteenth century.[24] The legends of Hugh and William were included in the *Nova Legenda Angliae*,[25] although their feasts failed to achieve greater than local fame.

The cults of the English ritual murder victims fed upon, and were in turn fed by, the growing anti-Semitism and escalating violence against the Jews that led to their expulsion from England in 1290. Evidence for the two most popular cults, William of Norwich and High of Lincoln, shows that after the use of the ritual murder charge to establish the victim's identity as a true martyr, no unusual circumstances differentiated the cults from those of other saints. After William of Norwich, none of the deaths were clearly connected with the Easter season, although several later became associated with that time. Reports of healing miracles survive for both William and Hugh, and are reported as general occurrences for the less well-known cults.

The charge of ritual murder first appeared on the Continent by 1171. From its initial manifestations in France, Spain and Germany, charges of child-murder were marked by extreme violence against Jewish communities, in some cases in the absence of any discernible crime. In France, beginning with the infamous Blois Incident of 1171, many Jews were killed and few cults formed. Only two cults of ritual murder victims, both dating from the late twelfth century, were generated from the many accusations. This may indicate that, far more than in England, the wish to persecute Jews outweighed the desire to worship their victims as saints.

The Blois Incident of 1171, in which some 31 Jewish men and women were burned at the stake, is the first recorded instance in which civil authorities were seen to act on the ritual murder charge, and the first such charge which saw the execution of Jews for the supposed crime. The charge itself may have appeared in France earlier. At Blois, no specific disappearance of any individual was claimed, no corpse was produced, and no cult was established. The incident seems to be one of purely anti-Semitic nature, with no connection to popular religious expectations.[26] The Jews of Worms were accused of the murder of a Christian for the purpose of poisoning the water supply during the First Crusade, in 1096.[27] In 1192 at Bray-sur-Seine, at least eighty Jews were burned by Philip Augustus for the scourging and hanging of a Christian, a murderer and thief whom they had allegedly paid the countess to obtain.[28] This incendiary charge occurred amidst the excitement of the Crusades. Pope Innocent III clearly believed the Jews of France capable of such acts; in 1205 he reported a current rumor that the body of a young man found in the latrines of Paris was the victim of

Jewish hatred.[29] In none of these cases, however, were popular cults formed. Charges made at Valréas in 1247, Troyes in 1288 and Chinon in 1317 also failed to generate cults, although at Valréas the body of a two-year-old girl named Meilla was produced.[30] Meilla disappeared on Tuesday, March 26th, five days before Easter; her body was found the next day in the town ditch, with marks on the hands and feet. She was said to have been seen in the Jewish section before her disappearance, and the Jews, being put to the question most effectively, confessed that her blood was to be used *quasi sacrificium*. The case prompted two papal bulls from Innocent IV to the Archbishop of Vienne, condemning the torture, robbery and murder of the Jews of the town. No cult formed around the relics of the child.[31] This pattern was repeated in other countries as well. In 1261, a seven-year-old girl in Pforzheim was supposedly sold to the Jews and killed for ritual purposes.[32] The evidence was flawed, relying as usual upon torture, but the incident, reported to Thomas of Cantimpré by two Dominicans who claimed to have been in the area within three days of the crime, included a number of minor miracles. The child's corpse refused concealment, although weighted with stones and thrown into the river, and her wounds began to bleed in the presence of Jews. When the Jews were taken to view the corpse a second time, the face flushed and the arms rose up. Although the same effect was produced upon the arrival of the Margrave of Baden, he was not suspected of any complicity in the murder.[33] The cult of *Il Santo Niño de la Guardia*, which appeared in Spain in 1487, generated extensive veneration despite the absence of any corporeal remains or proof that a crime had been committed.[34] The ritual murder charge thus spawned bodies without cults, and cults without bodies.

The cult of Richard of Pontoise at Paris was the first successful cult of this type to be established outside of England. His death is dated at 1179 by the Bollandists,[35] but by others at 1171 and possibly as early as 1163.[36] The first mention of Richard's death was in 1180, and was simply reported as a crucifixion and martyrdom at the hands of the Jews. The body was placed in the Church of the Holy Innocents in Paris, where it produced miracles for those who prayed to it.[37] The story of Richard's death was related in a much later *passio* by Robert Gaguin[38], and relied heavily on the themes of youthful innocence and willing martyrdom. Beyond the endurance of flagellation and crucifixion in imitation of the suffering Jesus, Richard bore up under his tortures with a remarkable strength of faith reminiscent of child martyrs of the early Church. At one point, he even exclaimed, *"Nolite timere eos, qui corpus occidunt,"* the phrase used many centuries earlier by little St. Flocel to encourage his companions in martyrdom. The Jews in this case only laughed at him.[39] The cult of Richard of Pontoise remained extremely popular, and in connection with the Blois incident, may have contributed to the climate which triggered the first expulsion of the Jews from France in 1182. Rigordus claimed that Philip Augustus was convinced of the veracity if these and many other charges, and was influenced by a holy zeal when he ordered the expulsion of the Jews, but others cited the more mundane grounds of usury.[40] The shrine of William the Infant, although established in the same atmosphere as that of Richard, may not have been accompanied by the murder of Jews. The cult was established in Paris in 1177; few details survive beyond the attribution of murder by Jews on Good Friday. William is included in the Gallican Martyrology.[41]

The death of Dominic del Val in 1250 marked the first appearance of the blood accusation in Spain, and its development relied heavily on previously established hagiographical motifs as well as vilification of the Jews. The alleged victim was a seven-year-old altar boy and chorister, who was kidnapped by Jews and nailed against a wall. The crime was revealed by a miraculous light which shone over his hidden grave, a motif similar to that found in the lives of William of Norwich and Hugh of Lincoln, as well as earlier medieval child saints. The case was considered one of ritual murder, although the saint's feast day is August 31, far removed from the Easter season. Dominic's cult was quickly established in Aragon.[42] As the *Bibliotheca Sanctorum* remarks, however, "*Certo il culto, leggendario il resto.*"[43]

The same remark could apply to the cult of Christopher of Guardia. Christopher, also known as Il Santo Niño de la Guardia, was allegedly killed in 1487, although the first written account of his martyrdom did not appear until 1544. The remains of the murdered child were never produced before the Inquisition or at any later time, although they were ardently desired. The execution of the Jews at Guardia for the unproven crime had been preceded by accusations at Valladolid in 1454 and Sepulveda in 1468, but neither resulted in the establishment of a cult to the victim. Fifteen Jews were either burned or hanged at Sepulveda.[44] The use of torture at Guardia is heavily credited with the production of confessions despite the absence of a *corpus delecti.*

In the Guardia incident, a converted Jew named Benito Garcia was handed over to the authorities after a consecrated Eucharistic wafer was found among his possessions. He was subjected to diverse tortures, including the lash, the water torture, and the garrote, and finally confessed that had engaged, with other *conversos* and several Jews, in magical rituals with the wafer and a human heart. All of the participants named under torture were arrested and brought before the Inquisition. One of the prisoners allegedly confessed that the group had crucified a child in order to procure its heart for the magical ritual.[45]

The confessions, obtained under torture, contradicted each other and could not be verified. No child was ever reported missing, and no body of a child was ever found. The child was allegedly murdered in a cave, and his body buried near La Guardia. The alleged burial site was revealed to the Inquisitors by one of the accused after torture, but it did not contain a body or any physical evidence proving that a crime had occurred. Despite this, the Jews were torn with hot pincers and burned to death. The repentant *conversos* were treated more mercifully by being strangled before their bodies were thrown on the flames. Three defendants who had died during the trial were burnt in effigy.[46]

One official connected with the case expressed, on the day following the executions of the alleged murderers,

> [T]he hope that God will miraculously make manifest the bones of the martyr, and he begs the magistrate not to allow the spot pointed out by Juan Franco as the place of burial to be ploughed over, for it is a place for Ferdinand and Isabella, for the cardinal, and for the whole world to gaze upon. Rather should there be a monument built there in memory of the *sagrada pásion* of the martyr.[47]

The cult, lacking physical remains, flourished instead through veneration of the sites of the child's passion. The house where the child was supposedly kept prisoner before his murder was torn down, and a church erected on the spot. The cave where he was martyred was also transformed into a church with attached convent. The grave, which was never proven to have held a body, was honored with a chapel erected over it. The nonexistent martyr was named as Patron Saint of La Guardia.[48]

In the attempt to establish the validity of their cults, the characters of child martyrs were, from the beginning, presented as unusually pious; increasingly, the theme of crucifixion generated a more complete identification with the sufferings of Christ, often exaggerated to stress the piety of the child in enduring them. The cult of Christopher of Guardia generated a passion play, in which the child was made to endure all the torments of Jesus and more. During the play, the child endured 5,495 lashes of the whip in silence, and only cried out during the last five. When asked the reason, he replied, "Because you have given me five more than to my Divine Lord."[49] When the Jew who slit his breast to remove his heart cut at first into the right rather than the left side, the holy child advised him of his error, whereupon the Jew was able to successfully complete his task. The alleged removal of the heart of the victim was one of the elements which originally identified this case with charges of magic rather than ritual murder, although no dismembered heart was found in the possession of any of the accused.[50]

Manifestations of the blood libel in Italy were infrequent, not appearing until the fifteenth century; only two cults besides the highly publicized and popular case of Simon of Trent in 1475 were created.[51] The cult of Sebastian Novello developed near Bergamo in 1480,[52] and that of Laurentinus Sossius in the countryside outside of Venice in 1485. The worship of Laurentinus led to the expulsion of the Jews from Venice and the surrounding countryside by the decree of Doge Marco Barbarigo in 1486.[53] Both victims, like those found in Spain, were venerated on the basis of their deaths rather than their preceding lives; in 1488 the body of the latter child was worshipped only as an "anonymous" victim of the Jews at the church of S. Sebastiano at Maristoca. Although this cult was officially disapproved of at the time, worship continued with the tacit approval of local authorities into the twentieth century. Pietro Barozzi, who visited the church in 1488 as a representative of the Church declared, in an attempt to suppress the cult, that he did not observe any miracles. The bishops of Padua and Venice, however, took no action against the cult. The confirmation process for Andrew of Rinn in 1755 noted the longstanding cult of Laurentinus, and his worship was confirmed on this basis in 1867, despite earlier disapproval.[54] No further cults to ritual murder victims were established in Italy. The Jews of Asti were accused of ritual murder in 1553, and imprisoned; Jews in Rome were subject to the charge in 1554. The next recorded instance of the accusation did not occur until 1705. None of the incidents spawned cults.[55]

In what is probably the first manifestation of the ritual murder charge in Germany, a pattern was set which despite the efforts of both secular and clerical authorities was to provide both the greatest number of popular cults and an even larger number of accusations and executions. Six Jews were executed in Erfurt in 1199 on a ritual murder charge, but no victim was produced and no evidence of a cult exists.[56] At Fulda in 1235, the five sons of a miller died on Christmas day, while their parents were at church. It was claimed that the children were killed by Jews, the blood of the children collected in waxed bags, and the house set on fire to cover up the crime. The appearance of the boys in a local martyrology as *V pueros* provides evidence of at least a brief popular veneration;[57] however, the popularity of the cult may have been diminished by the disapproval of Emperor Frederick II and Pope Innocent IV. Thirty-four Jews of both sexes were killed on December 28th in retribution for the crime.[58] Frederick II acquitted the Jews of Fulda, posthumously, and also the Jews of Germany, of this or any similar charges, and this case was cited by Innocent IV as one of the reasons for issuing a declaration against such accusations.[59]

The next popular cult to form in Germany, and the first with an identifiable victim, was that of Henry, a boy killed at Wassenburg in Bavaria in 1270. Leeches were put to his veins, and he was buried to hide the evidence of the crime.[60] Also in the thirteenth century, a child named Joannettus was supposedly killed by Jews in Cologne, and his relics venerated because of the miracles generated.[61] This was quickly followed by the development of two far more popular and influential cults, those of Werner of Trier, or Oberweisel, in 1275,[62] and Rudolf of Bern,[63] in 1287. Werner was a boy of fourteen who had gone to work for a Jewish family and was supposedly murdered by them after receiving Holy Communion on Maundy Thursday. The Jews, attempting to procure a sample of the Eucharist for magical purposes, tried to persuade Werner to supply it for them. When he refused, and they were unable to extract the Host by force, they murdered him. As well as emphasizing the boy's innocence and virginity, the story draws similarities between the martyrdom of Werner and that of Christ, and claims that Werner was targeted by the Jews for his Christlike purity and his veneration of the Virgin.[64]

Werner was immortalized in his *passio* as a *puer simplex, humilis, pius et timoratus*,[65] as well as *puer vere Catholicus & Christo devotus*.[66] According to his *vita*, demonstrations of miraculous piety occurred only after death, beginning with the refusal of the corpse to stay hidden after being submerged, and a miraculous fragrant odor which emanated from the body.[67] Before its discovery by a peasant, the body was miraculously preserved intact from the depredations of the beasts and birds,[68] as was the body of little William of Norwich. The body of Werner inspired numerous healing miracles among the pious, beginning immediately and extending into the seventeenth century. The first recorded miracle attributed to Werner involved the cure of Eberhard de Diepach, a blind boy, in 1287, whose sight was restored in one eye after holding vigil at his tomb. On the same day, a crippled merchant of good conduct and reputation was also cured, as well as a crippled scholar, two crippled boys, a blind woman, two crippled girls, a man named Henricus and two unnamed men and a woman.[69] While the shrine of Werner operated basically as a general healing shrine, the large proportion of children taken there, as well as the reporting of the first cure as visited on a child, may indicate a societal association with the healing of children. The beginning of the fifteenth century saw a renewed interest in the cult, with an unsuccessful attempt to have Werner beatified in 1427.[70]

The cult of Rudolph of Bern was less popular and less well documented. He is first mentioned in the *Martyrologium Germanico* in versions dating from 1562 and 1563, but no *passio* remains beyond a brief version of his martyrdom recorded in the seventeenth century.[71] His death came through torture and decapitation.[72] Descriptions of Rudolph do not extend beyond the characterization as *innocens puer et verus Dei Martyr*,[73] whose sanctity was assured by the many miraculous cures of old and young, men and women, performed at his shrine.

Although the murders were attributed to the late thirteenth century, popular veneration of the victims increased throughout the fifteenth century, as the number and intensity of ritual murder charges peaked in Germany.[74] The church honoring Werner of Trier was first built in 1428. The date of construction coincides with introduction of the process of beatification for the little saint. The cult spread in area and influence throughout the fifteenth and sixteenth centuries, as both his relics and his reputation spread. A chapel was built in Besançon in the mid-sixteenth century when relics of the child were obtained by a canon of that city. For some reason, he was honored as a patron of winegrowers in that region.[75] Relics of Rudolph were translated to the Church of St. Vincent in Lausanne in 1421, and the church containing the remaining relics was demolished and rebuilt on a grander scale in 1487.[76] Although the church at Trier was destroyed in 1601, and the relics contained there lost, relics of Werner were claimed in the early seventeenth century by churches in Belgium and Italy, making his cult unusually widespread for a saint of this sort.[77]

The cult of Conrad of Weissensee, the son of a soldier, was established at his death in 1303. A *passio* was written in the fourteenth century which described his death at the hands of the Jews, who were later unable to conceal the crime.[78] His "innocent martyrdom" inspired many miracles.[79] Ludwig von Bruck of Ravensburg was a Swiss boy of fourteen who came to Germany and was murdered; local Jews confessed after the use of torture, and the relics of the boy were preserved in the chapel of another boy martyr, St. Vitus. This was a popular rather than a liturgical cult. A chapel was erected in the woods at Haslach, where the body was discovered, to honor the martyr. The relics themselves were preserved at Ravensburg until the seventeenth century. [80]

The two most significant cults formed around the charge of ritual murder cult formation neighboring areas at virtually the same time. Andreus Oexner of Rinn was a three-year-old boy who was killed in 1462. Allegedly found hanged and mutilated in the woods outside the village, the crime is unusual in that it was originally attributed to the boy's lunatic uncle until the development of the cult of Simon of Trent in 1475.[81] At that time, it was realized that Andreus had actually been killed by Jews, miracles began to be associated with his burial site in the cemetery, and his body was translated into the church itself. Beyond the inscription marking the translation of the relics, the legend existed in an oral version for almost 200 years. The details of the legend were first set down in the seventeenth century by a local physician, who inspired the spread of the cult and the construction of a new church in the boy's honor in 1670.[82] The local cult was approved in 1753 by Benedict XIV, and a plenary indulgence granted to pilgrims visiting the church in 1754.[83]

Simon of Trent, a two-year-old boy who was killed in 1475, was the only ritual murder victim to be included in the Roman Martyrology.[84] Simon disappeared on Holy Thursday and his body was found on Easter Sunday; in this emotionally charged atmosphere, veneration of the body was assured, as well as the suffering of many Jews. The boy's father, a tanner, was afraid that his son had fallen into a ditch, and searched the city with friends, but was unable to locate the child. He reported Simon's disappearance to the Bishop on Good Friday, and asked for assistance. On Saturday, the father requested that the houses of the Jews be searched. The body was found in the cellar of a Jew, Samuel, on Easter Sunday. The Jews, who had previously searched their cellars in fear that the child's body would be planted in one of their homes, feared that a drainage ditch running through the cellar had carried the corpse inside to be discovered. When the body was brought before the assembled Jews, it bled, confirming to the authorities their guilt in his murder. Six Jews, including Samuel, were immediately arrested, with more following, and eight were executed for the crime.[85]

The cult of Simon of Trent is noteworthy for its wealth of documentation, including the accounts of the initial trial in 1475, a second trial in 1476, a third trial in Rome in 1477-78, and the papal inquiry leading up to canonization in 1588. During both the first and second trials, presided over by Church officials, evidence was presented that the Jews were framed by a Swiss named Zanesius who had lost a lawsuit against Samuel, the principal defendant in the murder case. Despite church attempts to treat the Jews fairly, "popular piety rapidly overtook the legal scruples of the ecclesiastical authorities: miracles began to be attributed to the little martyr boy, Trent became a pilgrimage site, and Simon was beatified by the Curia."[86] Popular enthusiasm for the cult of the little martyr outstripped the pace of justice. The report of the physician who examined Simon's body described the emotional as well as the physical suffering of the child. In addition to the catalogue of wounds, the *medicus* described how the beautiful child whimpered and wept, and called out the name of his mother.[87] Miracles attributed to the child began within a week of the discovery of the body, and one hundred twenty-nine miracles were reported by June 1476.[88] The story was promulgated through the new medium of print; it was included in the *Nuremburg Chronicle* of 1493,[89] and the cult achieved great popularity in Italy.[90] The legend of little Simon of Trent, like that of Hugh of Lincoln, also inspired popular ballads and poems celebrating his suffering.[91] A formal request for canonization was made in 1479, and the cult continued in popularity long after the request was granted in 1588. In 1965, Vatican II ordered the cult suppressed and Simon's name expunged from the Martyology.[92]

In addition to their widespread popularity and symbiotic relationship, Andrew of Rinn and Simon of Trent established the typology of the toddler as ritual murder victim.[93] Unlike earlier victims, for whom some effort was made to establish pious behavior as well as a martyr's death, these saints achieved fame simply through their youth and innocence. The emotional appeal of these cults may also have been instrumental in unleashing a stronger wave of anti-Semitism in Germany, as woodcuts, murals, plays and songs contrasted the savagery of the Jews with the extreme youth and helplessness of the victims. In Frankfurt, a mural depicting the evisceration of Simon was painted near the busiest of the city gates.[94]

Numerous attacks on Jews followed these highly publicized cases, but few later cults were established. Matthew Bader of Bensenhausen, a seven-year-old boy who was killed in 1504, was venerated as a ritual murder victim and saint despite the execution of his own father, a thief, for the crime. Matthew was an illegitimate child; the father, trying to escape punishment, claimed that he had sold the boy to the Jews, and that they were responsible for his death.[95] Michael Pisenharter of Sappenfeld was a three-year-old boy whose mutilated body was found in 1540. The body was put on display and bled miraculously five weeks later. Sappenfeld became a temporary pilgrimage site.[96] The pathos of his demise inspired an invective against the Jews; they had never been attacked by Christians, and certainly not "by innocent children and lambs."[97] A number of unnamed murdered children, such as a twelve-year-old boy killed in Wurzburg in 1570 whose corpse exhibited miraculous behavior in the presence of his alleged murderers, received passing mention but do not seem to have inspired cults.[98] The historian Joseph Jacobs records some thirty-nine accusations made between the Fulda incident of 1235 and a case at Frankfort-on-the-Main in 1593. These charges produced ten verifiable cults with named victims, plus cults at Fulda, Endingen, and Ratisbon where the children remained anonymous.[99]

The town of Regensburg alone leveled the ritual murder accusation at Jews in 1428, 1473 and 1475 without generating a cult to any of the alleged victims, but venerated six boys allegedly killed in 1486.[100] Between 1401 and 1597, thirteen additional charges, including the murder of two female children, were leveled at Jews in Central and Eastern Europe.[101] Although these cases are listed in the *Acta Sanctorum* as examples *de pluribus Innocentibus per Judaeos excruciatis*,[102] no evidence of popular cults has survived. The last recorded case of popular veneration of a child murder victim in Western Europe occurred in 1650, when the child Matthias was said to have been killed by Jews at Kaaden in Bohemia and was venerated as a martyr.[103]

Decline of the ritual murder charge in various areas was, to point out the obvious, directly linked with the expulsion of Jews from these areas. Expulsion from a particular region was often triggered by charges of ritual murder. Allegations of the crime in more modern centuries was found in Eastern Europe with great frequency, but only occasionally was a cult formed as a result. A ritual murder accusation made at Bjelistock in 1690 involving a six-year-old boy named Gabriel resulted in a cult in the Eastern Church,[104] but popular worship of such individuals in the West continued to center around older established cults. In fact, activity around many German cults increased in the eighteenth century, as seen in the attempt to canonize Andrew of Rinn, along with enhanced interest in other cults. Instances of the blood accusation, without the formation of poplar cults to the victim, have continued well into the twentieth century, and the accusation remains disturbingly active on various internet sites in the present day.

The cults of the ritual murder victims are the most famous and infamous of all child saints. Straddling the line between popular patronage and ecclesiastical exploitation, and condemned on both counts by the Church hierarchy, the cults failed to achieve official recognition but maintained sustained popularity. Despite the sensational charges of torture and murder by Jews, the purity and innocence of the victims remained a significant theme in their veneration. The proliferation of such cults in the later Middle Ages resulted in substantial harm to the Jewish communities of Europe, yet ironically the innocence of the victims remained an image with powerful emotional appeal. Joaff and Moses, two of the Jews hanged for the murder of Simon of Trent, invoked the intercession of "the boy and his innocent blood" before their execution.[105]

Medieval churchmen exploited many shrines and relics for prestige and financial gain besides those of the ritual murder victims.[106] Popular enthusiasm for the cult of the saints also gave rise to countless inventions and abuses over the centuries. No other group of saints, however, was created at the expense of so much innocent blood. For this reason, the boy martyrs of this group remain unique. In the face of heightened expectations of piety, popular sympathy for the death of innocent children remained so strong that it required an outlet which could be seen as legitimate. All male child saints whose cults developed between 1100 and 1600 either died of natural causes or were thought to have been murdered by Jews. Secular murder victims modeled after earlier saints Kenelm, Melor, Wistan and Edward did not emerge as objects of veneration. The newer model of martyrdom was far more exclusive than earlier concepts of the role. Adults allegedly killed by Jews escaped the dubious honor of popular veneration, as did young girls.

The identification of children with ritual murder, and the validity of popular veneration on that account, continued to be connected with societal beliefs of magic and of magical practices as were child murder victims of the early Middle Ages. The Jew was seen as a practitioner of magic for whom the flesh and blood of innocent children was a necessary ingredient;[107] such ideas may explain the focus on young boys as ritual murder victims. "Children are virginal and uncontaminated; by the special logic of magic 'innocent' blood should be most potent," noted Joshua Trachtenberg in his 1943 study of the blood libel charge.[108] Later examples of ritual murder, such as Christopher of Guardia and Werner of Trier, incorporated charges of host desecration with the earlier charge, first seen in the thirteenth century, of the blood of the victims being collected for magical purposes.[109] The alleged power of both substances in magical rituals, combined with the reputation of the Jews for prowess in magic and sorcery, were seen to provide a strong motivation for so heinous a crime. Both charges came to overshadow the original accusation of ritual crucifixion in mockery of Christ and hatred of Christians alleged by Thomas of Monmouth. The interrelation of magic and religion manifested through the cult of the saints can be seen in this idea as well.

If certain aspects of popular outlook serve to explain the impulse to worship young dead boys as ritual murder victims, there remains no explanation for the failure of cults to form in other localities under similar or identical circumstances. Such cults were initially formed with relatively little importance attached to the Jews allegedly involved. Later, after the establishment of the *topos*, accusation and execution of Jews was not necessarily connected with either the wish or the attempt to establish a cult to the victim, although every cult formed outside of England included the arrest, torture, or execution of Jews. The presence of relics was neither an influence nor a deterrent in cult formation. In many cases, actual murders occurred without the development of cults. On the other hand, a *corpus delecti* was not necessary to procure a conviction of accused Jews, and was not absolutely essential for the formation of a cult. As in the case of Christopher of Guardia, the absence of corporeal relics did not necessarily preclude the formation of a cult if the popular or official desire was strong. The failure of the majority of ritual murder accusations to generate cults, even though these involved the death of children, merits further historical research.

The cults of the ritual murder victims, in their own way, demonstrate the triumph of the papal agenda with regard to the popular worship of saints, despite papal disapproval of most of the cults.[110] Saints and their shrines functioned as conduits of miraculous healing and intercession between society and God, which was a form of magic. In rejecting the simple image of the victim of unjust death in favor of an image which directly invoked the martyrdom of Christ, medieval society demonstrated its acceptance of the papal promotion of stricter standards of piety in determining sanctity. Unjust death was no longer a satisfactory basis for veneration; further justification for worship was needed. Circumstances must be right. Miracles must be publicized. As it had done in earlier centuries, medieval society redefined martyrdom into a new form; this form was no more in conformance with ecclesiastical standards than was the earlier popular definition, but the greater emphasis on piety and a more conventional martyrdom were present. The medieval papacy may have lost the battle in trying to squelch those cults dedicated to a crime which did not exist, but it had won the ideological war. The magic of the saints, even of child saints, was placed more strongly within a standardized doctrinal framework.

Conclusion: *Vox Infantis*

In July of 1649, the inhabitants of the town of Leominster, England, discovered in a nearby field "a young child, which was wrapped up in swadling clouts, and to their judgements, appeared not to bee above a quarter of a yeere old."[1] Taken home by one of the laborers and fed a concoction of pap, the child "being therewith satisfied began to speake to all the people there present, and told them that it was the best meate he did ever eate, which Miracle in an Infant so young, bred admiration and astonishment in all the spectators."[2] The rest of his speech dealt with future political events, the duration of the war and the restitution of the monarchy, subjects much on the minds of men. Once delivered of his information, the child asked to be carried back to the spot where he was found, whereupon he vanished with the words, "Glory bee to God on high peace on earth &c."[3]

Roughly a millennium after the supposed appearance of the precociously loquacious St. Rumwald, infants were still accorded the power of miraculous speech. Child prophecy was not uncommon in the early modern period; the prophetical infant did not generate a cult in Protestant England, but other child visionaries attracted enthusiastic crowds. William Withers, an eleven-year-old boy, awoke from a ten-day trance in 1581 to deliver a series of prophetic utterances on sin and immorality that attracted "muche resort of people."[4] The child prophet Sarah Wight also garnered a popular following.[5] The Protestant Reformation abolished the veneration of saints' cults but promoted standards of pious behavior for children previously manifested only by the most dedicated of child saints. Children were presented with new forms of exemplary literature, such as *A Token for Children*, "being an account of the conversion, holy and exemplary lives; and joyful deaths of several young children."[6] Young readers were repeatedly exhorted to go to a corner and weep and pray for their sins, as they could die at any moment like the children in the book: "How do you know but that you may be the next Child that may die? and where are you then, if you be not God's Child?"[7] Keith Thomas in fact notes several instances of children who prophesied their own death,[8] and Gábor Klaniczay mentions the role played by children in prophecy in the late Middle Ages, while noting that this phenomenon needs yet to be examined.[9]

As with all themes in popular religion or popular culture, any choice of a chronological end for a study is more or less arbitrary. The religious and political upheavals of the early modern period do not provide a clear cessation of manifestations of religious or cultural significance attached to children who die. All manifestations of sanctity venerated in children by medieval society have survived in some form into the modern period. A renewed wave of missionary activity in the later sixteenth century led to the creation of a group of child saints almost identical in behavior to the child martyrs of late antiquity. The Martyrs of Japan numbered several children among their ranks. All, according to their passions, embraced martyrdom voluntarily along with other members of their families in behavior reminiscent of the earliest *passios*. One six-year-old boy was crucified with his mother, on a cross made especially small to fit his diminutive frame. Several children explicitly stated their wish to be crucified. Two boys, aged eleven and nine, changed into white garments before presenting themselves for execution with their grandmother. Family members expressed pride that their children chose to die with them.[10]

In a more exact parallel to the early child martyrs, the cult of St. Philomena, a child of twelve or thirteen supposedly martyred under Diocletian, was founded in 1802 when a set of bones was discovered behind an ancient and unintelligible inscription in a Roman catacomb. Three tiles reading "LUMENA PAXTE CUMFI" were believed arranged in error at the time of the burial, and so were rearranged to read "PAX TECUM FILUMENA."[11] Her *passio*, which was miraculously revealed to a Dominican tertiary in 1833, identified her as a virgin martyr who refused the hand of Diocletian in marriage. Her birth itelf was a miracle; her childless parents accepted baptism in exchange for the blessing of fertility, and were rewarded. Filumena, or Philomena, was baptized and pledged her virginity to Christ at an early age. When she was thirteen, the Emperor Diocletion became smitten by her beauty, and offered her marriage. Her father, "dazzled with an honor he was far from expecting," apostatized, but Philomena remained steadfast, despite being cast into prison in chains, tortured, and scourged. She was flung into the Tiber with an anchor around her neck, shot through with arrows, being shot at with heated arrows, but survived all trials. The baffled Diocletian accused her of being a magician. Finally, after converting many pagan onlookers through the miraculous demonstration of the power of God, she was pierced through the neck and died. The *passio* received the Imprimatur of the Holy Office in 1883.[12]

Philomena's relics were translated to the town of Mugnano in 1805. Her skull and bones were encased in a papier-maché body with a painted wax head, and dressed in sumptuous robes, for display.[13] An ampulla of dried blood found near her remains was said to miraculously transform into jewels before pious onlookers,[14] and a statue of the saint presented to the shrine by the Archbishop of Naples in 1823 was said to exude a miraculous liquid referred to as "manna."[15] Early promotion of the cult was spurred by reports of miraculous cures of many people, especially children. As with other local saints throughout the ages, Philomena's power was extended to people of all ages, but she was thought to have a special affinity for children, and for infertile couples.[16] She eventually acquired followings in France, England, Portugal, and several regions of the United States, where she was also renowned for her care of children.[17] She was canonized in 1837 by Pope Gregory XVI, but in 1961 her name was removed from all Church calendars and several of her shrines ceased activity. The shrine in Mugnano remains active, as does the shrine in Briggsville, Wisconsin. A new shrine to St. Philomena was established in 1987 in Dickinson, Texas.[18]

The medieval version of the child martyr, the ritual murder victim, has exhibited remarkable resilience in the modern age. Those who claim a decline of ritual murder charges cite the growth of rational thought associated with the Enlightenment and the modern era, but the decline more accurately represents shifting demographic patterns for Jewish communities rather than altered sensibilities of the Christian population. Areas from which the Jews had been expelled expressed anxieties about unseen threats to children by accusing witches of similar crimes.[19] Shrines of ritual murder victims continued to be venerated, especially in Germany and Italy, but no new cults were created after the sixteenth century. Ritual murder charges, however, continued unabated into the twentieth century and were prosecuted as secular crimes. Girls as well as boys, adults as well as children, were seen as victims of the blood accusation, although young male children still predominated. Popular veneration of the victim still occurred under some circumstances, although no cults wereofficially recognized. As the medieval cult of Christopher of Guardia demonstrated, the body of a victim was not always necessary for prosecution. Other cases ended in aquittal on lack of evidence even when a child had actually been murdered.

Hsia has noted that after 1540, accusations of ritual murder by Jews were replaced by accounts of secular child murder, usually by family members.[20] With few Jews remaining in Western Europe by the end of the sixteenth century, the blood accusation moved into Eastern Europe, where such accusations were rare in the Middle Ages, and into the Middle East. Daniel Trollet has documented one hundred and eleven cases of ritual murder accusations between 1500 and 1789 in the region of the Polish-Lithuanian

Commonwealth, of which only a handful generated cults; only two such charges were made before 1500.[21] Many of the incidents included the claim that the children were sold to the Jews by Christians, and although some of the charges led to the torture and execution of the accused, in many cases the Jews were protected by civil authorities or the Catholic Church. Some of the more notorious cases of the nineteenth and twentieth centuries resulted only in civil trials.

In the Damascus Affair, a Sardinian priest, Father Thomas, and his servant, Inbrahim Amara, disappeared mysteriously on February 5, 1840. Several Jews were arrested, and after torture confessed to a hideous crime. The priest had been murdered and his blood drained out of his body, after which his clothes were burnt, the flesh cut up, and the skull and bones crushed into tiny pieces and thrown into a conduit to prevent detection of the crime. Remains conforming to the description of the dismemberment, along with a scrap of cloth and a piece of scalp, were discovered in a conduit and identified as Father Thomas by the authorities. A month later, a subsequent search uncovered bones and a shoe in the same area that were identified as the remains of the servant.[22] At the same time, an eleven year old Greek Orthodox boy in Rhodes disappeared while on an errand. Although his body was never found, arrests of Jews were made, and after confession under torture incriminated others, arrests increased.[23] The paucity of evidence that any crimes had been committed, along with European diplomatic pressure and international outcry over the absurdity of the charge and the extended use of torture, resulted in the ultimate release of those arrested in both cases, but no fewer than six ritual murder accusations were made in Egypt between 1870 and 1892, and the charge recurred in Damascus in 1890.[24] The pattern also continued in Eastern Europe throughout the nineteenth century.

In Nagykálló, Hungary, in 1790, a ten year old shepherd boy named János Bujkus disappeared while tending a flock of geese owned by a local Jew. The ritual murder charge was made, and the owner of the flock sentenced to death and several other members of the Jewish community imprisoned before the boy turned up alive and unharmed.[25] In 1882, in Tiszaeslár, the disappearance of a fifteen-year-old servant girl names Esther Solymosi prompted the charge that she had been lured into a synagogue and murdered. A female corpse was retrieved from the Tisza River and identified as Esther, without corroborative evidence. The flimsiness of the charges and the evidence resulted in the acquittal of all defendants, but the popular reaction to the trial demonstrated deeply-rooted anti-Semitic prejudices.[26] Similar charges were made at Xanten in 1891 and Polna in 1899,[27] and in Kiev in 1911, with varying outcomes.

In Xanten in 1891, the body of a five year old boy, John Hegemann, was found dead in a neighbor's barn with his throat slit. Agitation by the local Catholic priest led to the arrest of the local butcher, Adolf Buschoff, who was Jewish, but he was acquitted of the charge on lack of evidence. A surge of popular anger over the acquittal led to Buschoff's re-arrest in 1892, but the charge was dismissed, again on lack of evidence.[28] The Hilsner Affair in Polna began with the discovery of the body of nineteen year old Anezka Hruzová on April 1, 1899. Her throat was also cut, and the absence of blood at the scene led to the charge that "the motive for the murder was neither robbery nor sexual perversion, but a desire to obtain blood from the body of an innocent Christian virgin."[29] Leopold Hilsner, a Jewish shoemaker's assistant who lived with his widowed mother, was arrested for having been seen near the scene of the crime. He was found guilty and hanged. The Beilis Case began similarly but ended far differently. On March 19, 1911, the body of thirteen year old Andrei Yushchisky, badly beaten and stabbed repeatedly, was found outside of Kiev. Almost immediately, the Jews were blamed for the death and "Andryushka" was popularly proclaimed a martyr by his mourners.[30] The charge of ritual murder necessitated the arrest of a Jew. Mendel Beilis, the manager of a brick factory near where Andryushka was found, was arrested four months after discovery of the body. The Beilis case, like the Damascus Affair, became an international cause, and Beilis was acquitted although the jury found that the child had indeed been the victim of ritual murder.[31]

The ritual murder accusation did not die out in Eastern Europe with the Beilis case,[32] nor did it remain confined to the Old World. In 1913, Leo Frank, the Jewish superintendent of a pencil factory in Atlanta, Georgia, was arrested for the murder of an employee, fourteen year old Mary Phagan, who was found dead in the factory basement.[33] The overt charge of ritual murder was not raised; instead, the case was made that Frank was guilty of sexual perversions, and that this was the motive for the girl's slaying. Five members of the grand jury that indicted Frank on the charge of murder were Jewish.[34] Frank was found guilty and sentenced to death, and when the Governor of Georgia commuted his sentence to life imprisonment, he was lynched. The story was made into a musical, "Parade," in 1998.[35] An often unremarked feature of the story was the massive popular reaction to the death of the innocent girl, which was said to have an "exalted, religious quality...For years after her burial, thousands of people made a solemn pilgrimage to her grave."[36]

Further examples of the blood libel in the United States occurred without victims or trials. A series of accusations during and after World War I, brought by immigrants from regions in which the blood libel flourished, reflected the continuing fear of Jewish involvement in ritual murder. In Clayton, Pennsylvania, in 1913, a sixteen year old servant girl named Anna Hansel became frightened by the sight of a large knife used by her employer, Mrs. Stein, and disappeared overnight. Neighborhood agitation that "the Jews killed the Christian girl" dissipated when she reappeared unharmed.[37] In Fall River, Massachusetts, in 1913 and Pittsfield, Massachusetts, in 1919, little Polish boys who were injured told their parents that the Jews had attacked them; the parents told the priest, who told the police. In both cases the charge was fabricated. The Fall River boy was beaten up in a fight. The Pittsfield boy later admitted that he fell out of a tree.[38] In Massena, New York, in 1922, the disappearance of four-year-old Barbara Griffiths was attributed by a Greek luncheonette owner of being the work of the Jews until she was located unharmed a few days later in the woods near where she first disappeared. In the meantime, a Jewish boy and the rabbi of the local Jewish community were questioned by police.[39] The Massena Incident is perhaps the most famous of the blood libel charges in the United States.

As disturbing as these modern incidents are, they demonstrate ongoing societal fears for the innocence and vulnerability of childhood. More positive manifestations of the veneration of children have also continued into the modern period. In the sixteenth and seventeenth centuries, the Church promoted cults of the Infant Jesus in the form of El Santo Niño de Atocha and the Holy Infant of Prague. El Niño de Atocha originally appeared in Spain in the fifteenth century, as a miraculous visitation to starving Christians under siege from Moslems. The child, dressed in the garb of a pilgrim, brought them food and water. The cult of the Niño spread throughout Spain, and was exported to the New World, especially Mexico and New Mexico. The Holy Infant of Prague, not a vision but a statue, also originated in Spain. It was sent to Prague as a gift in 1556, and became one of the most famous cult statues of the period. Its popularity endures to this day.[40]

After the Reformation, the popular desire to venerate the innocence of the child was increasingly satisfied by Jesus Himself rather than by sacral underlings, but the pious infant has reappeared in several forms in the modern era. Marian apparitions of the nineteenth and twentieth centuries frequently appeared to children, such as the visions seen at Lourdes by fourteen-year-old Bernadette Soubirous in 1858, the year of her first communion. The body of St. Bernadette, who died in 1879 at the age of thirty-five after a lifetime of ill health, has been preserved incorrupt.[41] The Marian apparitions at Fatima in Portugal first appeared in 1915 to three young shepherd children, eight-year-old Lucia dos Santos, and her younger cousins Francisco and Jacinta Marta. Francisco died of influenza in 1919 at the age of ten, and Jacinta died the following year at the age of nine. Jacinta, especially, was noted during her brief lifetime for piety, asceticism, and charity, and she also predicted her own death. The process for beatification was begun for Francisco in 1949, and for Jacinta in 1979, notwithstanding an admonition by the Virgin Mary that although both children would go to heaven, Francisco would have to say many rosaries first.[42]

In 1922, Anne de Guigné died of meningitis at the age of eleven after several years of unusually pious behavior. This young girl, who showed "every sign of naughtiness from earliest infancy,"[43] evinced a miraculous change of heart at the age of four, upon the death of her father in battle in 1915. From then on, her every waking moment was marked with piety, purity, and prayer. She fervently desired First Communion from an unusually early age, and was approved for the sacrament at age five, after successfully navigating "a rigorous examination by...the Superior of the Jesuits, who was by no means disposed in her favor."[44] Her champions compared her to "the great pioneers of the Liturgy...in those early days when Christianity was young,"[45] and stoutly denied that she was in anyway "pushed into sanctity... those who think children can be forced or persuaded into sanctity show that they have had very little experience with children."[46] Anne was noted for her obedience, her concern with purity, and her frequent prayers. In hindsight, she was said to have divined her approaching demise. Her death from meningitis, "longer and more terrible than many a martyrdom,"[47] was quickly followed by a succession of miraculous cures and other interventions. Her nine-year-old brother had the presence of mind to create dozens of relics from his sister's body by "collecting everybody's prayerbooks and holy pictures,"

> and brought them all down to Anne's room, where he piled then in a heap beside the bed and then proceeded to press each thing against her hand....the little boy looked round at them and said firmly, "Someday you will be very glad I have done this." And he went on making relics![48]

Laid to rest in the family vault, her remains attracted popular veneration, "for the whole countryside knew the sweet little girl who 'prayed so well.'"[49] She became known as "The Apostle of the Nursery" for her miraculous favors toward children. An investigation into Anne's life was begun in 1932; in 1933 her relics were exhumed and her body was found to be incorrupt.[50] The beatification process was begun in 1955, "but like many other causes of children and youths, the process became stalled;" in 1990, Pope John Paul II approved a decree recognizing Anne's Heroic Virtue. "Before this decree was possible there had been a long discussion on the question of whether children from age seven to fourteen were capable of practicing the virtues in an extraordinary, heroic way."[51]

While Anne's life has been narrated to fit the conventions of the pious infant, her popular cult may also be traced to the early medieval practice of venerating the dead children of the nobility; she was the eldest daughter of Jacques, Count de Guigné, and his wife Antoinette de Charette. A similar cult to Guy de Fontgalland, a young man who died of diphtheria in 1925 at the age of ten, after exhibiting extraordinary piety following his First Communion, failed to win papal approval despite the laudatory biography written by his mother, the Comtesse de Fontgalland. The impulse to venerate the dead children of the powerful is not confined to Europe. In the town of Richard, Louisiana, the body of a twelve-year-old girl who died of leukemia in 1959 was reported, thirty years later, to be working miraculous cures. The local priest was reportedly pursuing the possibility of canonization. The child's family name is Richard.[52]

The human capacity for veneration of children who died unjustly, and through no fault of their own, continues into the present. The outlook which in previous centuries encouraged the growth and spread of the cults of Reginswinde, Panacea, Edward, Kenelm, and other child victims of violent crime can also be seen in such popular phenomena as the 1991 report from Chula Vista, California, that the face of a murdered nine-year-old girl had appeared on a billboard two miles from the site where her body was discovered.[53] The modern Catholic Church has formally embraced the veneration of child murder victims; Maria Goretti, a young Italian peasant girl who died at the age of eleven in 1903 after being raped and stabbed by the adolescent son of a neighboring farmer, was canonized in 1950. She lived long enough to forgive her assailant, who later in life showed much remorse for the crime.[54] Simon of Trent did not survive the purifications of Vatican II, but Maria Goretti did.

Once the details of their cults are known, the veneration of child saints can strike Catholics in the modern world as odd or even repulsive. During one presentation I gave on child saints at a conference in 1992, a woman in the audience remarked that she found the veneration of St. Maria Goretti particularly appalling. What kind of spiritual example, she asked indignantly, did a twelve year old rape victim represent? The modern age is taught to look to the saints for spiritual inspiration and examples of heroic Christian living, to inspire greater closeness to God. Spontaneous veneration of the victims of random criminal violence belongs to a forgotten era. A visit to Norwich Cathedral in 1994 and a simple query about the shrine of William of

Norwich-denuded, unmarked, and shrouded in obscurity-prompted a similar reaction. "We never talk about it," hissed the elderly female docent. "It's shameful-shameful."

And yet, the example of the child saint surfaces in surprising ways. One day, while concluding a class on medieval popular religion, I sketched the survival of many popular practices into the modern age, and included the example of little Maria Goretti. After class, one of my students shared an anecdote. She had attended an all-female Catholic high school, and on the morning of the senior dance, to be held with the boys' Catholic school across town, the principal, an elderly nun, spoke over the intercom to address her young pupils. On this important day, she told the girls, they should all bow their heads and pray to St. Maria Goretti.

"She never told us why," said my student. "Now I know."

Notes

Abbreviations

AASS	*Acta Sanctorum*
Anal. Boll.	*Analecta Bollandiana*
CCLS	*Corpus Christianorum, seies Latina*
EETS e.s.	*Early English Text Society, extra series*
EETS o.s.	*Early English Text Society, old series*
EETS s.s.	*Early English Text Society, supplementary series*
MGH	*Monumenta Germaniae Historica*
PG	*Patrologia cursus completes, series Graeca*
PL	*Patrologia cursus completes, series Latina*
Rolls Series	*Rerum Brittanicum Medii Aevi Scriptores, or Chronicles and Memorials of Great Britain and Ireland during the Middle Ages*
VCH	*Victoria History of the Counties of England*

Introduction

1. E. C. Brewer, *A Dictionary of Miracles, imitative, realistic, and dogmatic* (Philadelphia: J.B. Lippincott, 1884) xxxii–iii.

2. L. von Hertling, "Utrum pueri canonizari possint?" *Periodica de re morali, canonica, liturgica* 24 (1935): 66–73.

3. Camillus Baccari, "Beatification and Canonization," *Catholic Encyclopedia* (New York: The Encyclopedia Press, 1907) 2:364.

4. Ibid., 365.

5. Pierre DeLooz, "Towards a sociological study of canonized sainthood," in *Saints and their Cults: Studies in Religious Sociology, Folklore, and History*, ed. Stephen Wilson (Cambridge: Cambridge University Press, 1983, repr. 1987) 193.

6. Richard Kieckhefer and George Bond. eds., *Sainthood: its Manifestations in World Religions* (Berkeley: University of California Press, 1988) viii. See also Marc Garneau, "The cult of saints among the Muslims of Nepal and northern India," in *Saints and Their Cults*, 291–308.

7. See Donald Weinstein and Rudolph Bell, *Saints and Society: The Two Worlds of Western Christendom 1000-1700* (Chicago: University of Chicago Press, 1982) 1–13, and Wilson, *Saints and their Cults*, 1–41.

8. Weinstein and Bell, 8.

9. Delooz, 191–2; Jonathan Sumption, *Pilgrimage: an Image of Medieval Religion* (Totowa, NJ: Rowman and Littlefield, 1975) 148.

10. Sumption, 22.

11. Ibid., 148.

12. Baccari, 366.

13. Delooz, 192.

14. Baccari, 364.

15. Sumption, 22.

16.   Luke 2:46–7, *The New Oxford Annotated Bible* (New York: Oxford University Press, 1977) 12–45.

17. In the Gospel of Thomas, Jesus does not resurrect the children he kills in anger, but in the Gospel of Pseudo-Matthew he is better behaved. *The Apocryphal New Testament*, ed. M.R James (Oxford: Clarendon Press, 1927) 38–90. See also O. Cullmann, "Infancy Gospels," in Edgar Hennecke, *New Testament Apocrypha*, tr. R. McL.Wilson (Philadelphia: Westminster Press, 1963) 1:363–417, and M. R. James, ed., *Latin Infancy Gospels* (Cambridge: Cambridge University Press, 1927.)

18. Philippe Aries, *Centuries of Childhood: a Social History of Childhood* tr. Robert Baldrick (New York: Knopf, 1962) 39.

19.   Nicholas Orme, *Medieval Children* (New Haven and London: Yale University Press, 2001) 4–6; Egle Becchia and Dominique Julia, eds, *Histoire de l'enfance en occident*, Vol. I: De l'Antiquité au xviie siècle ,tr. Jean-Pierre Bardos (Paris: Éditions du Seuil, 1998) 14–33.

20. Shulamith Shahar, *Childhood in the Middle Ages* (London: Routledge, 1990) 1.

21.   Barbara Hanawalt, *Growing up on Medieval London: the Experience of Childhood in History* (Oxford: Oxford University Press, 1993) 5.

22. J.A. Burrow, *The Ages of Man: A Study in Medieval Writing and Thought* (Oxford: Oxford University Press, 1988); Michael Goodich, *From Birth to Old Age: the Human Life Cycle in Medieval Thought* (New York, 1989); Elizabeth Sears, *The Ages of Man: Medieval Interpretations of the Life Cycle* (Princeton: Princeton University Press, 1986). See also Thomas Wiedemann, *Adults and Children in the Roman Empire* (New York and London: Yale University Press 1989), 114, and Lynn Thorndike, *A History of Magic and Experimental Science* (New York: Columbia University Press, 1923) 2:409–14.

23.   Joseph de Ghellinck, "Iuventis, gravitas, senectus", *Studia Mediavalia in Honorem Admodem Reverendi Patris Raymondi Josephi Martin* (Bruges, 1948) 3959; Pierre Riché, "L'enfant dans le haut moyen age," *Études: Enfant et sociétés*, 95. See also Ariès, 15–32.

24. Jerome Kroll, "The concept of childhood in the Middle Ages," *Journal of the History of the Behavioral Sciences* 13 (1979): 388.

25. Ghellinck, 41. Wiedemann, 114, gives the age of seventeen as the end of *adolescentia* in the Roman world, and as the age of eligibility for army service; Jean-Pierre Nérandau, "L'enfant dans la culture Romaine," *Histoire de l'enfance en occident*, 74, fixes eligibility for military service at fourteen. Kroll, 388, notes the ages of eighteen to twenty-one as legal definitions for the attainment of maturity.

26. Usuardus, *Le Martyologe d'Usuard: texte et commentaire*, ed. Jacques DuBois (Bruxelles: Société des Bollandistes, 1965) 296. The *Martyrologium Romanum, Propylaeum ad Acta Sanctorum Decembris* (Bruxelles: Société des Bollandistes, 1940) 377, condensed the entry to read "Antoninus, a boy [Antonini pueri]."

27. Usuard, 153. The *Martyrologium Romanum*, 3, also identifies Marcellinus as a *puer*, but the modernized *Roman Martyrology*, ed. J.B. O'Connell (Westminster, MD: The Newman Bookshop, 1962) 2, identifies him as a young man.

28. Alexandre-Bidon and Lett, 21; Nérandau, 73.

29. Egle Becchia, "Le Moyen Age," in Becchia and Julia, eds, *Histoire de l'enfance en occident*, 104.

30. Frances Arnold-Forster, "Child Saints," in *Studies in Church Dedications* (London: Skeffington and Sons, 1899) 1:168–76.

31. Brewer, xxxii–xxxiii.

32. Michael Goodich, "Childhood and Adolescence among the Thirteenth-Century Saints," *History of Childhood Quarterly* I (1973): 285–309; "Une enfant sainte, une sainte des enfants: l'enfance de sainte Élisabeth de Hongrie (1207–1231)" in Becchia and Julia, eds, *Histoire de l'enfance en occident*, 134–159; Weinstein and Bell, Saints and Society, 19–47.

33. Anna Benvenuit Papi and Elena Ginannarelli, eds., *Bambini Santi: rapprezentazioni dell'infanzia e modelli agiographici* (Turin: Rosenberg & Sellier, 1991)

34. Michael Goodich, "Il fanciullo come fulcro di miracoli e potere spirituale (XIII e XIV secolo)," *Poteri carismatici e informali: chiesa e societá medioevali*, ed. Agostino Paravicini Bagilani and André Vauchez (Palermo: Sellerio, 1992): 38–57.

35. Orme, 200236. Specific discussion of child saints, 211 and 233–235.

36. Diana Wood., ed. *The Church and Childhood* (London: Blackwell, 1994.)

37. Francesco Scorza Barcellona, "Infanzia e martiria: la testimonia della più antica letteratura cristiana." *Bambini Santi:rapprezentazioni dell'infanzia e modelli agiographici*, ed. Anna Benvenuit Papi and Elena Ginannarelli. Rosenberg & Sellier: Turin, 1991) 61.

38. Goodich, "Childhood and Adolescence," 292.

39. Weinstein and Bell, 28.

40. Barbara Hanawalt, *The Ties that Bound: Peasant Families in Medieval England* (Oxford: Oxford University Press, 1989) 187.

41. Rosalind and Christopher Brooke, *Popular Religion in the Middle Ages: Western Europe 1000–1300* (London: Thames and Hudson, 1984) 59.

42. Gábor Klaniczay, *The Uses of Supernatural Power*, tr. Susan Singerman (Princeton, Princeton University Press, 1990) 2–3; Peter Brown, *The Cult of the Saints: its Rise and Function in Latin Christianity* (Chicago: University of Chicago Press, 1981) 48, questions the value of constructing a two-tiered model of popular versus elite spheres of belief.

43. Klaniczay, 15.

44. Ibid.

45. Jean-Claude Schmitt, *The Holy Greyhound: Guinefort, healer of children since the thirteenth century*, tr. Martin Thom. (Cambridge: Cambridge University Press, 1983.)

46. Brooke and Brooke, 61. See also Valerie Flint, *The Rise of Magic in Early Medieval Europe* (Princeton: Princeton University Press, 1991) *passim*.

47. Gábor Klaniczay, "Witchcraft and Sainthood: Anthropological Problems and Structural Comparison," Plenary address delivered at the 27th International Congress on Medieval Studies, Kalamazoo, MI, May 9, 1992. See also Klaniczay, 4.

48. Klaniczay, 2. See also Keith Thomas, 232–4, 325–6, 342–4 for examples of the impact of belief in magic upon the political structure, and Richard Kieckhefer, *Magic in the Middle Ages* (Cambridge: Cambridge University Press, 1989) 15356, for discussion of the role played by the clerical elite in the practice and spread of magic and superstition.

49. Gustav Henningsen, *The Witch's Advocate: Basque Witchcraft and the Spanish Inquisition 1609–1614* (Reno: University of Nevada Press, 1980) 390.

50. David Marshall Lang, *Lives and Legends of the Georgian Saints* (New York: MacMillan, 1953) 40–43.

1. *Christianus Sum:* Child Martyrs of the Early Church

1. Maurice M. Hassatt, "Martyr," *Catholic Encyclopedia* 9:739.

2. For a general introduction to early developments in popular worship of the martyrs, see Peter Brown, *The Cult of the Saints*, (Chicago: University of Chicago Press, 1981); Robin Lane Fox, *Pagans and Christians* (New York: Alfred A Knopf, 1989) 419–92, and Hippolyte Delehaye, *Les Origines du Culte des Martyres* (Brussels: Société des Bollandistes, 1933).

3. See Francesco Sforza Barcellona, "Infanzia e martirio: la testimonianza della più antica litteratura Christiana, *Bambini Santi*, 59–83.

4. Roland Bainton, *Early Christianity* (New York: Van Nostrand, 1960) 21.

5. Pliny, *Ep.* 10:96, *Letters of the Younger Pliny*, ed. and tr. Betty Radice (Harmondsworth: Penguin Books, 1963) 293. See also Fox, 421, for specific examples of obstinacy.

6. Fox, 434, 457; Bainton, 27.

7. Fox, 422.

8. Pliny, *Ep.* 10:96, *Letters,* 293.

9. Bainton, 26.

10. Mark Golden, *Children and Childhood in Classical Athens* (Baltimore: Johns Hopkins University Press, 1990) 6.

11. Wiedemann, 17–21.

12. Ibid., 21–4. Of the child-martyrs treated in this chapter, boys outnumber girls by somewhat more than two to one (29 to 13.) This number is skewed by the exclusion of adolescent girls of marriageable age who were martyred in defense of chastity; nevertheless, it was less common for girls than for boys to show the heroic qualities of the *puer senex*. For this reason, girls who performed heroic deeds in defense of their faith were considered especially worthy of notice.

13. Ibid., 41.

14. Suzanne Dixon, *The Roman Mother* (Norman: University of Oklahoma Press 1988) 168–203, provides an overview of many of the famous and infamous mother-son relationships of the Republic and the Empire; mothers and daughters frequently experienced lifelong close relationships devoid of the manipulation to gain power and prestige characteristic of the mother-son bond. For father-child relationships, see Wiedemann, 87, and Dixon, 29

and *passim*. Dixon refutes Veyne's contention that Roman men systematically resented their fathers because of the strength of the *patria potestas*.

15. Suzanne Dixon, *The Roman Family* (Baltimore: Johns Hopkins University Press, 1992) 119–20.

16. Ibid., 117.

17. Wiedemann,11.

18. Dixon, *Roman Mother*, 141–5.

19. Dixon, *Roman Family*, 104–5.

20. Dixon, *Roman Mother*, 219–20.

21. Jean-Pierre Nérandeau, "L'enfant dans la culture romaine," *Histoire de l'enfance en occident I: de l'Antiquité au XVIIe siècle* (Paris: Editions du Seuil, 1998) 74.

22. Paul Veyne, "The Roman Empire", *A History of Private Life, Volume 1: From Pagan Rome to Byzantium*, tr. Arthur Goldhammer (Cambridge, MA: Belknap Press, 1987) 79; Dixon, *The Roman Mother*, 112. Wiedemann, 31, takes issue with the interpretation of the *deliciae* as a sexually exploited group in general, and instead places Latin pederastic poetry in a class outside the normal standards of society.

23. Tacitus, *Germania* 19–20, *Complete Works of Tacitus*, tr. Alfred John Church and William Jackson Brodribb (New York: Modern Library, 1942) 71–8.

24. Richard B. Lyman, Jr., "Barbarism and Religion: Late Roman and Early Medieval Childhood," *The History of Childhood*, ed. Lloyd DeMause (New York: Psychohistory Press, 1974) 84, sees a continuation of classical "ambivalence" toward children in the Roman Christian world.

25. Fox, 666 and *passim*., John Boswell, in *The Kindness of Strangers: the Abandonment of Children in Western Europe from Late Antiquity to the Renaissance* (New York: Pantheon Books, 1988) does much to dispel the myth that the advent of Christianity ended or even seriously curtailed the practice of abandonment, although such actions need no longer be seen as simply a form of infanticide.

26. Bainton, 49.

27. Wiedemann, 193. He also notes, 159–200, that no Christian curriculum developed to supersede the pagan *artes liberales*, and that the continued participation of Christian youths in pagan education was the subject of some debate, indicating that many parents continued to provide such education for their sons.

28. Ibid., 101.

29. C. John Sommerville, *The Rise and Fall of Childhood*, 2nd ed. (New York: Vintage Books, 1990) 61.

30. Lyman, 90. While Boswell, in *The Kindness of Strangers*, claims that the majority of exposed children were claimed by other adults, and survived by being raised as either slaves or alumni, most ancient and modern sources agree that exposure of infants was likely to result in death. See W.V. Harris, "Child-exposure in the Roman Empire," *Journal of Roman Studies* 84 (1994) 1–22; Louise Tilly et. al., "Child Abandonment in European History: a Symposium," *Journal of Family History* 17, no. 1 (1992) 1–23.

31. Lloyd DeMause, "The Evolution of Childhood," *The History of Childhood*, 47.

32. Lyman, 90.

33. Wiedemann, 98.

34. Claudian, *Panegyric* 7.85–86, praising the Emperor Honorius as a child.

35. Burrow, 94–5.

36. See Hippolyte Delehaye, *The Legends of the Saints*, 4th ed., tr. Donald Attwater (New York: Fordham University Press, 1962) 86–100, for general guidelines on the interpretation of hagiographical texts.

37. *Liber Pontificalis*, ed. L. Duchesne (Paris: E. de Bocard, 1955), 1:180, for the basilica dedicated to Agnes by Constantine at the request of his daughter; Liberius 1:208; Symmachus 1:263; Honorius 1:323.

38. Florian Jubaru, *Sainte Agnèse: Vierge et martyre de la Voie Nomentane* (Paris: J. Dumoulin, 1907) 1.

39. Thierry Ruinart, *Acta Martyrum Sincera et Selecta* (Ratisbon: G.J. Manz, 1859) 488. Prudentius, *Peristephanon* 14, calls her a young girl, employing the term *puella* in line 2, and *puellula* in line 11. Prudentius, *Aurelii Prudentii Clementis Carmina*, ed. Maurice Cunningham, CCSL 126 (Turnholt: Typographi Brepols, 1966).

40. Ambrose, *De Virginibus*, 1.2.5, *PL* 16:189.

41. Ambrose, "Vita S. Agnetis," *AASS* Jan. II, 351.

42. *Martyrologium Romanum*, 29.

43. Prudentius, *Peristephanon* 14, line 8.

44. *AASS* Jan. II, 351–52.

45. Prudentius, *Peristephanon* 3, CCSL 126.

46. Ibid., lines 161–65; Gregory of Tours, *Glory of the Martyrs*, tr. Raymond Van Dam (Liverpool: Liverpool University Press, 1988) 114.

47. *Bibliotheca Sanctorum* 5:207. The earliest surviving version of the legend, as well as that of the similarly tortured Eulalia of Barcélona, dates only from the seventh century. See also Carmen Garcia Rodriguez, *El Culto de los Santos en la España Romana y Visigoda* (Madrid : CSIC, 1966), 284–303.

48. Jerome, *Martyrologium*, *PL* 30:478.

49. *AASS* Oct. III, 264.

50. *AASS* Maii III, 21. Although the baptism was supposed to have been performed by Pope Cornelius (251–3), his martyrdom allegedly occurred under Diocletian.

51. Ibid. Although the word *infantia* is used, Diocletian later addresses Pancras as *adolescentule*.

52. *Liber Pontificalis*, 1:262, 324.

53. Gregory of Tours, *Glory of the Martyrs*, 60.

54. Gregory I, *Homilia 23, 40 Homiliarum in Evangelia*, *PL* 76:120–4–10.

55. *AASS* Maii III, 21. One of the more unreliable aspects of the passio is that he was supposedly brought to Diocletian himself for his hearing after his arrest. If one accepts this as an indication of confusion with his martyrdom during the reign of Diocletian, however, the story remains plausible. The story does not, for instance, contain any incidents of miraculous survival of tortures, or other examples of divine intervention.

56. Jubaru, 20.

57. *AASS* Feb. II, 515.

58. *AASS* Maii II, 519.

59. Ibid.

60. *Comam,* Ruinart, 422; *AASS* Maii II, 519, gives the word *collam* [neck], which Ruinart lists as a variant, but it would not make sense to begin a list of threats with a fatal action.

61. *AASS* Maii II, 519. Some versions omit this threat altogether.

62. Ibid.

63. Delehaye, *Legends,* 114–16; *Origines,* 386–88.

64. *AASS* Jun. III, 24.

65. *AASS* Jun. III, 29–30.

66. *AASS* Jul. I, 642.

67. Ibid., 641. Some confusion as to the identity of the child has resulted from the variations in the story. In one version, he is martyred with a man named Paul; in another version, he appears alone and unnamed. A third version contains the martyrdom of Paul, along with the wives and children of Mark and Mucianus. Because of these divergent renditions, the child is sometimes given the name of Paul.

68. Usuard, 359. The *Martyrologium Romanum,* 582, differentiates Dioscorus from the first three.

69. *Martyrologium Romanum,* 519. Paulillus is not mentioned by Usuard.

70. *Martyrologium Romanum,* 259.

71. *AASS* Sept. II, 669.

72. Their relics were translated to Sens in 273 or 274. *Vies des Saints et des Bienhereux,* 7th ed., ed. Paul Guérin (Paris, 1882) 10:527.

73. *Roman Martyrology,* 233. Lisping speech is developmentally appropriate for five-year-olds, as this is the time when the front baby teeth begin to fall out, and pronunciation is affected.

74. Mary R. Lefkowitz and Maureen B. Fant, ed. and tr., *Women's Life in Greece and Rome* (Baltimore: Johns Hopkins Press, 1982) 268.

75. Goodich, "Childhood and Adolescence," 298. For parallel behavior in the modern era, Goodich cites Edwin Starbuck, *The Psychology of Religion* (London: W Scott, 1899.) See also Weinstein and Bell, 52–67.

76. 2 Maccabees 7.1–42. *The Apocrypha of the Old Testament, New Oxford Annotated Bible,* 274. Several folkloric *passios* popular in the Middle Ages, such as the story of Faith, Hope and Charity, and their mother Wisdom, St. Symphorosa and her seven sons, and St. Felicitas and her seven sons, directly copy this motif.

77. Prudentius, *Peristephanon* 10, line 663. Barulas is not named by Prudentius, but is described, line 666, *Da septuennem circiter puerum aut minus,* and in line 676 as *infans.*

78. Ibid., line 681.

79. Ibid., lines 736–40.

80. Ibid., lines 776–80.

81. Ibid., lines 791–5.

82. *AASS* Oct. VIII, 338–9.

83. *AASS* Aug. I, 30–38.

84. *AASS* Aug. IV, 419–21.

85. *AASS* Aug. I, 16–19.

86. Ruinart 72–4 and 70–71, respectively.

87. *AASS* Maii VII, 4–10. The version of the story which survives contains many miraculous occurrences, but the martyrdom of a son with his father is not implausible.

88. *AASS* Sept. IV, 351–3.

89. *AASS* Jul. V, 137.

90. *AASS* Maii V, 7.

91. *AASS* Jan. I, 570–87.

92. *AASS* Sept. V, 481.

93. Luke 12.4–5; G. Rivain, *Saint Flocel, Martyr; sa vie et son martyre, son culte et sa dévotion* (Paris: Bloud & Gay, 1932) 11.

94. *AASS* Jan. II, 297.

95. *AASS* Aug. II, 154–5.

96. *Bibliotheca Sanctorum* 7:53.

97. The brothers are traditionally considered children, and are listed in the *Martyrology* of Usuard as suffering under the persecution of Decius *cum essent pueri*, 240. The *passio* included in the *AASS*, however, uses the term *viri*. *AASS* Jun. I, 272–3. The acts of these martyrs date from the sixth or seventh century. *Bibliotheca Sanctorum* 10:489.

98. *AASS* Jan. II, 616–17.

99. *AASS* Jun. II, 1013–25.

100. *Bibliotheca Sanctorum* 4:331.

101. *AASS* Jul. V, 524–5.

102. *AASS* Jan. II, 770–1.

103. *AASS* Maii VII, 428–30. Their *passio* has been attributed to St. Ambrose, but may in fact date from the early fifth century.

104. *AASS* Jan. II, 185–7. For Claudius and persecution, see *Acts* 18.2.

105. *Martyrologium Romanum*, 211. A twelfth-century *passio* is contained in the *AASS* Maii VI, 664–8.

106. *Bibliotheca Sanctorum* 4:103–6.

107. *AASS* Jan. I, 753–64.

108. *Bibliotheca Sanctorum* 1:132–3.

109. Cyril is described in *AASS* Maii VII, 17 as *puer* and *juvenis*.

110. Ruinart, 289–90. .

111. Identified as *filia* rather than *puella*, she was probably a young unmarried adolescent. *AASS* Maii III, 188–90. The *Martyrologium Romanum*, 186, does not identify her as a child.

112. *AASS* Maii III, 189–92.

113. Her shrine was visited by the Emperor Maurice in 591. *Bibliotheca Sanctorum* 7:57.

114. *Martyrologium Romanum*, 139. Her passio is in *AASS* Jul. II, 268–79.

115. *Bibliotheca Sanctorum* 11:596.

116. Ibid. The *AASS* Maii V, 173, contains only a terse mention of the cult.

2. Infant Saints: The Cult of the Holy Innocents

1. Matthew 2:16, *New Oxford Annotated Bible* (New York: Oxford University Press, 1977) 1173.

2. Estimates of infant mortality in the first year of life range from 20–50%, with an average of 30%. Schulz, 46; Alexandre-Bidon and Lett, 32.

3. Ambrose, *Ep.* 83, *Letters*, tr. M. M. Beyenka (Washington D.C., 1967) 285.

4. René Aigrain, *L'hagiographie: ses sources, ses méthodes, son histoire* (Paris: Bloud & Gay, 1953) 20–22.

5. Frederick Holweck, "Holy Innocents," *Catholic Encyclopedia* 7:419.

6. Suetonius, *Augustus* 94. *The Twelve Caesars*, tr. Robert Graves, rev. Michael Grant (London: Penguin, 2000) 104.

7. Suetonius, *Nero* 36. *The Twelve Caesars*, 234.

8. David Hugh Farmer, *The Oxford Dictionary of Saints*, 2nd ed. (Oxford: Oxford University Press, 1990), 209, estimates between six and twenty-five victims, based upon the population of Bethlehem at the time. The *Bibliotheca Sanctorum* approximates the population of males under age two at thirty to forty. *Bibliotheca Sanctorum* 7:820.

9. Peter Chrysologus, *Sermo* 152.9, *Sancti Petri Chrysologi Collectio Sermonum*, ed. Alexander Olivar, *CCSL* 24 (Turnholt: Brepols, 1975–82) 3:955.

10. Cyprian, *Ep.* 56.6, *Opera Omnia*, *PL* 4 (Paris, 1844) 354.

11. Chrysologus, 3:952.

12. Louis Bouyer, *The Spirituality of the New Testament and the Fathers*, tr. M.P. Ryan (New York: Desclee Co., 1963) 190–210.

13. For a general introduction to the debate on infant baptism in the early centuries of the Church, with a bibliography of references to infant baptism in patristic writings, see Joachim Jeremias, *Infant Baptism in the First Four Centuries*, tr. David Cairns (Philadelphia: Westminster Press, 1960) but also see Kurt Aland, *Did the Early Church Baptize Infants?* (Philadelphia: Westminster Press, 1963) for an alternate interpretation and criticism of Jeremias. See also Joachim Jeremias, *The Origins of Infant Baptism, a Further Study in Reply to Kurt Aland* (London: SCM Press, 1963).

14. P. J Toner, "Limbo," *Catholic Encyclopedia* 9:256–9.

15. Chrysologus, 3:952.

16. Ibid., 954.

17. Ibid. For a discussion of the iconography of this scene, see *Bibliotheca Sanctorum* 7:823–31.

18. *Bibliotheca Sanctorum* 7:54; see also Brown, *The Cult of the Saints*, 70–76, for a discussion of the perceived efficacy of burial near the relics of a martyr.

19. Paulinus of Nola, Hymn 31, *The Poems of St. Paulinus of Nola*, tr. P.G. Walsh (New York: Newman Press, 1975) lines 578–90.

20. Ibid., lines 592–5.

21. Chrysologus, 3:952–3.

22. Pseudo-Ambrose, *AASS* Jan. II, 353, and the *Martyrologium Romanum*, 32, use the word *catechumena* to describe Emerantiana.

23. *AASS* Jan. II, 458. See also Jubaru, 181–201.

24. *AASS* Jan. II, 353. Pseudo-Ambrose, the author of the *passio,* can be established as writing in the fifth century. *Bibliotheca Sanctorum* 4:1165.

25. *AASS* Jul. V, 136.

26. Sabine Baring-Gould, *The Lives of the Saints*, new and rev. ed. (Edinburgh: J Grant, 1914) 2:83.

27. *AASS* Feb. I, 465.

28. A third translation took place in 1882. Ibid., 466.

29. Gregory of Tours, *Glory of the Confessors*, tr. Raymond Van Dam. (Liverpool: Liverpool University Press, 1988) 94.

30. Gregory of Tours, ibid., notes that he died in the white robes of baptism, but does not identify him as a child. The *Martyrologium Hieronymien, PL* 30:480, lists the cult of *sancti Lusoris pueri et confessoris*, but does not mention the white robes.

31. M. de Langardière, *L'église de Bourges avant Charlemagne* (Bourges, 1951), 24–7.

32. L. Duchesne, *Fastes episcopaux de l'ancienne Gaule* (Paris : A. Fontemoigne, 1907–15) 2:104–17. See also *Bibliotheca Sanctorum* 7:9–10. The Bollandists, in obvious disapproval of the cult, identify Justinianus as an invention based upon a scribal error; the feast of St. Julianus, confessor, is listed on the same day. *AASS* Jul. IV, 172–3.

33. *Vita Beati Antonii Abbatis, PG* 26:842.

34. Sulpicius Severus, *Vie de saint Martin*, ed. and tr. Jacques Fontaine (Paris: Editions du Cerf, 1967–69) 1:254.

35. Gregory I, *Dialogi,* ed. De Vogué, *Sources Chrétiennes* 265 (Paris, 1980) 70–72. See also *AASS* Apr. I, 94.

36. Gregory I, *Dialogi,* 72–4.

37. *AASS* Apr. I, 94, lists her inclusion in several martyrologies on the strength of Gregory's mention of her, but no relics or church dedications are specifically cited.

38. *AASS* Jan. II, 297.

39. *AASS* Feb. III, 375–7.

40. Fox, 446; Brown, *The Cult of the Saints*, 7.

3. Translations and Inventions: The Veneration
of Child Martyrs in Medieval Europe

1. Jacobus de Voragine, *The Golden Legend*, tr. William Granger Ryan (Princeton: Princeton University Press, 1992) vii–x.

2. Patrick Geary, *Furta Sacra: The Theft of Relics in the Central Middle Ages*, 2d. ed. (Princeton: Princeton University Press, 1990). See also Jonathan Sumption, *Pilgrimage: An Image of Medieval Religion* (Totowa, NJ: Rowman and Littlefield, 1975) 31–40.

3. Geary, 63 and 34.

4. Ibid., 7.

5. Brooke and Brooke, 19. The collection, also included the swaddling clothes in which Jesus was wrapped, and pieces of the bread from which Jesus fed the five thousand—another relic, like bones of the Holy Innocents, capable of almost infinite multiplication.

6. Ibid., 26; Geary, 151.

7. Gregory of Tours, *Glory of the Confessors*, 47.

8. Gregory of Tours, *Glory of the Martyrs*, 60. The cult at Rome has left no archaeological trace. Charles Pietri, *Roma Christiana* (Rome: École Francaise de Rome, 1976) 613 n. 4.

9. *Golden Legend* 1:311. Voragine attributes this custom to the tradition recorded by Gregory of Tours.

10. Gregory gave a homily to Pancras on the anniversary of his martyrdom (12 May; *Hom.* 27, *PL* 76:1204–10) and founded a monastery in his honor .(*Ep.* 4.18, *PL* 77:687–8.)

11. *PL* 80:95.

12. Arthur Stanley, *Historical Memorials of Canterbury* (New York: E.P. Dutton, 1892) 43.

13. Ep. 49, *PL* 78:834.

14. Arnold-Forster 1:169–70.

15. *Bibliotheca Sanctorum* 8:82, 85.

16. *AASS* Maii III, 19.

17 *Golden Legend*, 1:311.

18. Ibid.

19. *Bibliotheca Sanctorum* 10:89.

20. Aelfric, *Lives of the Saints*, ed. Walter Skeat, *EETS* o.s. 76 (London, 1881), 170–94; Hrosvitha, *The Non-Dramatic Works of Hrosvitha*, tr. Sister M. Gonsalva Wiegand (Saint Louis, MO, 1936) 237–62.

21. *Cild-lic on gearum*. Aelfric, 170, line 9.

22. *Golden Legend*, 1:102.

23. Hrosvitha, 246, lines 178–80.

24. *Golden Legend* 1:103.

25. See *AASS* Jan. II, for an account of her relics and their translations, 354–61; a list of miracles is recorded on 361–3.

26. *AASS* Jun. II, 1020.

27. *Golden Legend* 1: 322.

28. Ibid., 1:323.

29. St. Vitus' Dance, or rheumatic chorea, affects children of both sexes, but more commonly girls. It is most likely to occur in summer and early autumn; recovery is generally spontaneous and complete in about three to six months, thus making the disease a prime candidate for successful cure at a healing shrine. H. Winter Griffith, M.D., *Complete Guide to Symptoms, Illness and Surgery* (Tucson: Body Press, 1985) 532.

30. *Butler's Lives of Patron Saints*, ed. Michael Walsh (San Francisco: Harper and Row, 1987) 432. The circumstances of his association with this particular disease are unknown, but his general efficacy in the cure of nervous diseases may derive from his legendary cure of the son of Diocletian from an infestation of demons.

31. The translation occurred under Abbot Fulraed (d. 784). Frederick George Holweck, *A Biographical Dictionary of the Saints, With a General Introduction on Hagiology* (St. Louis and London: B Herder, 1924) 1028.

32. *AASS* Jun. II, 1015–16.

33. Ibid., 1034–6.

34. Ibid., 1036–7.

35. Holweck, 380; Geary, 26.

36. Geary, 59–60.

37. See *Liber Miraculorum Sancte Fidis*, ed. Luca Robertini (Spoleto: Centro Italiano di studi sull'alto medievolo, 1994.)

38. She is addressed in the legend as *O juvenis puella*. *AASS* Oct. III, 288–89.

39. *AASS* Oct III, 281–4; Medieval English paintings of the saint, however, do not portray her as a child.

40. Ibid., 302.

41. The cult of St. Mamas, a third-century shepherd boy honored in the Eastern Church, was imported to Europe in Merovingian times by Radegund. *Vies de Saints*, 9:635–6. The legend of Mamas promoted at that time still identified him as a boy who was stoned to death, but Usuard, 285, lists him as a martyr without noting his age, and he is assigned a "prolonged martyrdom from childhood to old age" by the *Martyrologium Romanum*, 343.

42. *AASS* Jun. III, 29.

43. *Golden Legend* 1:324.

44. Ibid.

45. *AASS* Jun. III, 20. Ruinart, 503, also notes the antiquity of the cult in Gaul.

46. W. J. Rees, *Lives of the Cambro-British Saints*, (London: Longman, 1853) 609.

47. *AASS* Jun. III, 22.

48. Ibid., 35.

49. *Golden Legend*, 1:58. Voragine cites St. John Chrysostom, who believed that Herod might have murdered all children over the age of two rather than under.

50. Holweck, 506.

51. Another derivation for the name may come from the identification of the relics with a namesake associated with the titular patron of the church, *Petragorica civitate, natale beati Memorii, innocentis et martyris quem beatus Fronto, cum esset in Aegypto, relevante Domino, reperit. Bibliotheca Sanctorum* 9:316. The *AASS* Maii VI, 370, lists Memorius as a confessor rather than a martyr, but notes the belief that he was one of the Holy Innocents.

52. *AASS* Maii I, 183–4. See also *Bibliotheca Sanctorum* 11:1021–2.

53. *Vies des Saints* 6:178 for Memorius; 5:237 for Sicarius.

54. Delehaye, *Origines*, 185.

55. The Provençal relics were located at St. Chapelle de Bourges. *Vies des Saints* 5:237.

56. *Bibliotheca Sanctorum* 7:822.

57. Jocelyn Rhys, *The Reliquary: a Collection of Relics* (London: Watts, 1930) 41.

58. Gregory of Tours, *History of the Franks*, tr. Lewis Thorpe (London and New York: Penguin, 1974) 81; Bede, *Martyrologium, AASS* Maii I, xlii.

58. Peter Abelard, "In Festo SS Innocentum," *Hymnarius Paraclithensis Text and Notes*, ed. Joseph Szovérffy (Albany, NY: Classica Folia Editions, 1975) 214–17.

60. Paul Hayward, "Suffering and Innocence in Latin Sermons for the Feast of the Holy Innocents, c. 400–800," *The Church and Childhood*, ed. Diana Wood (London: Blackwell, 1994) 67.

61. Edward F. Rimbault, "Two Sermons Preached by the Boy Bishop," *The Camden Miscellany*, n.s. 14 (1875): vi–x.

62. Caen appointed a girl-abbess in 1423. *Bibliotheca Sanctorum* 7:822.

63. Baring-Gould, *Lives of the Saints* 15:311–14.

64. *Micrologus de ecclesiasticis observationibus*, attr. to Bernold of Constance, *PL* 151:1005–6.

65. Bernard of Clairvaux, "Sermo in nativiate Innocentum," Opera Omnia, *PL* 183 (Paris, 1854), 129–32.

66. *Golden Legend* 1:56.

67. Ibid.

68. Amalarius, *Liber Officialis* 1.41 (Vatican City: Biblioteca apostolica vaticana, 1948)

69. *"Non haec martyr ab Eulalia Emeritensi diversa sit, non est huius loci inquere."* *Bibiotheca Hagiographica Latina Antiquiae et Mediae Aetatis* (Brussels: Société des Bollandistes,1898–1901) 1:404.

70. Enrique Florez, *España sagrada* (Madrid: M. F. Rodriguez, 1754–59) 29:371–75.

71. *Bibliotheca Sanctorum* 5:208.

72. Florez, 13:390.

73. Ibid., 29:308–09.

74. Ibid., 13:392–98. At the moment of her death, a white dove flew from her throat.

75. Aldhelm, "De Virginitate," *Aldhelm: The Prose Works*, tr. Michael Lapidge and Michael Herron (Totowa, NJ: Rowman and Littlefield 1979) 113; neither Eulalia nor Agnes, 112, are identified as children. Bede, *Martyrologium*, xli, gives Eulalia's age as thirteen.

76. Gregory of Tours, *Glory of the Martyrs*, 90–91.

77. "El santo niño Augusto," Florez 13:322–6. Neither the age of the child nor the date of his death is given, but his story is related by Paul of Mérida.

78. Ibid., 325.

79. *Bibliotheca Sanctorum* 7:25.

80. Flint, 204–7.

81. Arnold-Forster, 2:547–9.

82. *Annales Monasterii de Wintonia, Annales Monastici*, ed. H.R. Luard, vol. 2, *De Wintonia et Waverleia*, Rolls Series 36 (London: Longman, 1865) 10.

83. *AASS* Oct. VIII, 333–4.

84. *Bibliotheca Sanctorum* 5:24.

85. *AASS* Oct. VIII, 333–4.

86. St. Just in Roseland, Falmouth, and St. Just in Penworth, Land's End. Arnold-Forster, 2:547–9.

87. *AASS* Oct. VIII, 330.

88. The first mention of his existence appears in the Martyrology of Usuard. Usuard, 277, and *Bibliotheca Sanctorum* 5:20.

89. *Bibliotheca Sanctorum* 4:1165.

90. *AASS* Jan. II, 353; Jubaru, 332.

91. *Bibliotheca Sanctorum* 4:1166.

92. *Golden Legend* 1:103.

93. *AASS* Maii VII, 413.

94. Baring-Gould, *Lives of the Saints* 5:429–30.

95. *AASS* Maii VII, 432.

96. Although her cult can be traced from the fourth century, her passio dates only from the ninth. *Bibliotheca Sanctorum* 4:330–32.

97. *AASS* Jul. V, 499–500.

98. Ibid., 518.

99. Ibid., 517–18.

100. A church was dedicated to Agapetus by Felix III (483–492); *Liber Pontificalis* 1:252. Pope Leo III (795–816) restored this basilica, ibid., 2:33, and another dedicated to Agapetus, ibid., 2:29. Agapetus became patron of Parma, Toledo, and the monastery of Kremsmunster in what is now Austria, *Bibliotheca Sanctorum* 1:313.

101. *AASS* Aug. III, 528.

102. Rivain, 25–38.

103. Ibid., 24.

104. Ibid., 37.

105. Ibid., 43.

106. Ibid., 41.

107. *AASS* Jan. II, 770. Some relics were translated to Corsica, her birthplace, in 1637 by the Jesuits.

108. Gregory of Tours, *Glory of the Confessors*, 94.

109. Laugardière, 27.

110. *Bibliotheca Sanctorum*, 4:105; her cult was particularly strong in Rimini, and her relics were venerated in Rimini in the eighteenth century although claimed by Bari in the seventeenth century.

111. *AASS* Sept. II, 671.

112. *Bibliotheca Sanctorum*, 9:78

113. Gregory of Tours, *Glory of the Martyrs*, 70.

114. *Golden Legend* 2:19.

115. *Bibliotheca Sanctorum* 9:783.

116. *AASS* Maii VII, 4–5.

117. *AASS* Sept. IV, 352. Other relics were moved to Tortosa in 1606.

118. *AASS* Jul. II, 269.

119. Gregory of Tours, *Glory of the Confessors*, 104.

120. Gregory of Tours, *Glory of the Confessors*, 47. Those who would scoff at the gullibility of an uncivilized age should review the cult of St. Philomena.

121. *AASS* Aug. II, 148–52.

122. Ibid., 152. The inventory was made in 1568.

123. Ibid., 148.

124. Ruinart, 424–26; *AASS* Aug. I, 19; *Golden Legend*, 1:185–86.

125. *AASS* Aug. I, 18.

126. *Golden Legend* 1:185.

127. Delehaye, *Origines*, 326 n. 7.

128. *AASS* Aug. I, 17. Usuard, who composed an elegy in honor of Spes, lists her before her sisters. Usuard, 276–77.

129. Hrosvitha [Hrotwitha] of Gandersheim, *Hrotwitha Opera*, *PL* 137: 1045–52. Tr. Katharina Wilson, *The Plays of Hrotsvit of Gandersheim* (New York: Garland Publishing, 1989) 123–49.

130. Hrosvitha, *Plays,* 37–49.

131. Ruinart, 70–71.

132. Ibid., 72–74.

133. Baring-Gould, Lives of the Saints 9:4.

134. *Bibliotheca Sanctorum* 7:132.

135. *AASS* Jul. IV, 225–26.

136. *Bibliotheca Hagiographia Latina* 2:1006 nn. 6908–12; *AASS* Jan. II, 36. The *Bibliotheca Sanctorum* 10:1072, give his age as thirteen or fourteen.

137. *Bibliotheca Sanctorum* 10:1073.

138. Ibid., 1:1324.

139. Ibid. 12:137–38; the *AASS* Aug. III, 201, gives virtually no information on the cult.

140. *Bibliotheca Sanctorum* 7:118. Gordian is generally depicted as an adult man with a wife, who was converted and baptized by St. Januarius; the medieval tendency to impute youth to saints where evidence of youth does not exist could indicate that some advantage might be found in such a move. The passio is found in the *AASS* Maii II, 551–55.

141. Bede, *Martyrologium*, xxxiv.

142. *Bibliotheca Hagiographica Latina* 2:1043, nn. 7183–89.

143. *Martyrologium Romanum*, 441; *AASS* Oct. IV, 39–40.

144. *Bibliotheca Sanctorum* 11:124, and *Bibliotheca Hagiographica Latina* 2:1043, nn. 7188–89.

145. *AASS* Maii VI, 664–66. The church was consecrated by Pope Paschal II. Arcy in France later claimed the relics of the martyr, but Sora insisted that she had not been moved. The church was destroyed by earthquakes in 1654 and again in 1915. *Bibliotheca Sanctorum* 11:135. The relics of St. Restituta were impartially examined in 1683, lending credence to the claims advanced by the original site of her cult. *AASS* Maii VI, 673.

146. *AASS* Maii VI, 668–72.

147. *AASS* Jan. II, 184–87.

148. " 'Alors, tu es un magicien!' 'Non, je suis un chrétien...'" Rivain, 14, for Saint Flocel. For Vitus, *AASS* Jun. II, 1022 and 1025. For Justus of Beauvais, *AASS* Oct. VIII, 338. Symphronius the Prefect accuses St. Agnes of practicing magical arts, *AASS* Jan. II, 352. St. Potitus was accused by the emperor of practicing *maleficium*, *AASS* Jan. I, 756.

149. Eli Edward Burris, *Taboo, Magic, Spirits: a Study of Primitive Elements in Roman Religion* (New York: MacMillan, 1931) 47–71. See also E.S. McCartney "The Role of the Child in Supplications," *Classical Weekly* 22 (1928/1929): 151.

150. Wiedemann, 179–180. See also Georg Luck, *Arcana Mundi: Magic and the Occult in the Greek and Roman Worlds* (Baltimore: Johns Hopkins University Press, 1985) 173–75.

151. Wiedemann, 185–86.

152. Hrosvitha, *Plays*, 143; Wilson, n. 7, 154–5, quotes Hrosvitha's use of the term *maleficia*, but identifies it as "the beneficent sorcery of God."

153. Hrosvitha, *Plays*, 143. For the significance of the goddess Diana in medieval ideas of witchcraft, see Carlo Ginzburg, *Ecstasies: Deciphering the Witches' Sabbath*, tr. Raymond Rosenthal (New York: Pantheon Books, 1991) 89–121 and *passim*.

4. Martyrdom and Murder:
Child Saints of the Early Middle Ages

1. David Herlihy, *Medieval Households* (Cambridge and London: Harvard University Press, 1985) 54.

2. Sally Crawford, *Children in Anglo-Saxon* England (Stroud: Sutton, 2000) xiv.

3. "The whole weight of the newly-elaborated Christian rites fell on early childhood." Janet L. Nelson, "Parents, Children, and the Church in the Earlier Middle Ages," *The Church and Childhood*, ed Diana Wood (London: Blackwell, 1994) 99.

4. "Although infanticide was known among the Germans, it seems never to have been systematically practiced." Herlihy, *Medieval Households*, 54. Crawford, 92–93, notes the many causes of infant mortality in Anglo-Saxon society.

5. Suzanne Wemple, *Women in Frankish Society* (Philadelphia: University of Pennsylvania Press, 1985) 59.

6. James Brundage, *Law, Sex, and Christian Society in Medieval Europe* (Chicago and London: University of Chicago Press, 1987) 102–103; 113.

7. Lyman, 76.

8. John T. McNeill and Helena M. Gamer, *Medieval Handbooks of Penance* (New York: Columbia University Press, 1938; repr. 1990) 197, 254, 304; punishments were more severe for clergymen and their wives.

9. Wemple, 24.

10. Crawford, 92.

11. Dhuoda, *Handbook for William: a Carolingian Woman's Counsel for her Son*, tr. Carol Neel (Lincoln: University of Nebraska Press, 1991) 99.

12. Ibid., 2.

13. Ibid., 13, 95.

14. Ibid., 91.

15. Ibid., 28.

16. Ibid., 75.

17. Frances and Joseph Gies, *Marriage and the Family in the Middle Ages* (New York: Harper and Row, 1987) 61.

18. Nelson, 91.

19. Ibid., 93.

20. Gregory of Tours, *History of the Franks*, 296, quoted in Gies & Gies, 60, and Alexandre-Bidon and Lett, 34. The excessive grief of Queen Fredegund after the death of her young sons is cited by Gies and Gies, 60–61, and Wemple, 59, as examples of maternal love for children, but Fredegund once tried to murder her daughter Rigunth by slamming the lid of a chest onto her neck. Gregory, *History* 521–22.

21. Wemple, 100.

22. Patricia Quinn, *Better than the Sons of Kings: Boys and Monks in the Early Middle Ages* (New York: Peter Lang, 1989) 32.

23. Danièle Alexandre-Bidon and Didier Lett, *Children in the Middle Ages: Fifth-Fifteenth Centuries*, tr. Jody Gladding (Notre Dame: University of Notre Dame Press, 1999) 49.

24. Mary Martin McLaughlin, "Survivors and Surrogates: Children and Parents from the Ninth to the Thirteenth Centuries," *The History of Childhood*, ed. Lloyd DeMause, 169, nn. 170–171.

25. Alexandre-Bidon and Lett, 49.

26. Guibert of Nogent, *Self and Society in Medieval France:The Memoirs of Abbot Guibert of Nogent*, tr. John Benton (Toronto: University of Toronto Press) 44.

27. Alexandre-Bidon and Lett, 50.

28. Orme, 225.

29. Alexandre-Bidon and Lett, 39.

30. Eadmer, *The Life of St. Anselm, Archbishop of Canterbury*, tr. Richard Southern (London and New York: T. Nelson, 1962) 36–39.

31. McNeill and Gamer, 253.

32. Ibid., 98–99.

33. Ibid., 113–114. McNeill and Gamer have translated *ludis* as "misdemeanors;" the connotation of the word with games, play, or amusements argues even more strongly than McNeill's translation indicates that such offenses were viewed relatively lightly. Taking into consideration that thirteen of the twenty-one provisions deal with offenses of a sexual nature, this suggests a strong tolerance for the frailties of youth.

34. *AASS* Belgii 3:130–136.

35. *Ex translatione SS Livini et Brictii, MGH Scriptores* 15 (Hanover, 1887–88) 2:611–614.

36. *Bibliotheca Sanctorum* 1:197.

37. *Vies des Saints* 9:453–54.

38. *AASS* Sept. III, 70–71.

39. *Vies des Saints* 10:548.

40. *Vies des Saints* 10:346–347. The Huguenots burned the relics of St. Gaudins in 1569.

41. Clayton J. Drees, "Saints and Suicide: the motives of the martyrs of Córdoba, A.D. 850–859," *Journal of Medieval and Renaissance Studies* 20, no. 1 (Spring 1990): 59–89.

42. Kenneth Baxter Wolf, *Christian Martyrs in Muslim Spain* (Cambridge: Cambridge University Press, 1988) 1–2.

43. *Martyrologium Romanum*, 542.

44. Ibid., 224.

45. Wolf, 34.

46. Norman Daniel, *Islam and the West: the Making of an Image* (Edinburgh: University Press, 1966) 141–143.

47. *AASS* Jun. V, 207.

48. Holweck, 788.

49. *Bibliotheca Sanctorum* 10:441.

50. *AASS* Jun. V, 209–13. English translation, Wiegand, 128–157. For date of legend, Alban Butler, *Lives of the Saints*, ed. Herbert Thurston and Donald Attwater , 2nd ed. (London: Burns and Oates, 1956) 3:649.

51. Ann Lyon Haight, ed., *Hrotswitha of Gandersheim: Her Life, Times and Work* (New York: Hroswitha Club, 1965) 18–19.

52. Hrosvitha, *Passio Sancti Pelagii*, lines 225–250.

53. Ibid., lines 271–273.

54. Bede, *Ecclesiastical History*, 131.

55. Gregory of Tours, *History of the Franks*, 288.

56. Ibid., 298.

57. Crawford, 89.

58. Baring-Gould, *Lives of the Saints* 7:323.

59. Gregory of Tours, *Glory of the Confessors*, 47.

60. Baring-Gould, *Lives of the Saints* 7:323.

61. *Bibliotheca Sanctorum* 4:569.

62. *Vies des Saints* 3:344.

63. The date of Rumwald's death is based on the claim that he was the grandson of Penda. John Capgrave, *Nova Legenda Angliae*, ed. C. Horstmann, (Oxford: Clarendon Press, 1901) 1:345–350.

64. Bede, *Ecclesiastical History of the English People*, tr. Leo Sherley-Price, rev. R.E. Latham (London and New York: Penguin, 1990) 177.

65. *Nova Legenda Angliae* 1:345–50.

66. Ibid. 1:346.

67. Ibid., 1:347.

68. Ibid., 1: 349.

69. Arnold-Forster 1:172–174.

70. *Victoria History of the Counties of England, History of the County of Kent*, ed. William Page (London: Oxford University Press, 1932) 428.

71. Arnold-Forster 1:174.

72. *Bibliotheca Sanctorum* 11:384.

73. Arnold-Forster, 1:173.

5. Murder as Martyrdom: Child Victims of Violent Crime

1. McNeill and Gamer, 419–420.
2. D.W. Rollason, "The Cults of Murdered Royal Saints in Anglo-Saxon England," *Anglo-Saxon England* 11 (1983) 1. Rollason includes a number of the saints discussed in this chapter, but provides a different interpretation of the recognition of holiness which is essentially based upon political considerations, and does not impute any special relevance to childhood.
3. André Vauchez, *La Sainteté en Occident aux derniers siècles du Moyen Age, d'après les proces de canonisation et les documents hagiographiques* (Rome: École Francaise de Rome, 1981) 173–183, discusses several similar cases of popular sanctity in the High Middle Ages, and notes their predominance in England and the German-speaking regions of Europe to the exclusion of the Mediterranean world..
4. "Child murder was viewed, however, as a particularly unpleasant crime." Crawford, 92.
5. Rollason, 1.
6. *Two of the Saxon Chronicles Parallel*, ed. Charles Plummer (Oxford: Clarendon Press, 1929) 26. Not all versions of the Chronicle contain this entry.
7. *Handbook of British Chronology*, 3d ed., ed. E.B. Fryde, P.E. Greenway, S. Porter, I. Roy (London: Offices of the Royal Historical Society, 1986) 13.
8. Rollason, 5.
9. *Nova Legenda Angliae*, 1:429–32.
10. William of Malmesbury, *Gesta Regum Anglorum*, ed. Thomas Duffus Hardy (London, 1840) 1:362.
11. *Nova Legenda Angliae*, 429. See also *AASS* Oct. VIII, 90–103. A parallel situation can be seen in the accepted version of the death of St. Thomas of Canterbury, when the knights of Henry II "mistakenly" believed that their king wanted the archbishop killed.
12. *Nova Legenda Angliae*, 430–31.
13. William of Malmesbury, *Gesta Regum* 1:362. Thunor may be a derivative of Thor, and associated with pre-Christian occult beliefs.
14. Rollason, 18–19.
15. *Handbook of British Chronology*, 17.
16. Wilhelm Levison, *England and the Continent in the Eighth Century* (Oxford: Clarendon Press, 1946) 249–50.
17. Ibid., 251.
18. Ibid., 249.
19. Thomas Duffus Hardy, *Descriptive Catalogue of Materials Relating to the History of Great Britain and Ireland*, Rolls Series 26 (London: Longman, Green, Longman and Roberts, 1862) 1:508. The earliest surviving manuscripts date from the 11th or 12th century; vernacular versions appear in the 14th century.
20. William of Malmesbury, *Gesta Regum* 1:363–64.
21. *Nova Legenda Angliae* 1:110–14. Kenelm's miraculously prophetic gift could have been augmented by the observation that Askbert was digging a grave as the child napped.
22. J. Charles Wall, *Shrines of British Saints* (London: Methuen & Co, 1905) 209.

23. Arnold-Forster 1:174–75; R. M. Wilson, *The Lost Literature of Medieval England* (London: Methuen, 1952) 100.

24. Christina Hole, *Saints in Folklore* (New York: M. Barrows, 1965) 95.

25. *Nova Legenda Angliae* 1:465–67.

26. William of Malmesbury, *Gesta Regum*, 364, called him Berfertus, and did not designate him as Wistan's godfather; the *Nova Legenda Angliae* 1:465, called him Brithfardus. The claim to baptismal consanguinity occurs on page 466.

27. Rollason, 8.

28. *Gesta Regum*, 364.

29. Probably Wistow, Leicestershire; Farmer, 443, and Stanton, 249.

30. Roy Palmer, *The Folklore of Leicerstershire and Rutland,* (Wymondham: Sycamore Press, 1985) 193–95.

31. *Chronicon Abbatiae de Evesham*, ed. W. D. Macray, Rolls Series 29 (London, 1863), 325–37.

32. Arnold-Forster 1:175–76.

33. *Handbook of British Chronology*, 27. Farmer, 134, and Hole, *Saints in Folklore*, 92, give 979 as the year of his murder.

34. Frank M. Stenton, *Anglo-Saxon England*, 3rd ed. (Oxford: Clarendon Press,1971) 372–73.

35. Richard Stanton, *A Menology of England and Wales* (London, 1887) 122. Stenton, 372.

36. *Anglo-Saxon Chronicle*, ed. Dorothy Whitelock (New Brunswick, NJ: Rutgers University Press, 1961) 79. "He waes on life eordlic cing. He is nu aefter deade heofonlic sanct. Hine nolden his eordlican magas wrecan. Ac hine hafad his heofonlica faeder swide ge wrecen." *Two Saxon Chronicles*, 123. Not all versions contain this comment, although the murder itself is generally noted.

37. Stenton, 374.

38. *Memorials of Saint Dunstan, Archbishop of Canterbury*, ed. W. Stubbs, Rolls Series 63 (London: Longman & Co., 1874) 114.

39. Stanton,121.

40. Stenton, 372.

41. Alban Butler, *Lives of Eminent Saints* (Boston, 1880) 61.

42. Arnold-Forster 1:175.

43. Hole, *Saints in Folklore*, 95.

44. Rollason, 14.

45. Baring-Gould 1:44 for date of legend; Baring-Gould and Fisher 3:471 put date of death at 544.

46. F. Plaine, "Vita Inedita S. Melori Martyris," *Anal. Boll.* 5 (1886): 166–75, may date from the mid-ninth century, but this claim is disputed by Baring-Gould and Fisher, 3:471.

47. *AASS* Oct. I, 943 for Brittany; Jan. I, 136–37, for England. This version is taken from Capgrave, *Nova Legenda Angliae* 1:183–88. An English translation appears in G.H. Doble, *The Saints of Cornwall* (Chatham: Parrott & Neves, 1964) 3:20–54.

48. *Victoria History of the Counties of England, A History of Wiltshire* ed. R.B. Pugh and Elizabeth Crittall, vol. 3 (London, 1956) 242.

49. Christina Hole, *English Folklore* (London: B.T. Batesford, 1945) 171.

50. *Nova Legenda Angliae* 1:185–88.

51. Baring-Gould and Fisher, 3:472.

52. *VCH History of Wiltshire* 3:242..

53. Arnold-Forster 2:252–53. The prior possession of the relics may have suggested the site to the remorseful queen.

54. *VCH, History of Wiltshire* 3:243.

55. For Cornwall, Mylor near Falmouth; Linkenhorne near Liskeard. These churches claimed no relics of the saint. Doble, 3:34, and Arnold-Forster, 2:252–53.

56 Farmer, 311–12. Doble, 3:33, notes Aethelstan's general interest in the relics of Breton saints.

57. Arnold-Forster 2:252–53.

58. *VCH, History of Wiltshire* 3:243.

59. Baring-Gould and Fisher, 3:472.

60. *VCH, History of Wiltshire* 3:243.

61. *Bibliotheca Sanctorum* 6:293.

62. *AASS* Sept. IV, 264.

63. *Vies des Saints* 11:281–82; *AASS* Sept. IV, 259–63.

64. *AASS* Sept. IV, 268–9; *Anal. Boll.* 4 (1885): 2036.

65. Sabine Baring-Gould and John Fisher, *Lives of the British Saints* (London: C.J. Clarke, 1907) 2:356–59.

66. "L'aspetto é giovanile," according to the Italians. Perhaps. *Bibliotheca Sanctorum* 4:835–36. Also see photo in Baring-Gould and Fisher, 358.

67. *Bibliotheca Sanctorum* 12:647; Holweck, 988.

68. The legend is considered to be nothing more than a fragment of folklore. Tremorus is mentioned in the lives of Saint Gildas and Saint Brieuc, but the ancient Breton liturgy contained no mention of him. *Bibliotheca Sanctorum* 12:647.

69. *Bibliotheca Sanctorum* 10:791.

70. See Georges Duby, *The Knight, the Lady and the Priest: the Making of Modern Marriage in Medieval France*, tr. Barbara Bray (New York: Pantheon, 1983), *passim.*, for a general discussion of this often fatal conflict.

71. *Liber Landavensis*, ed. W. Rees (Cardiff, 1840) 127.

72. Baring-Gould, *Lives of the Saints* 16:202.

73. *AASS* Jul. IV, 90–96; *Bibliotheca Sanctorum* 11:80–82. Hubert was Bishop of Wurzburg 833–841.

74. *Bibliotheca Hagiographica Latina* 2:1033, n. 7101.

75. *Anal. Boll.* 54 (1936): 36; 79 (1961): 83.

76. *Bibliotheca Sanctorum* 11:81; *AASS* Jul. IV, 90–96.

77. *Bibliotheca Sanctorum* 12:119; *AASS* Oct. V, 122–23. Her age is not given.

78. St. Guinefort, the dog saint invoked by French peasants to justify folkloric ritual for the healing of children, presents a similar case. Schmitt, 18 and *passim.*

79. Hole, *English Folklore*, 148.

80. Luck, 29.

81. Fox, 446.

82. Ibid., 479–80.

83. Ibid., 448.

84. Luck, 92.

85. Marc Bloch, *Feudal Society*, tr. L. A. Manyon (Chicago: University of Chicago Press, 1961) 1:134–35.

86. Guibert of Nogent, *De Pignoribus Sanctorum*, PL 156:607–80. Quoted in Sumption, 146–47.

87. Caesarius of Heisterbach, *Dialogus Miraculorum*, ed. Joseph Strange (Cologne: H. Lempert, 1851; repr. Ridgewood, NJ 1966) 1:270.

88. William of Newburgh, *Historia Regum Anglicarum, Chronicles of the Reigns of Stephen, Henry II, and Richard II,* ed. R Howlett, Rolls Series 82, vol. 1 (London: Longman, 1884) 311.

89. Camillus Beccari, "Beatification and Canonization," *Catholic Encyclopedia* 2:366.

90. Schmitt, 4–5.

91. Schmitt, 31. See also H. C. Lea, "El santo niño de la Guardia," *English Historical Review* 4 (1889): 245. As in the case of Guinefort, outside ecclesiastical authorities rather than local clergy put a stop to a cult of questionable worth.

92. André Vauchez, *La Sainteté en Occident aux derniers siècles du Moyen Age, d'après les proces de canonisation et les documents hagiographiques* (Rome: École Francaise de Rome, 1981) 173–183.

93. Wiedemann, 178.

94. McNeill and Gamer, 339.

95. Luck, 73–75; Norman Cohn, *Europe's Inner Demons: an enquiry inspired by the great witch-hunt* (New York: Basic Books, 1975) 100, 228.

96. Kieckhefer, 63.

97. The blood of a maiden had the same power. Schulz, 53.

98. Kieckhefer, 59.

99. Ibid., 98.

100. Ibid., 196.

101. Golden 14, for Greece; for Rome, see Burriss, 47–71 and Wiedemann, 180.

102. Luck, 112.

103. Pliny, *Natural History* 20, 33; 22, 30; 28, 18–19.

104. Thorndike 1:418.

105. Wiedemann, 179.

106. Richard Kieckhefer, *Magic in the Middle Ages* (Cambridge, 1989) 43. Orme, 102–3, recounts several instances of young boys being used for purposes of divination.

107. John of Salisbury, *Policraticus,* tr. in Joseph B. Pike, *Frivolities of Courtiers and Footprints of Philosophers* (Minneapolis: University of Minnesota Press, 1938) 147.

108. Thorndike, 2:337.

109. William of Auvergne, *De Universo* 2.3.19, *Giulielmi Alverni Opera Omnia* (Paris, 1674; repr. Frankfurt: Minerva, 1963) 1:1053.

110. Sumption, 280–82. D.W. Rollason, "The Cults of Murdered Royal Saints," 16 ff, denies the connection between the veneration of murdered royal saints and any connection with pre-Christian notions of sacral kingship, and imputes the significance of their worship to ecclesiastical manipulation and political strife. Stenton, 374, however, credits popular veneration for Edward Martyr as contributing to the undermining of Aethelraed's power; this would argue for the influence of popular religion on political issues, rather than the influence of political issues on popular religion.

111. See C. Grant Loomis, *White Magic, an Introduction to the Folklore of Christian Legend* (Cambridge, MA: Medieval Academy of America, 1948); see also Hole, *Saints in Folklore*, and Wilson.

112. Bede, *History*, 86–87.

113. See Keith Thomas, *Religion and the Decline of Magic: Studies in Popular Beliefs in 16th and 17th Century England* (New York: Scribner, 1971); Carlo Ginzburg, *The Cheese and the Worms: the Cosmos of a Sixteenth-century Miller*, tr. John and Anne Tedeschi (New York: Penguin Books, 1982); Carlo Ginzburg, *The Night Battles: Witchcraft and Agrarian Cults in the Sixteenth and* Seventeenth Centuries, tr. John and Anne Tedeschi (New York: Penguin Books, 1983) for general works and specialized studies on this topic.

114. Crawford, 89–90.

115. Schmitt, 71–72.

116. See Janet and Colin Bord, *Sacred Waters: Holy Wells and Water Lore in Britain and Ireland* (London: Granada, 1985) and Hole, *Saints in Folklore*, 80–81. Also see Stith Thompson, *Motif-Index of Folk Literature* (Bloomington: Indiana University Press, 1932) 385–87, and Flint, 204–06.

117. Baring-Gould 8:321.

118. Alexander Chamberlain, *The Child and Childhood in Folk-Thought* (New York: MacMillan, 1896) 163–64.

119. Bord and Bord, *passim.*

120. Doble, 3:42.

121. Ibid.

122. Bord and Bord, 100–101.

123. *Bibliotheca Sanctorum* 11:384. The well at Sutton, known as "St. Rumbold's well," was located in the hamlet of Astrope. Arnold-Forster, 1:172–74.

124. Chamberlain, 286ff., "The Child as Judge." See also Wiedemann, 177–78, for observations on the prophetic role of children in the ancient world.

125. Juha Pentikainen, *The Nordic Dead-Child Tradition: Nordic Dead-Child Beings, a Study in Comparative Religions* (Helsinki, 1968), 73, 89–90.

126. Alexandre-Bidon and Lett, 22.

127. Thorndike 2:957.

128. Loomis, 28–29. Stith Thompson does not mention the column of light or similar motifs in connection with beliefs concerning the dead.

129. Bede, *Ecclesiastical History* 159, 219, 222, 249, 286.

130. Pentikainen, 141, 173. The word *myling* is Swedish; *gast* refers to an adult spirit.

131. Ibid., 138.

132. Ibid., 286. Most of the Nordic dead-child tradition deals with the act of infanticide, and the guilt attached to the furtive murder of helpless babies, but the parallels between Nordic folk-belief and early medieval child saints is striking.

133. Ibid., 139.

134. Ibid., 314.

135. Baring-Gould, *Lives of the Saints* 16:202.

136. Bede, *Ecclesiastical History*, 156.

137. Doble, 3:43–44.

138. McNeill and Gamer, 419–21, and passim.

139. Gustav Henningsen, *The Witch's Advocate: Basque Witchcraft and the Spanish Inquisition 1609–1614* (Reno, NV: University of Nevada Press, 1980), 155 and *passim.*, explores a more active role for children in both ritual and accusation than is usually presented, but for a later period than is considered here. For an anthropological approach to the question of the participation of children in accusations of magic, see Robert Brain, "Child-Witches," *Witchcraft Confessions and Accusations*, ed. Mary Douglas (London and New York: Tavistock, 1970) 161–79.

6. The Pious Infant: Child Confessors of the High Middle Ages

1. Shahar, *Childhood in the Middle Ages*, 13–14, 18.

2. David Herlihy, "Medieval Childhood," in *Essays on Medieval Civilization*, ed. Bede Karl Lackner and Kenneth Ray Philip (Austin: University of Texas Press, 1978) 127. In *Medieval Households*, 126, Herlihy notes that "in his writings, some have detected homosexual tendencies." On the subject of domestic harmony, Michael Goodich sees family life of the thirteenth century as a source of conflict and rebellion in the lives of saints of that period, which would not necessarily produce emotions sympathetic to childhood. Goodich, "Childhood and Adolescence," 286–287.

3. Bernard of Clairvaux, *In Conversione S. Pauli Sermo 2, PL* 183:365.

4. Herlihy, *Medieval Households*, 126–27.

5. Bartholomeus Anglicus, *De proprietatibus rerum*, ed. Georgius Bartholdus (Frankfurt: Minerva, 1964) 238–41.

6. Herlihy, "Medieval Chldhood," 124.

7. Shahar, 16.

8. Ibid., 163–64.

9. Philippe of Novara, *Les quatre ages de l'homme: Traité moral de Phillippe de Navarre* ed. Marcel de Fréville, (Paris: Librarie de Firmin Didot et Cie, 1888) 27.

10. Orme, 214–15.

11. André Vauchez, *La Sainteté en Occident aux derniers siècles du Moyen Age, d'après les proces de canonisation et les documents hagiographiques* (Rome: École Francaise de Rome, 1981) 25–30, traces the origins of pontifical involvement in the canonization process from the papal bull of Pope John XV issued in 993 in the case of Bishop Ulrich of Augsburg. Kemp, 57, agrees. The cult of the saints, however, was of only minor concern to the papacy until the late twelfth century; Innocent III was especially influential in extending papal control of the recognition of sanctity on a widespread scale.

The canonization process was not finalized in its present form until the pontificate of Pope Urban VIII (1623–44); at that time, all candidates for canonization who were not martyrs were required to demonstrate doctrinal purity, heroic virtue, and miraculous intercession after death. Weinstein and Bell, 141.

12. Vauchez, 173–183.

13. Weinstein and Bell, 142–43, find differences between the evolving patterns of sanctity in the high Middle Ages and the criteria of the canonization process, and assert that promotion of any cult had its basis in regional devotion to a particular individual.

14. Weinstein and Bell, 162; Vauchez, 450–51.

15. Delooz, 788, distinguishes between the *saint réel* and the *saint construit*.

16. Weinstein and Bell, 38–39; see 19–47 for a comprehensive discussion of pious behavior in children who later became saints. For Anthony of Padua, as well as numerous other examples, Goodich, "Childhood and Adolescence," 287–88, and Istvan Bejczy, "The *Sacra Infantia* in Medieval Hagiography," *The Church and Childhood*, ed. Diana Wood (London: Blackwell, 1994):143–151.

17. Guibert of Nogent, *Self and Society in Medieval France*, 46–50.

18. See Vauchez, 593–95; Goodich, 286–87, discusses the usefulness of the *vitae* in providing material for the study of medieval childhood despite the drawbacks inherent in hagiographical literature.

19. Quinn, 195–202. The presence of children in religious communities in large numbers in earlier centuries had not resulted in the formation of any cults; veneration of children in the early Middle Ages was a result of popular rather than ecclesiastic promotion. On the other hand, Goodich, 289–291, notes the continuation of a form of oblation in exposing children to the church through the agency of the mother's brother, who was often an ecclesiastic. Such children were often sent into an ecclesiastical environment at or even before the age of seven. Goodich estimates that of the thirteenth century saints whose age at profession of vocation is known, 25% were either oblates or may have been raised in a monastic setting.

20. Weinstein and Bell, 76; Goodich, 286, notes that the vast majority of thirteenth-century saints belonged to families of noble or elite status, and were often subjected to marriages of convenience.

21. Susan Ridyard, *The Royal Saints of Anglo-Saxon England: A Study of West Saxon and East Anglian Cults* (Cambridge: Cambridge University Press, 1988) 244–245.

22. Vauchez, 159–62, discusses the problem of conflict between the "universal view" of the Church and the "particularisms" of popular culture.

23. *AASS* Jun. I, 237. See also Weinstein and Bell, 60.

24. *AASS* Jun. I, 238–9.

25. Nicholas cured five women, one three-year-old girl, three boys [puer], one adolescent, and one man. Ibid., 247–252.

26. Nicholas was by no means the only saint to endure doubts of his sanity. Christina the Astonishing (1150–1224), who flew to the tops of trees and climbed into ovens to escape the odor of human sin, faced similar accusations of insanity by those unconvinced of her holiness. St. Catherine of Siena (1347–80), who began to receive mystical experiences at the age of six, faced accusations of fakery which, however, may have been engendered

by her habit of criticizing powerful officials. Public doubt of the sanity of Margery
Kempe was at least one significant factor in her failure to achieve sanctity.

27. *AASS* Sept. II, 417–434.

28. Ibid., 442.

29. Ibid., 434.

30. The miracles, most dating from the mid-fifteenth century just before her canonization,
include miraculous cures of seventeen men, thirty-two women, seventeen boys, fifteen
girls, and one horse. Several of the women were pregnant, and the intercession of the
saint saved both the women and their babies. *AASS*, Sept II, 445–66.

31. Vauchez, 297.

32. Peter was born on July 2, 1369, and died on July 2, 1387. *AASS* Jul. I, 486, 489.

33. *Bibliotheca Sanctorum* 10:706.

34. Vauchez, 299.

35. *Bibliotheca Sanctorum* 10:705.

36. Vauchez, 94 n. 69.

37. *AASS* Jul. I, 516.

38. Ibid., 509.

39. *...et licet infantia in eo computaretur in annis, senectus tamen mentis erat immensa.* Ibid.,
510.

40. *Enciclopedia Cattolica* (Vatican City, 1949–54) 3:587–89.

41. *AASS* Jul. I, 565–628.

42. *Bibliotheca Sanctorum* 10:705–706.

43. *AASS* Maii III, 184.

44. *Bibliotheca Sanctorum* 10:1076.

45. J.N.D. Kelly, *The Oxford Dictionary of Popes* (Oxford: Oxford University Press, 1986)
296–97.

46. *Bibliotheca Sanctorum* 10:1076.

47. *AASS* Mar. II, 235.

48. Ibid., 236–238. The language used does not emphasize the youth of the saint, as she is
generally described in terms of the weakness of her gender rather than the innocence of
her age.

49. Ibid., 238. Vauchez, 113, places Fina in the category of local saints who were not
canonized. See Vauchez, Fig. 13 for a fifteenth-century depiction of the young, paralyzed
Fina on her deathbed.

50. *AASS* Mar. II, 238.

51. *AASS* Mar. II, 238–42.

52. J.P. Migne, *Dictionnaire Hagiographique* (Paris: Chez l'Editeur, 1850) 1:31. His feast
day is June 11.

53. *AASS* Sept. III, 311.

54. Ibid., 310.

55. Mattheus Rader, *Bavaria Sancta* (Monaco: Raphael Sadeler, 1615) 2:334.

56. Ibid., and picture, 335.

57. *Bibliotheca Sanctorum* 1:374.

58. Migne, *Dictionnaire Hagiographique* 2:272.

59. She is also known under the variants Reinheldis, Reinlidis, Reinhilde, and Sunte Rendel. *Bibliotheca Sanctorum* 11:91.

60. Ibid.

61. *Bibliotheca Sanctorum* 10:75.

62. *AASS* Maii I, 165.

63. *Bibliotheca Sanctorum* 10:76.

64. Holweck, 767.

65. *AASS* Maii I, 164.

66. *AASS* Aug. III, 93–96. The cults of some martyrs have been criticized because the subjects were killed by other Christians, not pagans, but at least they were human.

67. Migne, *Dictionnaire Hagiographique* 2:587. See also Vauchez, 174–175, for Radegund, Margaret, and Panacea.

68. *AASS* Sept. III, 259.

69. Vauchez, 174–178.

70. G. G. Coulton, *From St. Francis to Dante: Translations from the Chronicles of the Franciscan Salimbene* (Philadelphia: University of Pennsylvania Press, 1972) 22.

71. Shahar, 250–51.

72. Jean André, *In Tertium Decretalium librum novella commentaria*, ca. 1330. Quoted in Vauchez, 603.

7. Sacred Passions: Willian of Norwich
and the Origins of the Ritual Murder Accusation

1. Gavin Langmuir, "The Knight's Tale of Young Hugh of Lincoln," *Speculum* 47, vol 3 (1972) 462.

2. Hermann Strack, *The Jew and Human Sacrifice* tr. Henry Blanchamp. New York: Bloch Publishing, 1909), 259.

3. See Cecil Roth, *A History of the Jews in England*, 3rd ed. (Oxford: Oxford University Press, 1978) and Robert Chazan, *Church, State, and Jew in the Middle Ages* (New York: Behrman House, 1980), 323–28, for a general survey of Jewish-Christian relations in medieval society.

4. Vauchez, 181–2.

5. Joshua Trachtenberg, *The Devil and the Jews: the Medieval Conception of the Jew and its Relation to Modern Anti-Semitism* (New Haven: Yale University Press, 1943) 125, asserts that this number covers only a fraction of the cases. See also Joseph Jacobs, "Blood Accusation," *Jewish Encyclopedia* (New York: Funk and Wagnalls, 1901–1905) 3: 266–68.

6. Geoffrey Chaucer, *The Works of Geoffrey Chaucer*, 2nd ed., ed. F. N. Robinson (Boston: Houghton Mifflin, 1957) 161

7. Ibid., 162.

8. Cecil Roth, ed., *The Ritual Murder Libel and the Jew: the Report by Cardinal Lorenzo Ganganelli* (Pope Clement XIV.) (London: Woburn Press, 1935)

9. R. Po-Chia Hsia, *The Myth of Ritual Murder: Jews and Magic in Reformation Germany* (New Haven: Yale University Press, 1988) 127.

10. Trachtenberg, 124–29.

11. Weinstein and Bell, 28; Goodich, 292; Hanawalt, 187.

12. Magdalene Schulz, "The Blood Libel: A Motif in the History of Childhood," in *The Blood Libel Legend: a Casebook in Anti-Semitic Folklore,* ed. Alan Dundes (Madison, WI: University of Wisconsin Press, 1991) 273–303.

13. Marie-France Rouart, *Le crime rituel, ou le sang de l'autre* (Paris: Berg International, 1997) Ch. II, "Le mythe de l'enfant martyr : 'tué par les Juifs' " 161–254, provides a comprehensive overview of the development of the cults of William of Norwich, High of Lincoln, Werner of Oberweisel, Andreas of Rinn, Simon of Trent, and Christopher of Guardia.

14. Thomas of Monmouth, 50.

15. Ruggero Taradel, *L'accusa del sangue: Storia politica di un mito antisemita* (Rome: Editori Riuniti, 2002) 23.

16. Thomas of Monmouth, 19–22.

17. Cecil Roth, "The Feast of Purim and the Origins of the Blood Accusation," *Speculum* 8 (1933): 520–26.

18. Gavin Langmuir, "Thomas of Monmouth: Detector of Ritual Murder," *Speculum* 59 (1984), 824–27.

19. Ibid.,, 823; Rouart, 41–43.

20. Thomas of Monmouth., 93.

21. Rouart, 172, notes an entry in the Anglo-Saxon Chronicle, redacted around 1155, that in 1144 "the child William was crucified by the Jews at Norwich" before publication of the *Life* in 1172, but this entry undoubtedly reflects oral tradition emanating from Norwich, no doubt propelled by Thomas. His dedication to the boy martyr is credited with "transforming a simple unresolved case of homicide or accidental death into a celebration of a holy martyr and into an accusation of ritual murder." Taradel, 23.

22. Langmuir, 840–41.

23. Thomas of Monmouth, 93–94.

24. Ibid., 85–88.

25. Jessop and James, lxv.

26. Thomas of Monmouth, 97, 107–8.

27. Ibid., 49–50.

28. Ibid., 117–18.

29. Ibid., 96.

30. Ibid., 11–12.

31. Ibid.

32. Loomis, 17–18.

33. Thomas of Monmouth, 13.

34. Ibid., 13–14. Inexplicably, Jessopp and James, editors of the *Life*, fail to acknowledge Thomas's construction of William's piety, and instead state that Richard of Pontoise (d. 11832) may have been the first ritual murder victim to demonstrate his adherence to a tradition of Christian virtue before his murder. Ibid., lxxv.

35. Ibid., 15.

36. Ibid., 40.

37. Ibid., 17–35.

38. Ibid., 31–32.

39. Jessopp and James, in Thomas of Monmouth, lxxxv.

40. M.D. Anderson, *A Saint at Stake: The Strange Death of William of Norwich 1144* (London: Faber and Faber, 1964) 191.

41. Thomas of Monmouth, 52.

42. Ibid., 67.

43. Ibid., 43–44.

44. Ibid., 64–65. Italics mine.

45. Ibid., 64.

46. Ibid., 121.

47. Ibid., 59.

48. Ibid., 61.

49. Ibid., 85.

50. Ibid., 87–88. Pantaleon, a physician and one of the Fourteen Holy Helpers, is not identified elsewhere as a child martyr.

51. Ibid., 85–86.

52. Ibid., 175–76.

53. Ibid., 16.

54. Ibid., 88.

55. Ibid., 84.

56. Ibid., 29.

57. Ibid., 97–98.

58. Ibid., 33.

59. Langmuir, "Thomas of Monmouth: Detector of Ritual Murder," 841.

60. Thomas of Monmouth, 99.

61. Ibid., 51.

62. Ibid., 166.

63. Ibid., 173.

64. Ibid., 192–93.

65. Ibid., 185–86.

66. Ibid., 221.

67. Ibid., 231.

68. Ibid., 262.

69. Orme, 221.

8. Holy Innocents and Sacrificial Lambs:
Child Saints and Ritual Murder

1. Joseph Jacobs, "Blood Accusation-List of Cases," *Jewish Encyclopedia* (New York: Funk and Wagnalls, 1902) 3:266–7. This list is incomplete and contains many inaccuracies concerning whether Jews were executed for any particular crime. The accompanying article, 260–266, was written by Hermann Strack.

2. *Historia et Cartularium Monasterii Sancti Petri Gloucestriae*, 1:20–21.

3. Ibid.

4. Ibid.

5. Joseph Jacobs, *The Jews of Angevin England* (London, 1893) 46.

6. *Historia et Cartularium Monasterii Sancti Petri Gloucestriae*, 1:20–21.

7. Ibid.

8. Jocelin of Brakelond, Chronica *Jocelini de Braeklonds de Rebus Gestis Samsonis Abbatis Monasterii Sancti Edmundi,* ed. J.G. Rokewood, Camden Society o.s., 13 (London: Camden Society, 1840) 12.

9. Stanton, 132.

10. *Bibliotheca Sanctorum* 9:233.

11. Vauchez, 176; *Similiter, apud Huntodinam de alio puero Herberto nomine nova contigerunt, quem proprius pater ad stipitem impie ligavit et in aqua que iuxta ipsam villam decurrit miserabiliter extinxit.* Jessopp and James, lxxv–vi, note that "he may as well drop out of the list."

12. Matthew Paris, *Chronica Majora*, ed. H.R. Luard, Rolls Series 57, vol. 4 (London, 1877), 377–378.

13. Jessopp and James, lxxxii. By 1312, nearly a quarter-century after the expulsion of the Jews from England, they had dropped to the level of 11 s. 10 1/2 d., and by 1343 they had shrunk to only 4 d. Hugh of Lincoln's shrine "seemed to have been popular in its early days," but by 1420 this most famous of child martyrs attracted a paltry 10 1/2 d. J.W.F. Hill, *Medieval Lincoln* (Cambridge, 1948) 229.

14. Denis Bethel, "The Making of a 12th Century Relic Collection," Popular Belief and Practice, *Studies in Church History* 8, ed. G.J. Cuming and Derek Baker (Cambridge, 1972), 68.

15. *Annales de Burton, Annales Monastici*, ed. H.R. Luard, Rolls Series 36, vol. 1 (London: Longman, 1864) 340–44.

16. Matthew Paris, *Chronica Majora*, ed. H.R. Luard, Rolls Series 57, vol 5 (London: Longman, 1880) 137–139.

17. Joseph Jacobs, "Little St. Hugh of Lincoln: Researches in History, Archaeology and Legend," *Transactions of the Jewish Historical Society of England* 1 (1893–94) 110.

18. Langmuir, "Knight's Tale," 466–467.

19. Thomas of Monmouth, 23–24.

20. The child was held for ten days, and fattened with milk for the duration of the confinement; Matthew Paris, 5:140. He was held for twenty-six days, and starved; *Burton Chronicle*, 341.

21. *Annales de Waverleia, Annales Monastici*, ed. H.R. Luard, Rolls Series 36, vol. 2 (London, 1865) 346.

22. Jacobs, "Little St. Hugh," 90–91; Langmuir, "The Knight's Tale," 477.

23. Although I have largely ignored the literature of literary criticism of the "Prioress's Tale" as essentially unhelpful to this study, see Carleton Brown, *Study of the Miracle of Our Lady Told By Chaucer's Prioress* (London: Trench, Trubner & Co, 1910); Margaret H. Statler, "The Analogues of Chaucer's 'Prioress' Tale;' The Relation of Group C to Group A," *Publications of the Modern Language Association* 65 (1950): 896–910; R.J. Schoeck, "Chaucer's Prioress: Mercy and Tender Heart," *Chaucer Criticism*, ed. Richard Schoeck and Jerome Taylor (Notre Dame: University of Notre Dame Press, 1960) 1:245–258. See also Rouart, 182–88.

24. Francisque Michel, *Hugues de Lincoln: Recueil de ballades Anglo-Normande et ecossoises relatives au meurtre de cet enfant commis par les Juives in MCCLV* (Paris: Silvestre, 1834) 1, 39, 47; the author of this compilation believed faithfully in the veracity of the accusations. For the New York example, Jacobs, "Little St. Hugh," 110.

25. William, 1:452–455; Hugh, 2:39–41.

26. Robert Chazan, "The Blois Incident of 1171: a Study in Jewish Intercommunal Organization," *Proceedings of the American Academy for Jewish Research* 36 (1968): 13–15.

27. Trachtenberg, 144.

28. Rigordus, 119.

29. Langmuir, 462–63.

30. Auguste Molinier, "Enquete sur un meurtre imputé aux Juifs de Valréas," *Le Cabinet Historique* 29 (1883) : 121–1, 127.

31. Strack, *The Jew and Human Sacrifice*, 179–82.

32. *AA SS* Apr. II, 838.

33. Strack, *The Jew and Human Sacrifice,* 182–83.

34. Isidore Loeb, "Le Saint Enfant de la Guardia," *Revue des Études Juives* 15 (1887): 250.

35. *AASS* Mar. III, 591.

36. Langmuir, "The Knight's Tale," 462, cf. Rigordus, *Gesta Philippi Augusti, Oevres de Rigord et Guillaume le Breton,* ed. H.F. Delaborde (Paris: Librarie Renouard, 188285) 1:15.

37. *AASS* Mar. III, 591.

38. The *passio* dates from 1498, and is reproduced in *AASS* Mar. III, 593–594.

39. *AASS* Mar. iii, 594.

40. Rigordus, 15; Trachtenberg, 138.

41. *Vies des Saints*, 4:554.

42. *Bibliotheca Sanctorum* 4:348; Lea, 231.

43. *Bibliotheca Sanctorum* 4:348. This may be an oblique reference to the absence of corporeal existence in the case of Christopher of Guardia. Notwithstanding this harsh judgment, the *AASS* Aug. VI, 777–83, provides an anonymous *passio* along with other documentation of his cult.

44. Henry Charles Lea, "El Santo Niño de la Guardia," *English Historical Review* 4 (1889): 232.

45. Ibid., 236–8.

46. Ibid., 243.

47. Ibid., 246, quoting Fidel Fita, "El Proceso de Jucé Franco," *Boletin de la Real Academia de la Historia* 11 (1887).

48. Ibid., 249.

49. Ibid., 247. The number 5,490 as the number of lashes endured by Christ was determined by the Carthusian Rudolf of Saxony.

50. Ibid. The alleged removal of the heart of the victim was one of the elements which originally identified this case with charges of magic rather than ritual murder.

51. Hsia, 55, notes the importance of the case of Simon of Trent in both the spread of the idea of the ritual murder victim and the standardization of the victims into "boys between infancy and age seven, the age of childhood."

52. The boy is referred to as blessed in at least one anthology without attribution. B.Freimut, *Die Judischen Blutmorde* (Munster: A. Russell, 1895) 22.

53. *Bibliotheca Sanctorum* 11:1318. The cult is sometimes conflated with that of St. Laurentius, a young martyr in the fifth century with the same feast day. *AASS* Apr. III, 76–64.

54. *Biblilotheca Sanctorum* 11:1319.

55. Jacobs, "Blood Accusation," 267.

56. Ibid., 266. Trachtenberg, 135, postulates that a charge against Jews of Tauber was made in 1234, as a prelude to an attack on the Jewish community there on New Years Day, 1235.

57. *Cronica S. Petri Erfordensis mod. A, Monumentum Erphesfurtensia saec. XII, XIII, XIV*, ed. O. Holder-Hegger, *MGH Scriptores rerum Germannicarum* 42 (Hanover, 1899) 233; Strack, *The Jew and Human Sacrifice*, 178–9; S. Salfeld, *Das Martyrologium des Nurnberger Memorbuches* (Berlin: L. Simion, 1898), 13, 122ff.

58. *Cronica S. Petri Erfordensis* 233.

59. Strack, 179.

60. Rader 2:333. Henry's feast was celebrated on June 29, indicating that at least part of the ritual murder legend was never fully applied in his case. Holweck, 470.

61. *AASS* Mar. III, 502. The version of his legend contained therein is from the seventeenth century, and the cult itself cannot be dated with accuracy.

62. *AASS* Apr. II, 699–701. Jacobs, 266, lists the crime as occurring in 1286.

63. *AASS* Apr. II, 504–505.

64. Kenneth Stow, *Jewish Dogs: An Image and Its Interpreters, Continuity in the Catholic-Jewish Encounter* (Stanford: Stanford University Press, 2006) 60–61.

65. *AASS* Apr II., 701.

66. Ibid.

67. Ibid., 700–701.

68. *Gesta Boemundi archepiscopi Treverensis*, ed. G. Waitz, MGH Scriptores24:470, reproduced in Stow, 188–9.

69. *AASS* Apr. II, 704.

70. Ibid., 714ff. See also Rouart, 200–212.

71. *AASS* Apr. II, 504–505.

72. Rouart, 80.

73. *AASS* Apr. II, 504.

74. Anna Esposito, "La morte di un bambino e la nascita di un martire: Simonino da Trento," *Bambini santi*, 99; R. Po-Chia Hsia, *The Myth of Ritual Murder: Jews and Magic in Reformation Germany* (New Haven: Yale University Press, 1988) 4.

75. *Bibliotheca Sanctorum* 12:956–57.

76. Ibid., 11:285.

77. *AASS* Apr. II, 739.

78. *Bibliotheca Sanctorum* 4:210. See *Anal. Boll.* 47 (1929): 390. Conrad is briefly mentioned in *AASS* Apr. II, 505, in conjunction with Rudolph of Bern.

79. *AASS* Apr. II, 505.

80. *Bibliotheca Sanctorum* 8:311–312.

81. *Bibliotheca Sanctorum* 1:1148–1149.

82. Hsia recounts the legend that the boy was sold to merchants by his godfather, and that particulars of the story were altered in 1475. R. Po-Chia Hsia, *The Myth of Ritual Murder*, 219–21. The story, with illustrations, is included in the *AASS* Jul. III, 462–470.

83. Hsia, 222.

84. *Tridenti, passio sancti simeonis pueri, a Iudaeis saevissime trucidati, qui multis posea miraculis coruscavit. Martyrologium Romanum*, 110. Recent literature on Simon and his cult is extensive. See Esposito, "La morte di un bambino e la nascita di un martire: Simonino da trento," *Bambini santi*, 99–118; Anna Esposito, "Das Stereotyp des Ritualmordes in den Trientiner Prozessen un die verehrung des 'Seligen' Simone," *Ritualmord: Legenden in der europäischen Geschichte, ed. Susanna Buttaroni and Stanislaw Musial* (Vienna: Böhlau Verlag, 2003): 131–172; Anna Esposito and Diego Quaglioni, *Processi contro gli ebrei di Trento (1477–1478.) I:Il processi del 1475* (Padova: CEDAM, 1990); Wolfgang Treue, *Der Trienter Judenprozeß: Voraussetzungen —Abläufe—Auswirkungen* (Hanover: Verlag Hahnsche Buchhandlung, 1996); R. Po-Chia Hsia, *The Myth of Ritual Murder: Jews and Magic in Reformation Germany* (New Haven: Yale University Press, 1988) and *Trent 1475: Stories of a Ritual Murder Trial* (New Haven: Yale University Press, 1992); Rouart, 223–238.

85. Hsia, *Trent: 1475*, 1–3.

86. Hsia, *Ritual Murder*, 43.

87. *AASS* Mar. III, 496–97.

88. Hsia, *Trent: 1475*, 52.

89. Hsia, *Ritual Murder*, 48.

90. *AASS* Mar. III, 498–500.

91. Hsia, *Ritual Murder*, 44–45.

92. Esposito, "La morte di un bambino," 101.

93. After these cases, the martyrs became standardized as young boys between infancy and age seven. Hsia, Ritual Murder, 55.

94. Ibid., 57–65.

95. Ibid., 91ff.

96. Ibid., 126; see also Mattheus Rader, *Bavaria Sancta* 3:176–180.

97. Rader, 176.

98. Hsia, *Ritual Murder*,202.

99. Jacobs, "Blood Accusation," 266–267.

100. Rader 3:172.

101. *AASS* Apr. II, 838–839.

102. The list was compiled in 1602. Ibid., 838.

103. Holweck, 685.

104. Holweck, 409. The relics were preserved in Sluzk monastery.

105. Hsia, *Trent: 1475*, 104.

106. Geary, *Furta Sacra,* passim, for the "pious" theft of relics and the various motivations for such actions. On the specific subject of profit to shrines, see Trachtenberg, 243, n. 2. This aspect of a martyr's cult provides a logical explanation for the early interest shown in the body of William of Norwich by the prior of St. Pancras.

107. Trachtenberg, 146; Hsia, *Ritual Murder,* 146, 209. Individual cases in which Jews are accused of needing the body for magical rituals have been mentioned throughout; see especially the cases of Dominic and Christopher.

108. Trachtenberg, 146.

109. Hsia, *Ritual Murder*, 8–12 and *passim*.

110. See Stow, *Jewish Dogs,* for an intriguing analysis of the attitudes of the Bollandists in the study of the cults of ritual murder victims.

Conclusion: *Vox Infantis*

1. "Vox Infantis, or the Prophetical Child," (London, 1649) repr. in Rev. George Townsend, *The Town and Borough of Leominster* (London: A Hall, 1863) 124.

2. Ibid., 124–25.

3. Ibid., 125.

4. Alexandra Walsham, "'Out of the Mouths of Babes and Sucklings': Prophecy, Puritanism, and Childhood in Elizabethan Suffolk," *The Church and Childhood*, ed. Diana Wood (London: Blackwell, 1994) 285–87.

5. Susan Hardman Moore, "'Such Perfecting of Phrase out of the Mouth of a Babe': Sarah Wight as Child Prophet," *The Church and Childhood, ed. Diana Wood* (London: Blackwell, 1994) 313ff.

6. James Janeway, *A Token for Children* (London: Dorman Newman, 1673; repr. New York and London: Garland Publishing, 1977) 1.

7. Ibid., preface.

8. Thomas, 132, in reference to pious children who divined their own deaths, a motif found in late antiquity and the early medieval period.

9. Klaniczay 33 and 194, n. 10.

10. St. Alphonsus de Ligouri, *Victories of the Martyrs*, tr. Eugene Grimm (New York, 1954) 313–431.

11. Sister Marie Helene Mohr, *Saint Philomena: Powerful With God* (Rockford, IL: TAN Books and Publishers, 1988) 3–6.

12. Ibid., 120–26.

13. Ibid., 25.

14. Ibid., 8–9.

15. Ibid., 44.

16. Ibid., 33–34.

17. Ibid., 71–72.

18. Ibid., vii–ix.

19. Hsia, *Ritual Murder*, 146.

20. Ibid., 155.

21. Daniel Trollet, *Acccuser pour convertir: Du bon usage de l'accusation de crime rituel dans la Pologne catholique à l'époque moderne* (Paris : Presses Universitaires de France : 2000) 227–246.

22. Jonathan Frankel, *The Damascus Affair: "Ritual Murder," Politics, and the Jews in 1840* (Cambridge: Cambridge University Press, 1997) 20–27.

23. Ibid., 69–70.

24. Jacob M. Landau, "Ritual Murder Accusations in Nineteenth-Century Egypt," *The Blood Libel Legend*, 198–205.

25. Andrew Handler, *Blood Libel at Tiszaeszlar* (New York: Columbia University Press, 1980) 117.

26. Ibid., 70–71 and *passim.* See also Edith Stern, *The Glorious Victory of Truth: The Tiszaeszlar Blood Libel Trial, 182–3* (Jerusalem: Rubin Mass, 1998)

27. Frankel, 4.

28. "Xanten," *Jewish Encyclopedia*, 12:574..

29. Frantisek Cervinka, "The Hilsner Affair," *The Blood Libel Legend*, 141–42.

30. Albert S. Lindemann, *The Jew Accused: Three Anti-Semitic Affairs (Dreyfus, Beilis, Frank) 1894–1915* (Cambridge: Cambridge University Press, 1991)177.

31. Ibid., 190–191.

32. Cases occurred in Uzbekistan in 1961 and 1962,in Soviet Georgia in 1962, and Lithuania in 1963. Abraham G Duker, "Twentieth-Century Blood Libels in the United States," *The Blood Libel Legend*, ed. Dundes, 234.

33. Lindemann, 240. See also Leonard Dinnerstein, *The Leo Frank Case* (New York: Columbia University Press, 1963) 2–3.

34. Ibid. 251.

35. "Parade," 1998. Music and Lyrics Jason Robert Brown. Book by Alfred Uhry. Both artists won Tony awards in 1999 for the work. My reaction to the performance of this work was that making a musical of this incident shows a lack of taste rivaling the fictional plot of "The Producers."

36. Lindemann, 240–41.

37. Duker, 235.

38. Ibid., 236–49.

39. Saul Friedman, *The Massena Incident: The Blood Libel in America* (New York: Stein and Day, 1978)

40. Mary Lee Nolan and Sidney Nolan, *Christian Pilgrimage in Modern Western Europe* (Chapel Hill, NC and London, 1989), 190–91.

41. Joan Carroll Cruz, *The Incorruptibles* (Rockford, IL: TAN Publishing, 1977), 288.

42. Msr. Joseph A. Cirrincione, "Venerable Jacinta Marto of Fatima," booklet (Rockford, IL: TAN Publishing, 1992) 6, 30, 58, 70–71 and *passim*.

43. *Anne: The Life of the Venerable Anne de Guigné 1911–1922 by a Benedictine Nun of Stanbrook Abbey* (Rockford, Ill: Tan Books and Publishers, 1932, repr. 1997) 2.

44. Ibid., 16.

45. Ibid., 44.

46. Ibid., 80–81.

47. Ibid., 84.

48. Ibid., 96–97.

49. Ibid., 97.

50. Ibid., 118.

51. Ibid., 119.

52. "Citing 'Miracles,' Louisiana Catholics Seek to have Cajun Girl Canonized," *Atlanta Journal and Constitution*, Aug 19, 1989, C12.

53. "Vision inhabits billboard," *Binghamton, N.Y. Press & Sun-Bulletin*, July 20, 1991, A3. The image of the victim, Laura Arroyo, was accompanied by a murkier shape believed to be the child's killer. To my knowledge, no miraculous cures have been reported.

54. *Bibliotheca Sanctorum* 8:1072–76. Also see Monica Turi, "Il 'Brutto Peccato.' Adolescenza e controllo sessuale nel modello agiografico di Maria Goretti." *Bambini Santi* 119–46.

Bibliography

Abelard, Peter. *Hymnarius Paraclithensis Text and Notes,* ed. Joseph Szovérffy. Albany, NY: Classical Folia Editions, 1975.

Acta Sanctorum. Ed. J. Bollandus el.al., 62 vols. Brussels: Société des Bollandistes, 1965–.

Aelfric. *Lives of the Saints,* ed. Walter Skeat. EETS o.s. 76. London: N. Trübner, 1881.

Aigrain, René. *L'hagiographie: ses sources, ses methods, son histoire.* Paris: Bloud and Gay, 1953.

Aland, Kurt. *Did the Early Church Baptize Infants?* Tr. G.R. Beasley-Murray. Philadelphia: Westminster Press, 1963.

Aldhelm. *Aldhelm: The Prose Works.* Tr. Michael Lapidge and Michael Herron. Totowa, NJ: Rowman and Littlefield, 1979.

Alexandre-Bidon, Danièlle, and Didier Lett. *Childhood in the Middle Ages: Fifth-Fifteenth Centuries.* Tr. Jody Gladding. Notre Dame: University of Notre Dame Press, 1997.

Amalarius. *Liber Officialis.* Vatican City: Biblioteca apostolica vaticana, 1948.

Anderson, M.D. *A Saint at Stake: the Strange Death of William of Norwich, 1144.* London: Faber and Faber, 1964.

Anglicus, Bartholomeus. *De proprietatibus rerum,* ed. Georgius Bartholdus. Frankfurt: Minerva, 1964.

Anglo-Saxon Chronicle, ed. Dorothy Whitelock. New Brunswick, NJ: Rutgers University Press, 1961.

Annales de Burton. Annales Monastici, ed. H.R. Luard, Rolls Series 36, vol. 1. London: Longman, 1864.

Annales de Waverleia. Annales Monastici, ed. H.R. Luard, Rolls Series 36, vol. 2. London: Longman, 1865.

Annales Monasterii de Wintonia. Annales Monastici, ed. H.R, Luard, Rolls Series 36, vol. 2. London: Longman, 1865.

Apocryphal New Testament. Ed. M.R James. Oxford: Clarendon Press, 1927.

Ariès, Philippe. *Centuries of Childhood: a Social History of Family Life.* Tr. Robert Baldrick. New York: Knopf, 1962.

Arnold-Forster, Frances. *Studies in Church Dedications.* London: Skeffington and Sons, 1899.

Bainton, Roland. *Early Christianity.* New York: Van Nostrand, 1960.

Baring-Gould, Sabine. *The Lives of the Saints.* New and rev. ed. 16 vols. Edinburgh: J Grant, 1914.

——and John Fisher. *Lives of the British Saints.* 4 vols. London: C.J. Clarke, 1907.

Baudot, Jules. *Dictionnaire d'hagiographie.* Paris: Bloud and Gay, 1925.

Bede. *Ecclesiastical History of the English People,* tr. Leo Sherley-Price, rev. R.E. Latham. London and New York: Penguin, 1990.

Bernold of Constance. *Micrologus de Ecclesiasticis Observationibus*. Patrologia cursus completus, series Latina 183.

Bethel, Denis. "The Making of a 12th Century Relic Collection," *Popular Belief and Practice: Studies in Church History* 8, ed. G.J. Cuming and Derek Baker. Cambridge: Cambridge University Press, 1972.

Bibiotheca Hagiographica Latina Antiquiae et Mediae Aetatis. Brussels: Société des Bollandistes, 1898–1901.

Blaher, Damian Joseph. *The Ordinary Process in Cases of Beatification and Canonization: A Historical Synopsis and Commentary*. Washington, D.C.: Catholic University of America Press, 1949.

Bloch, Marc. *Feudal Society*. Tr. L. A. Manyon. Chicago: University of Chicago Press, 1961.

Bokenham, Osbern. *A Legend of Holy Women: Osbern Bokenham, Legends of Holy Women*. Tr. Shiela Delany. Notre Dame: Univeristy of Notre Dame Press, 1992.

The Book of Saints; a dictionary of persons beatified and canonized by the Catholic Church. New York: Crowell, 1966.

Bord, Janet and Colin. *Sacred Waters: Holy Wells and Water Lore in Britain and Ireland*. London: Granada, 1985.

Boswell, John. *The Kindness of Strangers: the Abandonment of Children in Western Europe from Late Antiquity to the Reniassance*. New York: Pantheon, 1988.

Bott. D.J. "The Murder of St. Wistan." *Transactions of the Leicestershire Royal Archæological Society 44* (1953): 30-41.

Bouyer, Louis. *The Spirituality of the New Testament and the Fathers*, tr. M.P. Ryan. New York: Desclee Co., 1963.

Brewer, E. C. *A Dictionary of Miracles, imitative, realistic, and dogmatic*. Philadelphia: J.B. Lippincott, 1884.

Brooke, Rosalind and Christopher. *Popular Religion in the Middle Ages: Western Europe 1000–1300*. London: Thames and Hudson, 1984.

Brown, Carleton. *Study of the Miracle of Our Lady Told By Chaucer's Prioress*. London: Trench, Trubner & Co, 1910.

Brown, Peter. *The Cult of the Saints: its Rise and Function in Latin Christianity*. Chicago: University of Chicago Press, 1981.

——*Society and the Holy in Late Antiquity*. Berkeley: University of California Press, 1982.

Brundage, James. *Law, Sex, and Christian Society in Medieval Europe*. Chicago and London: University of Chicago Press, 1987.

Burke, Peter. *Popular Culture in Early Modern Europe*. New York: New York University Press, 1978.

Burris, Eli Edward. *Taboo, Magic, Spirits: a Study of Primitive Elements in Roman Religion*. New York: MacMillan, 1931.

Burrow, J.A. *The Ages of Man: A Study in Medieval Writing and Thought*. Oxford: Oxford University Press, 1988.

Butler, Alban. *Butler's Lives of Patron Saints*. Ed. Michael Walsh. San Francisco: Harper and Row, 1987.

——*Lives of the Saints*, ed. Herbert Thurston and Donald Attwater, 2nd ed. London: Burns and Oates, 1956.

Buttaroni, Susanna, and Stanislaw Musial. *Ritualmord: Legenden in der europäischen Geschichte*. Vienna: Böhlau Verlag, 2003.

Caesarius of Heisterbach. *Dialogus Miraculorum*, ed. Joseph Strange. Cologne: H. Lempertz, 1851.

Capgrave, John. *Nova Legenda Angliae*, ed. C. Horstmann. 2 vols. Oxford: Clarendon Press, 1901.

Casey, James. *The History of the Family*. Oxford: B. Blackwell, 1989.

Chamberlain, Alexander .*The Child and Childhood in Folk-Thought*. New York: MacMillan and Co.,1896.

Chaucer, Geoffrey. *The Works of Geoffrey Chaucer*, 2nd ed., ed. F. N. Robinson. Boston: Houghton Mifflin, 1957.

Chazan, Robert. "The Blois Incident of 1171: a Study in Jewish Intercommunal Organization." *Proceedings of the American Academy for Jewish Research* 36 (1968): 13–31.

——*Church, State, and Jew in the Middle Ages*. New York: Behrman House, 1980.

Chronicon Abbatiae de Evesham ad annum 1448. W. D Macray, ed. London: Longman et. Al., 1883.

Chrysologus, Peter. *Sancti Petri Chrysologi Collectio Sermonum*, ed. Alexander Olivar, CCSL 24. Turnholt: Brepols, 1975–82.

Cirricione, Joseph. "Venerable Jacinta Marta of Fatima." Booklet. Rockford, IL: TAN Publishing, 1991.

Cohn, Norman. *Europe's Inner Demons: an enquiry inspired by the great witch-hunt*. New York: Basic Books, 1975.

Collins, Roger. *Early Medieval Spain: Unity in Diversity*. New York: St. Martin's Press, 1983.

Coulton, G. G. *From St. Francis to Dante: Translations from the Chronicles of the Franciscan Salimbene*. Philadelphia: University of Pennsylvania Press, 1972.

Crawford, Sally. *Childhood in Anglo-Saxon England*. Stroud: Sutton, 2000.

Cronica S. Petri Erfordensis mod. A, Monumentum Erphesfurtensia saec. XII, XIII, XIV, ed. O. Holder-Hegger, *MGH Scriptores rerum Germannicarum* 42. Hanover, 1899.

Cruz, Joan Carroll. *The Incorruptibles: a study of the incorruption of the body of various Catholic saints and beati*. Rockford IL: TAN Publishing, 1977.

Cullmann, O. "Infancy Gospels," Edgar Hennecke, *New Testament Apocrypha*, tr. R. McL.Wilson. Philadelphia: Westminster Press, 1963: 1:363-417.

Cuming, G.J., and Derek Baker, eds. *Popular Belief and Practice*. Cambridge: Cambridge University Press, 1972.

Cyprian. *Opera Omnia*. Patrologia cursus completus, series Latina 4.

Daniel, Norman. *Islam and the West: the Making of an Image*. Edinburgh: University Press, 1966.

Davidson, H.R. Ellis. *Myths and Symbols in Pagan Europe: Early Scandinavian and Celtic religions*. Syracuse: Syracuse Univeristy Press, 1988.

Delehaye, Hippolyte. *The Legends of the Saints*. Tr. Donald Attwater. New York: Fordham University Press, 1962.

——*Les Origines du Culte des Martyres*. Brussels, Société des Bollandistes, 1933.

——*Sanctvs, essai sur le cute des saints dans l'antiquité*. Brussels ; Société des Bollandistes, 1927.

Delooz, Pierre. *Sociologie et canonisations*. Liège : Faculté de droit, 1969.

——"Towards a sociological study of canonized sainthoon in the Catholic Church." *Saints and their Cults*, ed. Stephen Wilson. Cambridge: Cambridge University Press, 1983: 189–216.

DeMaitre, Luke. "The Idea of Childhood and Child Care in medical Writings of the Middle Ages." *Journal of Psychohistory* 4 (1977): 461–490.

DeMause , Lloyd, ed. *The History of Childhood*. New York: Psychohistory Press, 1974.

Dhuoda. *Handbook for William: a Carolingian Woman's Counsel for her Son*. Tr. Carol Neel. Lincoln: University of Nebraska Press, 1991.

Dixon, Suzanne. *The Roman Family*. Baltimore: Johns Hopkins University Press, 1992.

——*The Roman Mother*. Norman: University of Oklahoma Press, 1988.

Doble, G.H. *The Saints of Cornwall*. Chatham: Parrott & Neves, 1964.

Douglas, Mary, ed. *Witchcraft Confessions and Accusations*. London and New York: Tavistock, 1970.

Drees, Clayton J. "Saints and Suicide: the motives of the martyrs of Córdoba, A.D. 850–859," *Journal of Medieval and Renaissance Studies* 20, no. 1 (Spring 1990): 59–89.

Duby, Georges. *The Knight, the Lady and the Priest: the Making of Modern Marriage in Medieval France*. Tr. Barbara Bray. New York: Pantheon, 1983.

Duchesne, L. *Fastes episcopaux de l'ancienne Gaule*. Paris : A. Fontemoigne, 1907–15.

Dundes, Alan, ed. *The Blood Libel Legend: a Casebook in Anti-Semitic Folklore*. Madison, WI: University of Wisconsin Press, 1991.

Eadmer. *The Life of St. Anselm, Archbishop of Canterbury*. Tr. Richard Southern. London and New York: T. Nelson, 1962.

Esposito, Anna. "La morte di un bambino e la nascita di un martire: Simonino da Trento." *Bambini santi : rappresentazioni dell'infanzia e miodelli agiografici*. Ed. Anna Benvenuti Papi and Elena Giannarelli. Turin: Rosenberg & Sellier, 1991: 99–118.

——and Diego Quaglioni. *Processi contro gli ebrei di Trento (1475–1478.) I: Il processi del 1475*. Padova: CEDAM, 1990.

Fell, *Christine. Women in Anglo-Saxon England*. Oxford: Bsil Blackwell, 1986.

Flint, Valerie. *The Rise of Magic in Early Medieval Europe*. Princeton: Princeton University Press, 1991.

Florez, Enrique. *España sagrada*. 59 vols. Madrid: M. F. Rodriguez, 1754–59.

Folz, Robert. *Les saints rois do Moyen Age en Occident (vi-xiii siècles.)* Brussels : Société des Bollandistes, 1984.

Forster, Robert, and Orest Ranum, eds. *Ritual , Religion, and the Sacred*. Tr. Elborg Forster and Patricia Ranum. Baltimore: Johns Hopkins University Press, 1982.

Forsythe, Ilene. "Children in Early Medieval Art: Ninth Through Twelfth Centuries." *Journal of Psychohistory* 4: (1976): 31–70.

Fox, Robin Lane. *Pagans and Christians*. New York: Alfred A Knopf, 1989.

Freimut, B. *Die Judischen Blutmorde*. Munster: A Russell, 1895.

Friedman, Saul S. *The Incident at Massena: The Blood Libel in America*. New York: Stein and

Day, 1978.

Gaiffier, Baudouin de. *Études critiques d'hagiographie et d'iconologie.* Brussels: Société des Bollandistes, 1967.

Geary, Patrick. *Furta Sacra: The Theft of Relics in the Central Middle Ages,* 2d. ed. Princeton: Princeton University Press, 1990.

Ghellinck, Joseph de. "Iuventis, gravitas, senectus." *Studia Mediavalia in Honorem Admodem Reverendi Patris Raymondi Josephi Martin.* Bruges, 1948.

Gies, Frances and Joseph. *Marriage and the Family in the Middle Ages.* New York: Harper and Row, 1987.

Ginzburg, Carlo. *The Cheese and the Worms: the Cosmos of a Sixteenth-century Miller.* Tr. John and Anne Tedeschi . New York: Penguin Books, 1982

——*Ecstasies: Deciphering the Witches' Sabbath.* Tr. Raymond Rosenthal .New York: Pantheon Books, 1991.

——*The Night Battles: Witchcraft and Agrarian Cults in the Sixteenth and Seventeenth Centuries.* Tr. John and Anne Tedeschi. New York: Penguin Books, 1983.

Golden, Mark. *Children and Childhood in Classical Athens.* Baltimore: Johns Hopkins University Press, 1990.

Goodich, Michael. *From Birth to Old Age: the Human Life Cycle in Medieval Thought.* Lanham, MD: University Press of America, 1989.

——"Childhood and Adolescence among the Thirteenth-Century Saints." *History of Childhood Quarterly* 1 (1973): 285–309.

——"Il fanciullo come fulcro di miracoli e potere spirituale (XIII e XIV secolo)," *Poteri carismatici e informali: chiesa e societá medioevali.* Ed. Agostino Paravicini Bagilani and André Vauchez. Palermo: Sellerio, 1992: 38–57.

Gordon, Eleanora C. "Child Health in the Middle Ages as Seen in the Miracles of Five English Saints." *Bulletin of the History of Medicine* 60 (1986): 502–522.

Grabar, André. *Martyrium: récherches sur la culte des reliques et l'art chrétien antique.* London : Variorum Reprints, 1972.

Grant, Michael. *Herod the Great.*New York: American Heritage Press, 1971.

Gregory of Tours, *Glory of the Confessors.* Tr. Raymond Van Dam. Liverpool: Liverpool University Press, 1988.

——*Glory of the Martyrs.* Tr. Raymond Van Dam. Liverpool: Liverpool University Press, 1988.

——*History of the Franks.* Tr. Lewis Thorpe. London and New York: Penguin, 1974.

Griffith, H. Winter, M.D. *Complete Guide to Symptoms, Illness and Surgery.* Tucson: Body Press, 1985.

Guibert of Nogent. *Self and Society in Medieval France: The Memoirs of Abbot Guibert of Nogent.* Tr. John Benton. Toronto: University of Toronto Press, 1970.

Haight, Ann Lyon, ed. *Hrotswitha of Gandersheim: Her Life, Times and Work.* New York: Hroswitha Club, 1965.

Hanawalt, Barbara. *Growing up in Medieval London: the Experience of Childhood in History.* Oxford: Oxford University Press, 1993.

——*The Ties that Bound: Peasant Families in Medieval England.* Oxford: Oxford University Press, 1989.

Handbook of British Chronology, 3d ed.,ed. E.B. Fryde, P.E. Greenway, S. Porter, I. Roy. London: Offices of the Royal Historical Society, 1986

Handler, Andrew. *Blood Libel at Tiszaeszlar*. New York: Columbia University Press, 1980.

Hardy, Thomas Duffus. *Descriptive Catalogue of Materials Relating to the History of Great Britain and Ireland, to the End of the Reign of Henry VII*. Rolls Series 26. London: Longman, Green, Longman and Roberts, 1862.

Henningsen, Gustav. *The Witch's Advocate: Basque Witchcraft and the Spanish Inquisition 1609–1614*. Reno: University of Nevada Press, 1980.

Herlihy, David. "Medieval Childhood," in *Essays on Medieval Civilization*, ed. Bede Karl Lackner and Kenneth Ray Philip. Austin: University of Texas Press, 1978. 109–141.

——*Medieval Households*. Cambridge and London: Harvard University Press, 1985.

Herrmann-Mascard, Nicole. *Les reliques des saints: formation contumière d'un droit*.Paris : Klincksieck, 1975.

Herzfeld, George, ed. *An Old English Martyrology*. Early English Text Society o.s. 116. London: K. Paul, Trench Trübner & Co., 1900.

Hill, James William Francis. *Medieval Lincoln*. Cambridge: Cambridge University Press 1948.

Historia et Cartularium Monasterii Sancti Petri Gloucestriae. Ed. E. H. Hart. London: Longman et. al., 1863.

Hole, Christina. *English Folklore*. London: B.T. Batesford, 1945.

——*Saints in Folklore*. New York: M. Barrows, 1965.

Holweck, Frederick George. *A Biographical Dictionary of the Saints, With a General Introduction on Hagiology*. St. Louis and London: B Herder, 1924.

Hrosvitha. *Hrotsvithae Opera*. Ed. Helena Homeyer. Munich: Paderborn, Schöningh, 1970.

——*The Non-Dramatic Works of Hrosvitha*. Tr. Sister M. Gonsalva Wiegand . Saint Louis, MO, 1936.

——*The Plays of Hrotsvit of Gandersheim*. Tr. Katharina Wilson. New York: Garland Press, 1989.

Hsia, R. Po-Chia. *The Myth of Ritual Murder: Jews and Magic in Reformation Germany*. New Haven: Yale University Press, 1988

——*Trent 1475: Stories of a Ritual Murder Trial*. New Haven: Yale University Press, 1992.

Jacobs, Joseph. "Blood Accusation-List of Cases," *Jewish Encyclopedia*. New York: Funk and Wagnalls, 1902.

——*The Jews of Angevin England*. London: D. Nutt, 1893.

——"Little St. Hugh of Lincoln: Researches in History, Archaeology and Legend." *Transactions of the Jewish Historical Society of England* 1 (1893–94): 89–135.

Jacobus de Voragine. *The Golden Legend*. Tr. William Granger Ryan. 2 Vols. Princeton: Princeton University Press, 1992.

James, M.R., ed. *Latin Infancy Gospels*. Cambridge: Cambridge University Press, 1927.

Janeway, James. A *Token for Children:Being an Exact Account of the Conversion, Holy and Exemplary Lives, and Joyful Deaths, of several young Children*. London: Dorman Newman, 1676; repr. New York and London: Garland Publishing, 1977.

Jeremias, Joachim. *Infant Baptism in the First Four Centuries*. Tr. David Cairns. Philadelphia: Westminster Press, 1960.

——*The Origins of Infant Baptism, a Further Study in Reply to Kurt Aland*. London: SCM Press, 1963.

Jerome. *Martyrologium vetustissimum. Opera Omnia*, vol 11. Patroiogia cursus completus, series Latina 30: 435- 486.

Jocelin of Brakelond,.*Chronica Jocelini de Braeklonds de Rebus Gestis Samsonis Abbatis Monasterii Sancti Edmundi*, ed. J.G. Rokewood, Camden Society o.s., 13. London: Camden Society, 1840.

John of Salisbury. *Policraticus*, in *Frivolities of Courtiers and Footprints of Philosophers*. Tr. Joseph B. Pike. Minneapolis: University of Minnesota Press, 1938.

Jubaru, Florian. *Sainte Agnèse: Vierge et martyre de la Voie Nomentane*. Paris: J. Dumoulin, 1907.

Jung, C.G and C. Kerenyí. *Essays on a Science of Mythology: the Myth of the Divine Child and the Mysteries of Eleusis*. 2nd ed. Princeton: Princeton University Press, 1969.

Kelly, J.N.D. *The Oxford Dictionary of Popes*. Oxford: Oxford University Press, 1986.

Kemp, Eric. *Canonization and Authority in the Western Church* .London: Oxford University Press, 1948.

Kieckhefer, Richard. *Magic in the Middle Ages*. Cambridge: Cambridge University Press, 1989.

——*Unquiet Souls: Fourteenth-Century Saints and their Religious Milieu*. Chicago: University of Chicago Press, 1984.

——and George Bond. eds. *Sainthood: its Manifestations in World Religions*. Berkeley: University of California Press, 1988.

Klaniczay, Gábor. *The Uses of Supernatural Power*. Tr. Susan Singerman. Princeton, Princeton University Press, 1990.

Kroll, Jerome. "The Concept of Childhood in the Middle Ages," *Journal of the History of the Behavioral Sciences* 13 (1979): 384-93.

Lang, David Marshall. *Lives and Legends of the Georgian Saints*. New York: MacMillan, 1953.

Laugardière, M. de. "Le culte liturgique des saints à Bourges aux XIIe et XIIIe siècles." *Cahiers d'Archaeologie et d'Histoire du Berry* 15 (1968) : 12–17.

——*L'Église de Bourges avant Charlemagne*. Bourges: 1951.

Langmuir, Gavin. "The Knight's Tale of Young Hugh of Lincoln," *Speculum* 47, vol 3 (1972):459–82.

Lea, Henry Charles. "El Santo Niño de la Guardia." *English Historical Review* 4 (1889): 229–250.

Leather, Ella Mary. *The Folk-Lore of Herefordshire*. Wakefield: S.R. Publishers, 1970.

Lefkowitz, Mary R. and Maureen B. Fant, ed. and tr. *Women's Life in Greece and Rome*. Baltimore: Johns Hopkins Press, 1982.

Lett, Didier. *L'enfant des Miracles: Enfance et société au Moyen Age (XIIe-XIIIe siècle.)* Paris: Aubier, 1997.

Levison, Wilhelm. *England and the Continent in the Eighth Century*. Oxford: Clarendon Press, 1946.

Liber Miraculorum Sancte Fidis. Ed. Luca Robertini. Spoleto: Centro Italiano di studi sull'alto medievolo, 1994.

Liber Pontificalis. 2nd ed. 3 vols. Ed. L. Duchesne. Paris: E. de Boccard, 1955.

Ligouri, Alphonsus. *Victories of the Martyrs.* Brooklyn: Redemptorist Fathers, 1954.

Loeb, Isidore. "Le Saint Enfant de la Guardia," *Revue des Études Juives* 15 (1887): 203–32.

Loomis, C. Grant. *White Magic, an Introduction to the Folklore of Christian Legend.* Cambridge, MA: Medieval Academy of America, 1948.

Lotter, Friedrich. "Innocens Virgo et Martyr. Thomas von Monmouth und die Verbreitung der Ritualmordlegende im Hochmittelatler." *Die Legende vom Ritualmorder: Sur Geschichte der Blutbeschuldigung gegen Juden.* Ed. Rainer Erb. Berlin: Metropol-Verlag, 1993.

Luck, Georg. *Arcana Mundi: Magic and the Occult in the Greek and Roman Worlds.* Baltimore: Johns Hopkins University Press, 1985.

Llull, Ramon. *Doctrine d'enfant.* Ed. Armand Lllinarès. Paris: P.Klincksieck, 1969.

Martyrologium Romanum, Propylaeum ad Acta Sanctorum Decembris. Bruxelles: Société des Bollandistes, 1940.

McCartney, E.S. "The Role of the Child in Supplications." *Classical Weekly* 22 (1928/1929): 151

McNeill, John T. and Helena M. Gamer. *Medieval Handbooks of Penance.* New York: Columbia University Press, 1938; repr. 1990.

Memorials of Saint Dunstan, Archbishop of Canterbury. Ed. W. Stubbs. Rolls Series 63. London: Longman & Co., 1874.

Michel, Francisque. *Hugues de Lincoln: Recueil de ballades Anglo-Normande et ecossoises relatives au meutre de cet enfant commis par les Juives in MCCLV.* Paris: Silvestre, 1834.

Migne, J. P. *Dictionnaire Hagiographique.* Paris: Chez l'Editeur, 1850.

Mills, A.D. *Dictionary of English Place-Names.* Oxford: Oxford University Press, 1991.

Mohr, Marie Helene. *Saint Philomena: Powerful with God.* Rockford, IL: TAN Publishiing, 1988.

Molinier, A. "Enquête sur un meurtre imputé aux Juifs de Valréas," *Le Cabinet Historique* n.s. 2(1884): 121–34.

Monumenta Erphesfurtensia saec. XII, XIII, XIV. Ed. O. Holder-Hegger. *Monumenta Germaniae Historica Scriptores rerum Germanicarum* 42. Hanover: Haniani, 1899.

Musurillo, Herbert. *The Acts of the Christian Martyrs.* Oxford: Clarendon Press, 1972.

New Oxford Annotated Bible. New York: Oxford University Press, 1977.

Newall, Venetia, ed. *The Witch Figure.* London: Routledge and Kegan Paul, 1973.

Nolan, Mary Lee and Sidney Nolan. *Christian Pilgrimage in Modern Western Europe.* Chapel Hill: University of North Carolina Press, 1989.

Orme, Nicholas. *Medieval Children.* New Haven: Yale University Press, 2001.

Palmer, Roy. *The Folklore of Leicerstershire and Rutland* Wymondham: Sycamore Press, 1985.

Papi, Anna Benvenuti and Elena Giannarelli, eds. *Bambini sant : rappresentazioni dell'infanzia e miodelli agiografici.* Turin: Rosenberg & Sellier, 1991

Paris, Matthew. *Chronica Majora.* Ed. H.R. Luard. Rolls Series 57, vol. 4. London: Longman, 1877.

Parker, Roscoe. "The Reputation of Herod in Early English Literature." *Speculum* 8 (1933):

59–67.

Patrologiae cursus completus. Series Latina. Ed. J.-P. Migne. Paris: venit apud editorem, 1844–1880.

Paulinus of Nola. *The Poems of St. Paulinus of Nola.* Tr. P.G. Walsh. New York: Newman Press, 1975.

Pentikainen, Juha. *The Nordic Dead-Child Tradition: Nordic Dead-Child Beings, a Study in Comparative Religions.* Helsinki: Suomalainen tideakatemia, 1968.

Philippe of Novara. *Les quatre ages de l'homme: Traité moral de Philippe de Navarre.* Ed. Marcel de Fréville. Paris : Librarie de Firmin Didot et Cie, 1888.

Pietri, Charles. *Roma Christiana : recherches sur l'église de Rome, son organisation, sa politique, son idéologie de Miltiade à Sixte III (311–440).* Rome: École Francaise de Rome, 1976.

Plaine, F. "Vita Inedita S. Melori Martyris," *Analecta Bollandiana* 5 (1886): 166–175

Pliny. *Letters of the Younger Pliny.* Ed. and tr. Betty Radice .Harmondsworth: Penguin Books, 1963.

Plummer, Charles. *Miscellanea Hagiographica Hibernica.* Brussels: Société des Bollandistes, 1925.

——*Vitae Sactorum Hoberniae.* 2 vols. Oxford: Clarendon Press, 1910.

——*Two of the Saxon Chronicles Parallel.* Oxford: Clarendon Press, 1929.

Prudentius. *Aurelii Prudentii Clementis Carmina.* ed. Maurice Cunningham, CCSL 126 Turnholt: Typographi Brepols, 1966.

Quinn, Patricia. *Better than the Sons of Kings: Boys and Monks in the Early Middle Ages.* New York: Peter Lang, 1989.

Rader, Mattheus *Bavaria Sancta.* 4 vols. Monaco: Raphael Sadeler, 1615.

Reed, Olwen. *An Illustrated History of Saints and Symbols.* London: Spurbooks, 1976.

Rees, William. J. *Lives of the Cambro-British Saints.* London: Longman & Co., 1853.

——*Liber Landavensis.* Cardiff, 1840.

Rhys, Jocelyn. *The Reliquary: a Collection of Relics.* London: Watts, 1930.

Richard of Devizes. *Chronicle of Richard of Devizes at the time of King Richard the First.* Ed. John T. Appleby. London and New York: T Nelson, 1963.

Ridyard, Susan. *The Royal Saints of Anglo-Saxon England: A Study of West Saxon and East Anglian Cults.* Cambridge: Cambridge University Press, 1988.

Rigordus. *Gesta Philippi Augusti, Oevres de Rigord et Guillaume le Breton.* Ed. H.F.Delaborde. Paris, Librairie Renouard, 1882. Vol I.

Rimbault, Edward F. "Two Sermons Preached by the Boy Bishop," *The Camden Miscellany,* n.s. 14 (1875): vi-x.

Rivain, G. *Saint Flocel, Martyr: sa vie et son martyre, son culte et sa dévotion.* Paris: Bloud & Gay, 1932.

Rock, Daniel. *The Church of Our Fathers as seen in St. Osmund's Rite for the Cathedral of Salisbury.* London: Murray, 1905.

Rodriguez, Carmen Garcia. *El Culto de los Santos en la España Romana y Visigoda.* Madrid: CSIC, 1966.

Rollason, D.W. "The Cults of Murdered Royal Saints in Anglo-Saxon England," *Anglo-Saxon*

England 11 (1983): 1–22.

Roman Martyrology. Ed. J.B. O'Connell. Westminster, MD: The Newman Bookshop, 1962.

Roth, Cecil. "The Feast of Purim and the Origins of the Blood Accusation." *Speculum* 8 (1933): 520–526.

——*A History of the Jews in England*. 3rd ed. Oxford: Oxford University Press, 1978.

——ed., *The Ritual Murder Libel and the Jew: the Report by Cardinal Lorenzo Ganganelli (Pope Clement XIV.)* London: Woburn Press, 1935.

Rouart, Marie-France. *Le Crime Rituel ou le sang de l'autre*. Paris: Berg International, 1997.

Ruinart, Thierry. *Acta Martyrum Sincera et Selecta*. Ratisbon: G.J. Manz, 1859.

Salfeld S. *Das Martyrologium des Nurnberger Memorbuches*. Berlin: L. Simion, 1898.

Schmitt, Jean-Claude .The *Holy Greyhound: Guinefort, healer of children since the thirteenth century*. Tr. Martin Thom. Cambridge: Cambridge University Press, 1983.

Schoeck, Richard and Jerome Taylor, ed. *Chaucer Criticism*. Notre Dame: University of Notre Dame Press, 1960.

Schulz, James. *The Knowledge of Childhood in the German Middle Ages, 1100–1350*. Philadelphia: University of Pennsylvania Press, 1995.

Sears, Elizabeth. *The Ages of Man: Medieval Interpretations of the Life Cycle*. Princeton: Princeton University Press, 1986.

Sébillot, Paul. *Le Paganisme Contemporain Chez les Peuples Celto-Latins*. Paris: O. Doin, 1908.

Severus, Sulpicius. *Vie de saint Martin*. Ed. and tr. Jacques Fontaine. Paris: Editions du Cerf, 1967–69.

Shahar, Shulamith. *Childhood in the Middle Ages*. London: Routledge, 1990.

——"Infants, Infant Care, and Attitudes Toward Infancy in the Medieval Lives of the Saints." *Journal of Psychohistory* 10 (1982): 281–310.

Snell, F.J. *The Customs of Old England*. London: Methuen, 1911.

Sommerville, C. John. *The Rise and Fall of Childhood*. 2nd ed. New York: Vintage Books, 1990.

South-English Legendary. Ed. Charlotte d'Evelyn and Anna J. Mill. Early English Text Society 236–236, 244. London: Oxford University Press, 1956–1959.

Stanley, Arthur. *Historical Memorials of Canterbury*. London: J. Murray, 1855.

Stanton, Richard. *A Menology of England and Wales*. London: 1887.

Statler, Margaret H. "The Analogues of Chaucer's 'Prioress' Tale;' The Relation of Group C to Group A," *Publications of the Modern Language Association* 65 (1950): 896–910.

Stenton, Frank M. *Anglo-Saxon England*. 3rd ed. Oxford: Clarendon Press, 1971.

Stern, Edith. *The Glorious Victory of Truth: The Tiszaeszlar Blood Libel Trial, 1882–3*. Jerusalem: Rubin Mass, 1998.

Stocker, David. "The Shrine of Little St. Hugh." *British Archaeological Association Conference Transactions for the Year 1982: Medieval Art and Architecture at Lincoln Cathedral*. Leeds: W.S. Maney, 1986: 109–117.

Stow, Kenneth. *Jewish Dogs: An Image and Its Interpreters. Continuity in the Catholic-Jewish Encounter*. Stanford: Stanford University Press, 2006.

Stolfi, Casimiro. *Leggende di alcuni santi e beati venerati in S. Maria degli angeli di Firenze*.

Bologna: G. Romangoli, 1864.

Storms, Godfrid. *Anglo-Saxon Magic*. The Hague: M. Nijhoff, 1948.

Strack, Hermann. *The Jew and Human Sacrifice: human blood and Jewish ritual, an historical and sociological inquiry*. Tr. Henry Blanchamp. New York and London: Bloch Publishing, 1909.

Suetonius. *The Twelve Caesars*. Tr. Robert Graves, rev. Michael Grant. London: Penguin, 2000.

Sumption, Jonathan. *Pilgrimage: an Image of Medieval Religion*. Totowa, NJ: Rowman and Littlefield, 1975.

Taradel, Ruggero. *L'accusa del sangue: Storia politica di un mito antisemita*. Rome: Editori Riuniti, 2002.

Thacker, Alan, "Kings, Saints, and Monasteries in Pre-Viking Mercia." *Midland History* 10 (1985): 1–25.

Thomas of Monmouth. *The Life and Miracles of St. William of Norwich by Thomas of Monmouth*. Ed. Augustus Jessupp and Montague Rhodes James. Cambridge: Cambridge University Press, 1896.

Thomas, Keith. "Age and Authority in Early Modern England." *Proceedings of the British Academy* 62 (1976): 205–248.

——*Religion and the Decline of Magic: Studies in Popular Beliefs in 16th and 17th Century England*. New York: Scribner, 1971.

Thompson, Stith. *Motif-Index of Folk Literature*. Bloomington: Indiana University Press, 1932.

Thorndike, Lynn. *A History of Magic and Experimental Science*. New York: Columbia University Press, 1923.

Thurston, Herbert J. "Anti-Semitism and the Charge of Ritual Murder." *The Month* 91 (1898): 561–574.

Tollet, Daniel. *Accuser pour converter: Du bon usage de l'accusation de crime ritual dans la Pologne catholique a l'époque moderne*. Paris: Presses Universitaires de France, 2000.

Townsend, George Fyler. *The Town and Borough of Leominster*. London:: A Hall, 1863.

Trachtenberg, Joshua. *The Devil and the Jews: the Medieval Conception of the Jew and its Relation to Modern Anti-Semitism*. New Haven: Yale University Press, 1943.

Treue, Wolfgang. *Der Trienter Judenprozeß: Voraussetzungen-Abläuf-Auswirkungen*. Hanover: Verlag Hahnsche Buchhandlung, 1996.

Two of the Saxon Chronicles Parallel. Ed. Charles Plummer. Oxford: Clarendon Press, 1892–99.

Usuardus. *Le Martyologe d'Usuard: texte et commentaire*. Ed. Jacques DuBois. Bruxelles: Société des Bollandists, 1965.

Vauchez, André. *The Laity in the Middle Ages: religious beliefs and devotional practices*. tr. Margery J. Schneider. Notre Dame: University of Notre Dame Press, 1993.

——*La Sainteté en Occident aux derniers siècles du Moyen Age, d'après les proces de canonisation et les documents hagiographiques*. Rome: École Francaise de Rome, 1981.

Victoria History of the Counties of England, History of the County of Kent. Ed.William Page. London: Oxford University Press, 1932.

Victoria History of the Counties of England, A History of Wiltshire. Ed. R.B. Pugh and

Elizabeth Crittall. 3 vols. London: Oxford University Press, 1956.

Vies des saints et des bienhereux selon l'ordre du calendrier : avec l'historique des faetes. 13 vols. Paris: Librarie Letouzey et Anae, 1936–1955.

Von Hertling, L. "Utrum pueri canonizari possint?" *Periodica de re morali, canonica, liturgica* 24 (1935): 66–73.

Wall, J.Charles. *Shrines of British Saints.* London: Methuen & Co, 1905.

Wall, R. "The Age at Leaving Home." *Journal of Family History* 3 (1978): 181–210.

Weinstein, Donald, and Rudolph Bell. *Saints and Society: The Two Worlds of Western Christendom 1000–1700.* Chicago: University of Chicago Press, 1982.

Wemple, Suzanne. *Women in Frankish Society.* Philadelphia: University of Pennsylvania Press, 1985.

Westwood, Jennifer. *Albion: A Guide to Legendary Britain.* London: Granada, 1985.

Wiedemann, Thomas. *Adults and Children in the Roman Empire.* New York and London: Yale University Press, 1989.

William of Auvergne. *Giulielmi Alverni Opera Omnia.* Paris, 1674; repr. Frankfurt: Minerva, 1963.

William of Malmesbury. *Gesta regum Anglorum = The history of the English Kings.* Ed. And Tr. R.A. B Mynors. Oxford: Clarendon Press, 1998–1999.

William of Newburgh,. *Historia Regum Anglicarum, Chronicles of the Reigns of Stephen, Henry II, and Richard II.* Ed. R Howlett. Rolls Series 82, vol. 1. London: Longman, 1884.

Wilson, R. M. *The Lost Literature of Medieval England.* London: Methuen, 1952.

Wilson, Stephen., ed. *Saints and their Cults: Studies in Religious Sociology, Folklore, and History.* Cambridge: Cambridge University Press, 1983, repr. 1987.

Windeatt, Mary Fabyan. *Patron Saint of First Communicants: the Story of the Blessed Imelda Lambertini.* Rockford, IL: TAN Publishing, 1991.

Wolf, Kenneth Baxter. *Christian Martyrs in Muslim Spain.* Cambridge: Cambridge University Press, 1985.

Wood, Diana, ed. *The Church and Childhood.* London: Blackwell, 1994.

Wordsworth, Christopher. *Ceremonies and Processions of the Cathedral Church of Salisbury.* Cambridge: Cambridge University Press, 1901.

Index

Studies in Church History

General Editor: William L. Fox

This series in Church history offers a place for diverse scholarship that is sometimes too particularly calibrated for any other publishing category. Rather, the richness of the Church history series is in its scope, which variously mixes historical theology and historical hermeneutics, doctrine and practices of piety, religious or spiritual movements, and institutional configurations. Western Europe and the United States continue to provide grounds for exploration and discourse, but this series will also publish books on Christianity in Asia, Africa, and Latin America. Traditional periodization (Early Christian, Medieval, Reformation and Modern eras) grants maximum representation.

The particular focus of the series is the treatment of religious thought as being vital to the historical context and outcome of Christian experience. Fresh interpretations of classic and well-known Christian thinkers (e.g., Augustine, Luther, Calvin, Edwards, etc.) using multicultural perspectives, the critical approaches of feminist and men's studies form the foundation of the series. Meanwhile, new voices from Christian history need illumination and explication by church historians in this series. Authors who are versatile enough to "cross-over" disciplinary boundaries have enormous opportunity in this series to reach an international audience.

For additional information about this series or for the submission of manuscripts, please contact:

Peter Lang Publishing
Acquisitions Dept.
Peter Lang Publishing, Inc.
P.O. Box 1246
Bel Air, MD 21014-1246

To order other books in this series, please contact our Customer Service Department at:

(800) 770-LANG (within the U.S.)
(212) 647-7706 (outside the U.S.)
(212) 647-7707 FAX

or browse online by series at:

WWW.PETERLANG.COM